THE WOMEN'S RIGHTS MOVEMENT
AND THE FINGER LAKES REGION

The Heart of New York State

By Emerson Klees

Photography by C. S. Kenyon

Friends of the Finger Lakes Publishing, Rochester, New York

Front cover: Statues of James Mott, Lucretia Mott, Elizabeth Cady
Stanton, and Frederick Douglass at the Women's Rights
National Historic Park Visitor Center, Seneca Falls

Back cover: Trinity Church on Van Cleef Lake, Seneca Falls—Finger
Lakes Association (FLA) photograph

For information, write:

Friends of the Finger Lakes Publishing
P. O. Box 18131
Rochester, New York 14618

Library of Congress Catalog Card Number 97-78050

ISBN 0-9635990-9-7

Printed in the United States of America
9 8 7 6 5 4 3 2 1

PREFACE

THE WOMEN'S RIGHTS MOVEMENT AND THE FINGER LAKES REGION: The Heart of New York State tells the story of the Women's Rights Movement. The book also offers a guide to places to see and things to do within just over a twenty-five-mile radius of Seneca Falls, the site of the first Women's Rights Convention, which was held on July 19-20, 1848.

The Heart of New York State is bounded by the I-390 Expressway in the West, the New York State Thruway in the North, the I-81 Expressway and Route 13 in the East, and Route 17, the Southern Tier Expressway, in the South. The scenic Finger Lakes Region is comprised of fourteen counties, 264 municipalities, and 6,125 square miles.

The social conditions with which women lived in the mid-1800s are described in the Prologue. Looking back from today, it is difficult to comprehend the social status imposed upon half of the population in the nineteenth century. The Introduction provides a brief history of the Women's Rights Movement from the first demands for the vote to the ratification of the "Susan B. Anthony Amendment" to the Constitution in 1920.

The book highlights the leaders of the Women's Rights Movement who dedicated themselves to overcoming the obstacles in their way, including an unsympathetic society, an unresponsive government, and a hostile press. Eight stories of the pioneers of the Movement are included in addition to nine stories about the struggle. The Women's Rights Movement in England is described through a profile of the indomitable Pankhurst family.

The book also contains a brief description and history of Seneca Falls and its neighboring municipalities along Routes 5 and 20. Information is provided on seven places to see and things to do in Seneca Falls in addition to 143 places to see and things to do within just over a twenty-five-mile radius of the Village. These 143 places to see and things to do are divided into four quadrants: northwest, northeast, southeast, and southwest of Seneca Falls.

The status of American women in the 1990s and the 21st century is discussed in the Epilogue. This book contains some material reprinted from *Persons, Places, and Things In the Finger Lakes Region; Persons, Places, and Things Around the Finger Lakes Region*; and *People of the Finger Lakes Region*.

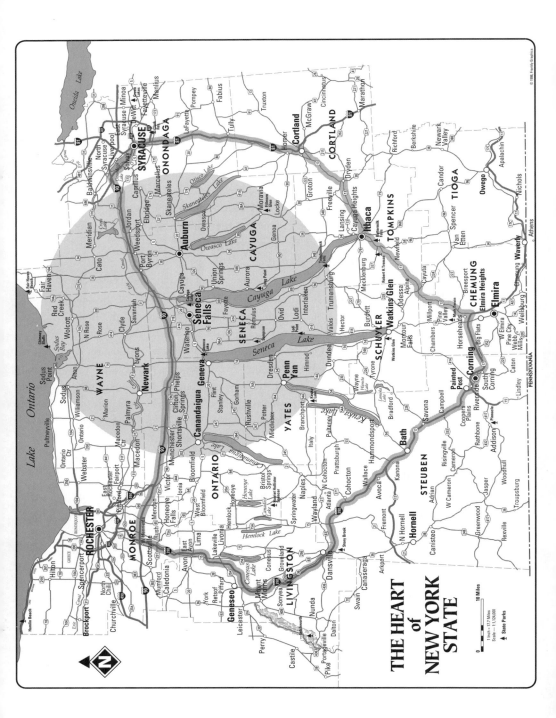

THE HEART of NEW YORK STATE

0   10 Miles

1 inch = 17.7 Miles
Scale — 1:1,124,000

▲ State Parks

TABLE OF CONTENTS

List of Photographs   **Page No.**

PROLOGUE

The Status of Women in the Mid-Nineteenth Century

"The most perfect social system can only be obtained where the laws that govern the sexes are based on justice and equality."

Sarah Moore Grimké

1

It is difficult for people living today to comprehend the conditions confronting women in the United States in the first half of the nineteenth century. The conditions addressed by the Women's Rights Convention on July 19-20, 1848, in Seneca Falls cried out to be changed. If women like Lucretia Mott and Elizabeth Cady Stanton had not insisted that they be addressed, nothing would have been done or action would have been delayed.

Women, along with African Americans and Native Americans, couldn't vote. Work outside of the home was limited for women; they could be a factory worker, a paid companion, a school teacher, a seamstress, or a servant. Other work options included running a boardinghouse, taking in laundry, or having a retail shop. Little else was available to women, regardless of how ambitious they were. Because women were not permitted to obtain a college education, the professions were closed to them.

If they did comparable work to men, such as a factory worker or a teacher, they were paid considerably less. Lucretia and James Mott taught in the same Quaker school. The men were paid 100-120 pounds a year; women earned 20-40 pounds a year. Men were paid a multiple of the salary of women for teaching the same material for the same length of school year. Similar imbalances existed in factory work.

Married women, in effect, forfeited their legal existence. They couldn't sign a contract, sue in court, or make a will. If a married woman worked outside of the home, her husband was entitled to all of her wages. She owned no property, not even her clothing. If she received an inheritance from a parent or relative, it became her husband's property. A father could contract to apprentice his children without consulting his wife, the children's mother.

Divorces were rare, but the husband automatically received custody of the children without any evaluation of his ability to raise them properly. If a married woman reported mistreatment by her husband, courts considered it unfortunate but did not take action.

Unmarried women had a little more freedom, but far less status than married women. "Old maids" were looked down upon for not fulfilling a woman's role of caring for a husband and having children. Single women usually lived with their parents and then lived with a male relative after their parents' death. A single woman's inheritance might be administered by a male guardian, who could spend it or invest it as he chose.

The church provided few opportunities for women. Generally, the church strived to keep a woman "in her proper sphere," that is, in the home. The Congregationalist ministers of Massachusetts declared that women should be "unobtrusive, mild, dependent." One exception was the Society of Friends, or Quakers, who had no ministers as such. Any church member, man or woman, could preach when he or she was motivated to do so. This was the exception to the general rule that women did not speak in public—especially before mixed audiences of men and women.

Women of the time had to fight unfair laws, biased religious belief, and long-term social customs. Most institutions were aligned against women, including the church, the government, colleges and schools, and certainly the press. For example, the Syracuse *Daily Star* referred to a women's rights convention as a "mass of corruption, heresies, ridiculous nonsense, and reeking vulgarities which these bad women have vomited forth for the past three days."

Women were often confronted with grossly unfair situations, which were considered completely legal. In 1856 in England, a woman established a milliner's shop when her husband failed in business. For many years, she was the sole support for her husband, herself, and their children. When she retired, they lived comfortably on her earnings as a milliner. When her husband died, he left all of his wife's earnings to his illegitimate children by another woman. His wife had no recourse in the courts.

Looking back on these conditions, it is difficult to believe that fifty percent of the population would be held back, not only from achieving their potential, but also from having the same rights that the male dregs of humanity, including drunkards and dropouts from society, enjoyed.

The women of Seneca Falls began an activist campaign that begged to be undertaken. One of their goals, obtaining the right to vote, wasn't obtained until 1920—seventy-two years later. For their determination and perseverance within a culture that limited their action, these women deserve our highest respect and admiration. For such women, Susan B. Anthony's prediction was correct: "Failure is impossible.'

INTRODUCTION

The Women's Rights Movement

"Hundreds of women gave the accumulated possibilities of an entire lifetime, thousands gave years of their lives, hundreds of thousands gave constant interest and such aid as they could. It was a continuous, seemingly endless, chain of activity. Young suffragists who helped forge the last links of the chain were not born when it began. Old suffragists who forged the first links were dead when it ended ... It is doubtful if any man, even among suffrage men, ever realized what the suffrage struggle came to mean to women before the end was allowed in America. How much of time, of patience, how much work, energy and aspiration, how much faith, how much hope, and how much despair went into it. It leaves its mark on one, such a struggle...."

Carrie Chapman Catt

Two of most prominent movements in the United States early in the nineteenth century in which women took an active role were the abolition movement and the temperance movement. Meetings were held, pamphlets were written, and societies were formed to address the evils of slavery and of drinking. Women became actively involved in both movements but were not welcomed into the antislavery or temperance societies, so they formed their own societies. Lucretia Mott was one of the founders of the Philadelphia Female Anti-Slavery Society and Susan B. Anthony founded the New York State Female Temperance Society after being denied the opportunity to speak at a Sons of Temperance meeting.

These female societies provided good training for those who later were active in the Women's Rights Movement. In fact, virtually all of the early women's rights leaders learned how to organize and to work together in the antislavery and temperance movements. They learned how to prepare and circulate petitions, how to plan and hold conventions, and how to handle the considerable volume of criticism that they received. Most importantly, they learned to speak before audiences. The early speeches were given to other women in parlors on the topics of antislavery and temperance.

Two of the earliest speakers were the Grimké sisters, Angelina and Sarah. In 1836, they were invited to work for the Anti-Slavery Society in New York, thus becoming the first two female abolitionist agents in the United States. Their first speaking assignments were to give talks to women in private homes. The sisters became effective speakers, especially Angelina, and were in demand by antislavery organizations outside of New York State. In 1837, the sisters made a speaking tour of Massachusetts.

Initially, they spoke to female audiences, but, increasingly, men attended their meetings when the society sponsoring their meetings began to invite men as well as women. Many New Englanders did not approve of women who spoke before mixed audiences. When the Grimké sisters began to debate men publicly, churches began to withhold permission to conduct meetings in their facilities.

Although the New England clergy came out strongly against Angelina and Sarah Grimké, the sisters made significant contributions to the early phases of the Women's Rights Movement, particularly through their pioneering of the right of women to speak in public.

In 1840, Lucretia Mott accompanied her husband, James, to London to attend the World Anti-Slavery Convention where she met Elizabeth Cady Stanton. Women were denied seating as delegates to the Convention. Lucretia Mott forced the issue of women's participation to the floor of the Convention instead of allowing it to be handled by the executive committee. However, her proposal to allow women to be active members was denied.

Lucretia Mott and Elizabeth Cady Stanton were relegated to the gallery with the other women to observe the activities of the Convention, not to participate in them. They agreed to call a meeting to address women's issues when they returned to the United States. The meeting that Mott and Cady Stanton had planned in London in 1840 while attending the World Anti-Slavery Convention finally occurred eight years later.

In early July 1848, Lucretia Mott visited her sister, Martha Wright, in Auburn and attended the Yearly Meeting of the Friends in Western New York. Mott contacted Elizabeth Cady Stanton in Seneca Falls, and they decided to continue the discussion of women's rights that they had begun in London.

Jane Hunt invited them to tea along with her friends, Martha Wright and Mary Ann M'Clintock. The five women discussed their frustration with the limited rights of women and the discrimination they had experienced in the antislavery and temperance movements. The planning for the first Women's Rights Convention was done in a meeting at the home of Jane and Richard Hunt in Waterloo. The five women prepared a notice about the Convention that appeared in the Seneca County *Courier* on July 14. They agreed to reconvene at the home of Mary Ann and Thomas M'Clintock in Waterloo on July 16 to prepare an agenda for the first Women's Rights Convention to be held in Seneca Falls on July 19-20.

At their meeting on July 16, the women decided to list their grievances and to propose resolutions for them. Elizabeth Cady Stanton was the principal author of the *Declaration of Sentiments* patterned on the *Declaration of Independence*. She wanted the right to vote to be one of the resolutions. The other women wanted to emphasize other women's rights first and postpone the right-to-vote issue as being too controversial. Cady Stanton prevailed, and the controversial right of women to vote became one of the resolutions.

James Mott called the Convention to order in the Wesleyan Chapel. Lucretia Mott stated the goals of the Convention and discussed the importance of educating women and elevating their social position. Mary Ann M'Clintock and Elizabeth Cady Stanton read prepared speeches and Martha Wright read newspaper articles that she had written about the plight of women.

After the *Declaration of Sentiments* was discussed, it was reread by Elizabeth Cady Stanton and adopted with some minor amendments. The only resolution that was not unanimously adopted was the ninth, which concerned the right of women to vote. Some attendees of the Convention thought that advancing the elective franchise of women at that time might reduce the probability of securing other rights for women. Thanks to Cady Stanton's and attendee Frederick Douglass' continued support, the ninth resolution eventually passed with a slight majority.

In the spring of 1851, Amelia Bloomer, now best remembered for popularizing the Bloomer costume, introduced two people to each other who were to have a significant impact on the Women's Rights Movement. Susan B. Anthony had come to Seneca Falls to attend an antislavery meeting and stayed at Bloomer's home. After the meeting, they waited for

Elizabeth Cady Stanton on the street corner, where Bloomer introduced two women who through their long working partnership served as principal forces in the Women's Rights Movement.

In 1854, Elizabeth Cady Stanton made her first address to the New York State Legislature on the Married Woman's Property Act and women's suffrage. Six years later she again addressed the New York State Legislature to request the expansion of married women's rights and women's suffrage.

In 1863, the National Woman's Loyal League was established by Susan B. Anthony and Elizabeth Cady Stanton. In 1868, the division between two factions of the Women's Rights Movement widened with the active discussion of the Fifteenth Amendment to the Constitution. The New Yorkers wanted the word "sex" added to the phrase "on account of race, color, or previous condition of servitude" in reference to guaranteeing rights to citizens. Lucy Stone and her New Englanders wanted to wait in the push for women's suffrage until the Fifteenth Amendment granting the vote to African Americans was ratified. The first Woman Suffrage Amendment was introduced to the U.S. Congress that year.

Also in 1868, Susan B. Anthony began to organize working women's organizations to further support the Women's Rights Movement. Lucy Stone was interested in the rights of women to control their own earnings and their own property, but she had no interest in the trade union movement. Also, she disliked some of the techniques, such as strikes, that labor organizations used.

In May 1869, the break between the two factions of the Women's Rights Movement occurred at a meeting of the Equal Rights Association. Differences in opinions about the Fifteenth Amendment were in the forefront at this convention.

Immediately after the meeting of the Equal Rights Association, the women who agreed with Susan B. Anthony and Elizabeth Cady Stanton met to organize the National Woman Suffrage Association to work for the passage of an amendment to the Constitution granting the vote to women. Lucy Stone and the New England wing of the Movement were not included in the planning session for the new organization.

In November 1869, Lucy Stone and the New Englanders formed the American Woman Suffrage Association, which focused on a narrower set of issues—specifically local and state suffrage. They avoided controversial issues. The National Association concentrated on obtaining a women's suffrage amendment to the Constitution and on issues affecting women's role in society. Also that year, the Territory of Wyoming became the first state or territory to give women the right to vote.

In 1872, Susan B. Anthony was arrested for attempting to vote in a national election in Rochester. Her trial in the Ontario County Courthouse in Canandaigua drew national attention because of the unjust treatment that she received. After sentencing, she refused to pay, saying, "I shall never pay a dollar of your unjust penalty." In 1878, the "Susan B. Anthony" Amendment was introduced to Congress in the final wording of the Nineteenth Amendment ratified in 1920. Two years later, Susan B. Anthony, Matilda Joslyn Gage, and Elizabeth Cady Stanton begin writing the first of six volumes of *The History of Woman Suffrage*.

In 1890, the American and the National Woman's Suffrage Associations reunited as the National American Woman's Suffrage Association (NAWSA). Elizabeth Cady Stanton was elected president, Susan B. Anthony became vice president, and Lucy Stone was the head of the executive committee. Two years later, Cady Stanton stepped down as president of the NAWSA and was succeeded by Anthony.

In 1890, Wyoming was admitted to the Union as a women's suffrage state. Three years later, New Zealand became the first country to grant women full suffrage.

In 1900, Susan B. Anthony was succeeded as the president of the NAWSA by Carrie Chapman Catt, who served for four years and passed the mantle to Anna Howard Shaw. In 1915, Carrie Chapman Catt, who had been active in the International Women's Rights Movement, resumed the presidency of the NAWSA from Anna Howard Shaw, who organized the participation of women in the war effort during World War I.

In 1918, the Woman Suffrage Amendment passed the U.S. House of Representatives. In the following year, the Amendment passed the U.S. Senate. In 1920, the Nineteenth Amendment was ratified by a majority of the states and became law. The struggle for women's rights took seventy-two years—from the first Women's Rights Convention in Seneca Falls in 1848 until 1920.

Note: Early in the Women's Rights Movement, the singular "woman or woman's" was used to describe "woman suffrage" and "woman's rights." Later in the Movement, the plural "women or women's" was used as in "Women's Rights Convention" and Women's Right's Movement." In this book the plural has been used throughout, so that singular and plural are not used alternately depending upon the point in time being discussed. Obviously, when a book is referenced, the actual title of the book is cited, such as *The History of Woman Suffrage*.

Wesleyan Chapel, Seneca Falls

CHAPTER 1

Leaders of the Women's Rights Movement

"Any consideration of woman's part in American history must include the protracted struggle of the sex for larger rights and opportunities, a story that in itself is one of the noblest chapters in the history of the American democracy."

Arthur Schlesinger

SUSAN B. ANTHONY

"Cautious, careful people, always casting about to preserve their reputation and social standing, never can bring about a reform. Those who are really in earnest must be willing to be anything or nothing in the world's estimation, and publicly and privately, in season and out, avow their sympathy with despised and persecuted ideas and their advocates, and bear the consequences."

Susan B. Anthony

In 1845, Susan B. Anthony's family moved from the Hudson River Valley to Rochester where her father, Daniel Anthony, became a successful farmer and insurance salesman. Two weeks after the first Women's Rights Convention on July 19-20, 1848, in Seneca Falls, another convention was held in Rochester.

Susan was working in Canajoharie, New York, as the girls' headmistress of the Canajoharie Academy and did not attend the convention in Rochester. However, her father, mother, and sister did; they signed petitions in support of the resolutions. When Susan heard that they had attended the convention and were in agreement with the sentiments, she wrote that, in her opinion, they were getting ahead of the times.

Within two years, Anthony was not only informed on the subject of women's rights, but she had discussed the subject with the abolitionists Frederick Douglass and William Lloyd Garrison, who were convinced that the women's rights cause should be pushed. Anthony's interest in the Movement was sparked by meeting Elizabeth Cady Stanton in Seneca Falls, after an antislavery meeting at which Garrison and the English abolitionist, George Thompson, spoke. It was the beginning of a friendship and a working relationship that lasted over a half century. Anthony's attention to detail and organizational skills were a perfect match with Cady Stanton's strengths as a philosopher and policy-maker.

Initially, Anthony supported three causes. The order of importance to her were first, temperance; second, abolition; and third, women's rights. Cady Stanton supported all of the liberal causes of the time, but concentrated upon women's rights and, in particular, women's right to vote.

Anthony was introduced to the role of women at a Sons of Temperance convention in Albany. She thought that she was attending as a member of the convention until she attempted to make a motion and was told by the chairman that "sisters were invited here not to speak, but to listen and learn." That incident motivated Anthony to organize the New York Women's Temperance Society in 1852 in Rochester. Cady Stanton was elected president of the society, and Anthony was elected secretary—a pattern that was repeated over the years.

Anthony attended her first women's rights convention in 1852; it was the Third National Women's Rights Convention. Cady Stanton didn't attend because she was at home awaiting the birth of her fifth child. However, she sent a letter to be read by Anthony at the Convention. Two thousand delegates attended, including Lucretia and James Mott from Philadelphia and Lucy Stone from New England.

The working relationship between Anthony and Cady Stanton was exemplified by their respective roles in preparing for a speech that Cady Stanton gave to the New York State Legislature in February 1854. In this speech, Cady Stanton addressed the right of women to keep the wages they earned and to own property in their own names. Cady Stanton was willing to give the speech; however, with her large, young family, she didn't have the time to prepare it. She sent a plea for help to Anthony, and the women reached an agreement. Anthony and a lawyer friend sympathetic to their cause would do the necessary research of discriminatory laws and would assemble the information, if Cady Stanton would prepare and present the speech.

The speech at Albany was well-received. It provided specific examples of the ways in which women were discriminated against and the means by which the law could be changed to end the discrimination. Anthony was well prepared; she obtained 6,000 signatures on petitions for women's property and wage reform as well as 4,000 signatures on a petition in support of women's right to vote. Changes to the law on women's property and wages would not come for another six years in New York; however, when the changes came, Anthony and Cady Stanton knew that they had contributed heavily to that reform. Cady Stanton's perception of their working relationship was:

> In thought and sympathy we were one, and in the division of labor we exactly complement-ed each other. In writing, we did better work together than either of us could have done alone. I am the better writer, she the better crit-ic. She supplied the facts and statistics, I the philosophy and rhetoric and together we have made arguments that have stood unshaken through the storms of thirty long years.... Our speeches may be considered the united prod-uct of two brains.

Anthony came to Seneca Falls frequently to take care of the Stanton children so that Cady Stanton could prepare a speech or give a speech. The children loved "aunt Susan," even though she was a stricter disciplinarian than their mother.

During the Civil War, Anthony and Cady Stanton differed on priorities. Cady Stanton wanted to concentrate on antislavery issues, but Anthony wanted to support both women's rights and abolitionism. Cady Stanton persuaded Anthony to focus on abolitionism, but she admitted later that Susan had been right because it delayed by four years the activity that eventually brought women's rights reforms.

An example of Anthony's quick thinking was her sharp exchange with Horace Greeley, editor of the New York

Tribune. Greeley asked, "Miss Anthony, you are aware that the ballot and the bullet go together. If you vote, are you also prepared to fight?" Anthony replied, "Certainly, Mr. Greeley, just as you fought the last war—at the point of a goose-quill."

The Fifteenth Amendment to the Constitution, which was adopted in 1870, stated, "The right of citizens of the United States to vote shall not be denied ... on account of race, color, or previous condition of servitude." The suffragists wanted the phrase "or sex" to be included in the Fifteenth Amendment. However, the phrase was not added, so women began to test the interpretation of their rights as citizens. Anthony wasn't the first woman to test whether the Fifteenth Amendment extended women the right to vote, but she certainly received more newspaper coverage than any other woman who did so.

On November 1, 1872, Anthony and her sisters decided to register to vote. The election inspectors told them that, according to New York State law, they would not be permitted to register. Anthony quoted from the Fourteenth and Fifteenth Amendments and insisted that she, as a citizen, had a right to vote. Anthony and her sisters were permitted to register, and they voted in the general election on November 5. She realized that they might have broken the law and could be liable for a $500 fine. On November 18th, a marshal came to Anthony's home and arrested her.

The Anthony sisters were arraigned and their bond set at $500 each. Her sisters posted the $500 bail, but Anthony refused to pay it. Her lawyer, Henry Selden, who did not want his client to go to jail, paid it for her. Anthony made many speeches describing what was happening to her, including speeches in Monroe County where her case was to be tried. Because of the intense public interest in her case in Monroe County, the trial was moved to Ontario County, south of Rochester.

On June 17, 1873, Anthony's trial began in Canandaigua, the county seat of Ontario County. Judge Ward Hunt, who had only recently been appointed to the bench, was selected to try her case. Selden conducted a skillful defense, pointing out that Anthony sincerely believed that she had been given the right to vote by the Fourteenth and Fifteenth Amendments. Judge Hunt refused to let her speak in her own defense.

Judge Hunt stated that it didn't matter what Anthony's beliefs were; she had broken the law. He took a note from his pocket, turned toward the jury, and read from it. The note concluded with the statement, "If I am right in this, the result must be a verdict ... of guilty, and I therefore direct that you find a verdict of guilty." An incensed Selden reminded the judge that he didn't have the right to instruct the jury in that manner and demanded that the jury be asked for their verdict. Judge Hunt ignored Selden, directed the court clerk to record the verdict, and dismissed the jury.

This shocking injustice was widely covered by the press. Even people who disagreed with Anthony's voting sided with her because of this unjust treatment in the courtroom.

Selden requested a new trial on the grounds that Anthony had been denied a fair trial by jury. Judge Hunt denied the request and stated her sentence—a $100 fine, considered very high for the offense. Anthony responded: "I shall never pay a dollar of your unjust penalty...." She never did pay the fine.

In 1880, Anthony and Cady Stanton began their monumental project, *A History of Woman Suffrage*. Cady Stranton wrote most of the first two volumes; Anthony verified the facts and assembled the material. Anthony had a major role in preparing volume three because Cady Stanton had just returned from visiting her daughter Harriot in England. Matilda Joslyn Gage of Syracuse was also a key contributor to the early volumes. The last three volumes were edited by Ida Husted Harper; they trace the history of the Movement through 1920. Harper was also Anthony's biographer; her *Life and Work of Susan B. Anthony* was published in 1898.

Anthony never retired from her lifelong efforts to secure women's rights. When the International Woman Suffrage

Alliance was formed in 1904, Anthony, at the age of eighty-four, was recognized as the leader. At their convention in 1906, she commanded the delegates, "The fight must not stop. You must see that it does not stop." At a dinner in her honor in Washington, D. C., she concluded her comments by stating, "Failure is impossible."

In 1920, the Nineteenth Amendment to the Constitution was ratified. It included the statement, "The right of citizens of the United States to vote shall not be denied or abridged by the United States or by any State on account of sex." It was called the "Susan B. Anthony Amendment." Anthony was right. Failure was impossible. In 1976, she was honored further by the United States government with the minting of the Susan B. Anthony dollar.

* * *

The Susan B. Anthony House, a National Historic Landmark at 17 Madison Street, Rochester, and the Visitor and Education Center at 19 Madison Street are open Thurday through Sunday 1-4 p.m.(closed holidays). A nominal admission fee is charged. Appointments may be made for group tours. Additional information may be obtained on (716) 235-6124.

CARRIE CHAPMAN CATT

"This world taught women nothing skillful and then said her work was valueless. It permitted her no opinions and said she did not know how to think. It forbade her to speak in public, and said the sex had no orators. It denied her the schools, and said the sex had no genius. It robbed her of every vestige of responsibility, and then called her weak. It taught her that every pleasure must come as a favor from men, and when to gain it she decked herself in paint and fine feathers, as she had been taught to do, it called her vain."

Carrie Chapman Catt, 1902

Carrie Clinton Lane Chapman Catt, the second of three children and only daughter of Lucius and Maria Clinton Lane, was born on January 9, 1859, in Ripon, Wisconsin. In 1866, the Lane family, attracted by the availability of prairie land, moved to a farm near Charles City, Iowa. Carrie was strongly influenced by growing up on the frontier. She was an active child who did many of the household chores, including cooking, and learned how to ride. She was self-reliant and did not consider females to be weak or inferior.

Carrie was a serious reader who graduated from Charles City High School in three years. Her father did not support her wish to go to college, so she obtained a teacher's certificate and taught school for a year to earn money for college. In the spring of 1877, she entered Iowa State College as a sophomore and supported herself by washing dishes and by working in the library. In November 1880, she graduated with a B.S. degree and worked in a law office for a year as preparation for attending law school.

In 1881, Carrie gave up her plans to go to law school and accepted the position of principal in the Mason City High School. Two years later she became the superintendent of schools, a position that was rare for a young woman at the time. On February 12, 1885, Carrie married Leo Chapman, owner and publisher of the Mason City *Republican*. She left her job with the school district to become assistant editor of the newspaper. She met Lucy Stone while attending a convention of the American Woman Suffrage Association that year.

In 1886, Leo Chapman sold the Mason City *Republican* and traveled to San Francisco to buy another newspaper. He contracted typhoid fever, and Carrie started for the West Coast to be with him. However, he died before she reached California. Carrie worked a year for a newspaper in San Francisco before returning to Charles City, Iowa, where she earned a living on the lecture circuit. In 1887, she joined the Iowa Woman Suffrage Association and became its unsalaried state organizer with only her expenses paid.

In 1890, Carrie, as a member of the Iowa Woman Suffrage Association, attended the first convention of the combined National and American Woman Suffrage Associations. She heard Elizabeth Cady Stanton speak as the president of the new organization, the National American Woman Suffrage Association. Carrie addressed the Convention and began to acquire a reputation as a gifted speaker.

In the summer of 1899, Carrie participated in a women's suffrage campaign in South Dakota, where she was appalled by the campaign's lack of organization. She wrote to South Dakota's campaign headquarters:

> With the exception of the work of a few women, nothing is being done. We have opposed to us the most powerful political elements in the State. Continuing as we are, we cannot poll 20,000 votes. We are converting women who "want to vote" by the hundreds, but we are having no appreciable effect on the men.

Of course, only men could vote. The results were 22,000 votes for women's suffrage and 45,000 votes against. Carrie defined the requirements for winning a referendum:

- endorsement by the large citizens' organizations
- endorsement by the two major political parties
- possession of a sufficiently large campaign fund

She vowed that she would never again participate in an effort doomed to failure because of lack of planning and adequate preparation.

On June 10, 1890, in Seattle, Carrie married George W. Catt, a structural engineer who became president of his own construction company. George Catt was a college acquaintance whom she had encountered in San Francisco. He was an advocate of women's rights, and, before they were married, he signed a legal agreement that Chapman Catt would have two months in the spring and two months in the fall each year to devote to suffrage work. He encouraged her to do the reforming for both of them while he earned a living to support them. They had no children.

In 1892, the Catts moved to New York City. That summer, Chapman Catt returned to Iowa to organize a Missouri Valley women's suffrage conference in Des Moines. Susan B. Anthony was impressed with the results of her efforts, and she was appointed finance chair of the National American Woman Suffrage Association.

In 1895, Chapman Catt suggested that the National American Woman Suffrage Association establish an organization committee to direct its work in the field. As chair of the committee, she operated as the executive secretary forming new branches, raising money, and dispatching organizers to the field organizations. She became known for careful planning, attention to detail, constantly searching for better ways of doing things, and organizational efficiency.

Chapman Catt was an attractive woman with a firm chin, a magnetic personality, a commanding stage presence, and an element of brashness that served her well. She delivered her well-conceived and logical speeches with a pleasant voice and clear enunciation. Because of her strong personal characteristics, she advanced to increasingly responsible positions within the Women's Rights Movement.

In February 1900, when Susan B. Anthony retired as president of the National American Woman Suffrage Association, Carrie Chapman Catt was elected to take her place. In her first speech as president, Chapman Catt said:

> The papers have spoken of the new president
> as Miss Anthony's successor. Miss Anthony
> will never have a successor. A president cho-

sen from the younger workers is on a level with the association.... The cause has gotten beyond where one woman can do the whole. I shall not be its leader as Miss Anthony has been; I can only be an officer of this association. I will do all I can, but I cannot do it without the cooperation of all of you.

Chapman Catt built up the national organization, expanded the treasury, and provided a foundation of sorely needed administrative procedures. However, in 1904, due to her husband's poor health, she announced that she would not stand for re-election.

In 1905, Chapman Catt was asked to direct a campaign in Oregon, but she declined: "All I have done for the suffrage cause during the last fifteen years, I have been able to do by my husband's generosity.... I would dearly love to undertake the work in Oregon, but my husband needs me now, and is going to need me more and more, and I will not leave him." George Catt died soon afterward at the age of forty-five, leaving Chapman Catt financially independent and able to focus her life on reform causes.

After her husband's death, Chapman Catt restricted her suffrage activities to New York City and New York State as well as the international movement. In 1909, she consolidated the splintered New York City groups into an Interurban Suffrage Council, which evolved in the following year into the Woman Suffrage Party. Also, she built up the International Woman Suffrage Alliance's membership from eight branches to twenty-five branches. In 1910-11, she traveled across Europe on behalf of the international Women's Suffrage Movement and met many notables.

In 1913-14, Chapman Catt chaired the Empire State Campaign Committee and led the effort to pass a State suffrage referendum. She resigned from the presidency of the International Woman Suffrage Alliance in 1915 to lead the

New York State campaign. The campaign failed but garnered forty-two percent of the vote. The New York *World* observed that this was "a revelation of the astonishing growth of the movement." The results of this campaign effort drew attention to her political skill.

In 1915, Chapman Catt was re-elected president of the National American Woman Suffrage Association, replacing Anna Shaw, who had led the Association for eleven years. Chapman Catt inherited a divided organization that was not clearly focused.

One division had begun in 1912, when Alice Paul had formed within the Association a Congressional Committee that two years later became an independent organization, the Congressional Union. In 1916, the Congressional Union became the Woman's Party. The new organization emphasized a federal suffrage amendment, an effort that had been neglected by the National American Woman Suffrage Association for years. Alice Paul and her organization blamed the incumbent Democratic Party for the failure to pass an amendment granting the vote to women.

Chapman Catt's efforts as the newly elected president of the National American Woman Suffrage Association were aided by a legacy of almost a million dollars from the estate of Mrs. Frank Leslie, widow of the publisher of *Leslie's Weekly*. Chapman Catt was directed to use the money "as she shall think most advisable to the furtherance of the cause of woman suffrage, to which she has so worthily devoted so many years of her life."

Chapman Catt placed the Association on a path that supported the passage of a federal amendment and simultaneously continued to push for obtaining the right to elective franchise for women in the states. The Association's efforts in the states took three different paths: via the amendment of state constitutions by referenda, by the vote of state legislatures in conferring suffrage, and by obtaining the right to vote in primaries.

With the United States entry into World War I, Chapman Catt directed the Association to push both the war effort and the women's suffrage cause. In Great Britain, the Women's Rights Movement had been set aside until the end of the war. Chapman Catt did not want to see that happen in the United States, since it would merely delay women's victory. Although some questioned her patriotism, she stayed with a decision that she believed was right. She served on the Women's Committee of the Defense Council while actively striving to achieve the Association's goals.

In January 1918, President Wilson made a commitment to the passage of a women's suffrage amendment. The evolution of his stance on this issue was based on his respect for the good judgment, stewardship, and tact of Carrie Chapman Catt and his appreciation of the series of state suffrage victories through 1917. The bill for the Amendment to the U.S. Constitution granting women the right to vote passed the House of Representatives on January 10, 1918, and the Senate on June 4, 1919.

The Nineteenth Amendment, the "Susan B. Anthony Amendment" was adopted on August 26, 1920, over seventy-two years after the first Women's Rights Convention in Seneca Falls. Its passage was the capstone to the life's work of Carrie Chapman Catt and of many other capable women.

Chapman Catt placed great demands on others, but she placed the greatest demands on herself. She was known for her leadership qualities, and she was widely loved despite her aloof personality. American women owe their right to vote to Carrie Chapman Catt, more than to any individual other than Susan B. Anthony, who devoted over fifty-five years of her life to the cause.

In 1920, Chapman Catt presented to the National American Woman Suffrage Association the idea of an organization that would become the League of Woman Voters. She proposed a nonpartisan political organization to educate women on how to use their newly gained rights. She envisioned a league that worked for child labor reform, for protective legislation for working women, and for the reduction and elimination of political corruption. The first president of the League of Woman Voters was Maud Wood Peck, who later wrote a biography of Carrie Chapman Catt.

After the passage of the Nineteenth Amendment, Chapman Catt continued with her international suffrage work, particularly with the International Woman Suffrage Alliance, which became the International Alliance of Women. She was also a strong supporter of the peace movement, including the effort to establish a League of Nations and later the effort to found the United Nations.

Chapman Catt and Nettie R. Shuler wrote *Woman Suffrage and Politics: The Inner Story of the Suffrage Movement.* Chapman Catt received honorary degrees from the University of Wyoming, Iowa State University, Smith College, and the Moravian College for Women. She received a citation of honor from President Roosevelt in 1936 and was awarded the gold medal of the National Institute of Social Sciences in 1940.

On March 9, 1947, Carrie Chapman Catt died of a heart attack at the age of eighty-eight in New Rochelle, New York. She was able to place winning the right to vote for women in perspective. She said: "Winning the vote is only an opening wedge. To learn how to use it is a bigger task."

MATILDA JOSLYN GAGE

"We demand political equality, for that lies at the base of all other kinds of equality; we demand political rights, that we may be able to protect all other rights."

Matilda Joslyn Gage

Matilda Joslyn Gage, who was born in 1826, was active in both the antislavery movement and the Women's Rights Movement. She was the daughter of a physician from the

Syracuse area and the wife of Henry Hill Gage, a wealthy Fayetteville, New York, dry goods merchant. Gage first attracted the attention of the leaders of the Women's Rights Movement when she asked permission to speak at the National Women's Rights Convention in Syracuse in 1852. Her forceful personality and gifts as a writer allowed her to make a significant contribution to the Movement.

The activist, who lived at 210 East Genesee Street in Fayetteville, was elected to the executive committee of the National Woman Suffrage Association upon its founding on May 11, 1869. Elizabeth Cady Stanton was elected president and Susan B. Anthony headed the executive committee. Later, Matilda Gage was elected vice president of the National Association.

The mother of four children, Matilda Gage was a strong-willed individual, and everyone knew her opinions on women's rights. She once wrote: "Women, if you will not be crushed, arise and fight your own battles. Man, your so-called protector, is your worst foe. Experience shows you cannot trust father, nor husband, nor brother, nor son ... " She was prominent in the Women's Rights Movement, but she spoke too softly to be an effective speaker. However, she was an effective organizer and writer.

Elizabeth Cady Stanton's mentor in the Women's Rights Movement, Lucretia Mott, urged Gage to write a history of the Movement. In 1876, Gage joined in a collaboration with Anthony and Cady Stanton "for the purpose of preparing and editing a history of the Woman Suffrage Movement." Gage's and Cady Stanton's tasks were to "write, collect, and arrange material," Anthony's responsibility was to "secure publication."

In November 1880, they began writing the history at Stanton's home in Tenafly, New Jersey. The first volume of *The History of Woman Suffrage* was published in May 1881; the second volume followed in May 1882. Gage's work on the third volume of the history was cut short in 1884, when her husband died. Ida Husted Harper, Susan B. Anthony's biographer, edited three later volumes of the work.

Matilda Joslyn Gage attempted unsuccessfully to vote in 1872. She was the first woman to vote in the school board elections in Fayetteville in 1880, forty years before women were granted the right to vote in national elections. This breakthrough came when women property owners convinced a majority of the New York State Legislature that they should have a voice in the activities of the school districts in which they paid taxes.

In 1881, Matilda Joslyn Gage wrote *Preceding Causes*, in which she placed the nineteenth-century Women's Rights Movement within the frame of reference of Western civilization. She contended that the two obstacles to human rights were the Church and the State. In Gage's view, women were the victim of the Church's stifling of free inquiry and the State's maintenance of artificial order through civil decree. She wrote that the pathway to progress in women's rights was by rational thinking and individual self-sufficiency.

In this book, Gage cited examples of "great women," who excelled in "free thinking, education, or professional work and those women who inaugurated the drive for progressive reform." Her examples included George Sand, Charlotte Brontë, George Eliot, and Harriet Beecher Stowe in literature; Elizabeth Barrett Browning in poetry; Dorothea Dix in prison reform; and Florence Nightingale and Clara Barton in nursing.

Gage left the National Woman Suffrage Association in 1890 and formed a more progressive organization, the Woman's National Liberal Union, which espoused broader platforms. In 1893, she wrote a book stating her view on women's rights entitled *Woman, Church and State*. Count Leo Tolstoy wrote her a letter praising the book and commenting that it proved that a woman could think logically. Poor health prevented her from becoming a nationally recognized figure in the Women's Rights Movement.

Gage's youngest daughter, Maud, married L. Frank Baum, the author of *The Wizard of Oz* and many other books. Maud had to overcome her mother's objections to marry the author. Gage died in 1898 while visiting the Baums. She wrote her own epitaph: "There is a word sweeter than mother, home, or heaven—that word is liberty."

LUCRETIA MOTT

"The question is often asked, 'What does woman want more than she enjoys?' I answer, she wants to be acknowledged a moral, responsible being. She is seeking not to be governed by laws, in the making of which she has no voice. She is deprived of almost every right in civil society, and is a cipher in the nation."

Lucretia Mott

Lucretia Coffin Mott was born to Thomas Coffin and Anna Folger Coffin on Nantucket on January 3, 1793. Three factors shaped her early life: being born into a Quaker family; growing up with the hardy, independent, and self-reliant people of Nantucket; and having a father who believed in educating his daughters. The Quakers gave women virtual equality with men, permitted them to speak at Quaker meetings, and allowed them to become ministers. Even as a young woman, Lucretia Mott was accustomed to speaking in public; she became a minister in her twenties. She was an accomplished speaker by the time she became active in the antislavery movement.

When Thomas Coffin, a whaler, was away on his sailing vessel, Anna Coffin ran their shop, kept the accounts, and made buying trips to Boston. Lucretia was used to seeing women in positions of responsibility on the Island. In 1804, the Coffin family moved to Boston; eventually, they moved to Philadelphia, the hub of Quaker life.

After completing elementary school at the age of thirteen,

Lucretia was sent to Nine Partners boarding school, an advanced Quaker academy near Poughkeepsie. The strong-willed Lucretia occasionally rebelled at the severity of the discipline. She could endure punishment for herself more easily than she could watch it inflicted on her classmates. The school building was divided into a "boys" side and a "girls" side, and boys and girls were not permitted to talk with one other. When a boy with whom she was friendly was confined to a closet on a diet of bread and water, Lucretia went to the boys' side of the school building to take additional food to him.

Lucretia received excellent grades at Nine Partners, and she taught at the school after she graduated. She met and fell in love with James Mott, who also taught there. Lucretia Coffin and James Mott were married on April 4, 1811 in Philadelphia, where James Mott had accepted a position in his father-in-law's mercantile business.

Lucretia and James had a strong, loving marriage. She said of their relationship: "Our independence is equal, our dependence mutual, and our obligations reciprocal." Later in life, Mott observed: "I owe the happiness of my own wedded life to the fact that my husband and I have always shared a deep interest in the sacred cause of wronged humanity."

Mott became a hard-working, nineteenth-century house-wife and eventually the mother of six children. She became known as an excellent hostess who was accustomed to entertaining large numbers of guests. She read widely, particularly history, philosophy, political economy, and theology. She also began to read about women's rights; Mary Wollstonecraft's *A Vindication of the Rights of Women* was a favorite book of hers.

Mott developed a keen memory and an analytical, independent intellect. As her children grew older and needed less direct attention, she became more active at Quaker meetings. In 1821, she was appointed a minister at the age of twenty-eight. In 1828, when the more liberal Hicksites split off from the Orthodox Friends, Lucretia and James Mott faced a very difficult decision. Ultimately, after much deliberation, they joined the Hicksites.

Mott believed strongly in "inward spiritual grace" and the following of an "inner light." She thought that there was a place for individual interpretation, not just following fixed creeds or rigid rituals. Her view of religion was based on justice and reason that expressed itself in "practical godliness;" that is, it must be lived rather than merely believed.

Occasionally, James Mott's business suffered a temporary reversal. On one such occasion, Lucretia Mott and a cousin established a school associated with the Quakers' Pine Street Meeting. The school was successful, and the income that she earned from the school helped the family get through its temporary financial difficulty. During this period of time, their son Thomas died of typhus, the same disease that had taken her father. Both parents had a difficult time recovering from the loss of their son at the age of two and a half.

The decade of the 1830s was a time of reform, and the Quaker community in and around Philadelphia was one of the earliest and most active in participating in the antislavery movement. The antislavery movement was one of the principal opportunities for practical godliness for the Motts. The Mott home on Arch Street became a station on the Underground Railroad, and the couple spent considerable time and effort helping escaped slaves. Mott stated clearly her view of the antislavery effort: "I endeavor to put my soul in [the slaves'] stead and to give all my power and aid in every right effort for their immediate emancipation. The duty was impressed upon me at the time I consecrated myself to the Gospel which anoints 'to preach deliverance to the captive, to set at liberty those that are bruised.'"

The Motts not only provided food, clothing, and shelter to fugitive slaves, but they also risked physical injury. On one occasion, a slave who was running away from his master sought refuge at the Motts' home. He ran into the house, through the parlor, and hid in the rear of the home. James Mott barred the door to the enraged master and "calmly stood at the door with a lighted lamp barring the way. He barely escaped death when the angry master threw a stone ... past his head and it crashed into the side of the door."

On another occasion, former slave Daniel Dangerfield, who had worked for years on a farm near Harrisburg, was brought to trial as a fugitive in Philadelphia. Mott rallied her friends in support of Dangerfield. In court, she sat directly behind the defendant. Edward Hopper, the Motts' son-in-law, who was the defense attorney for Dangerfield, called upon "witness after witness to testify Dangerfield's long residence in Pennsylvania." She spoke with the judge, a fellow Quaker, during the recess: "I earnestly hope that thy conscience will not allow thee to send this poor man into bondage."

After an all-night court session, Dangerfield was acquitted due to a technical error in the writ of accusation involving his height. Many of the people present at the trial credited Mott with having a major influence on the verdict. One of the men present observed: "She looked like an angel of light. As I looked at her, I felt that Christ was here."

On a third occasion, the Motts provided a refuge for Jane Johnson and her two sons. Jane, a slave belonging to John H. Wheeler, the U.S. Minister to Nicaragua, was attempting to take advantage of Pennsylvania's antislavery laws to gain freedom. William Still, a leader of the Underground Railroad, and Passmore Williamson, secretary of the Pennsylvania Anti-Slavery Society, helped her to escape from her master. Wheeler took legal action to obtain the return of his slaves.

An indictment was obtained against Williamson and his accomplices, who were accused of "conspired effort" to encourage Jane to run away. Mott accompanied Jane to the trial, attended all of the court sessions, and then took Jane to stay at the Mott home for several days. She convinced Jane to testify in her own behalf at the trial to show that she wanted to leave her master. Jane's testimony was a key factor in obtaining her release from bondage.

Williamson's accomplices were found by the jury to be not guilty of kidnapping and rioting charges, but they spent a week in jail for assault and battery because they had to pull Jane away from Wheeler, her master. Passmore spent three months in jail for contempt of court because he had told the court that he did not know where Jane was. Jane and her sons stayed several more days with the Motts and then were guided successfully via the Underground Railroad to Canada and freedom.

In December 1833, the American Anti-Slavery Society was formed in Philadelphia. Mott was one of four women invited to attend their first convention, but the women were not permitted to join the new organization. They formed the Women's Anti-Slavery Association, and Mott was elected president. When a Pennsylvania branch of the national society was established, James Mott was a charter member. Again, his wife was not invited to join, but two years later the rules were changed to allow women members. She became an active, influential member.

Lucretia Mott was a firm supporter of Angelina and Sarah Grimké in their early efforts to speak in public to mixed audiences of men and women. She provided them with advice and encouragement when they were being harassed for attempting to speak in public. Sex discrimination had existed from the beginning of the antislavery movement, but the prejudice against the Grimkés was more than she could bear. From this point onward, she was driven by the "women question." It became "the most important question of my life."

When Mott accompanied her husband to London to the World Anti-Slavery Convention in 1840, she was prepared as a woman delegate to be rejected. When she was rejected, being prepared didn't make it any less painful. Lucretia forced the issue of women's participation to the floor of the Convention and out of the secrecy the executive committee. However, she lost her proposal to let women be active members of the Convention. Mott had first met the young Elizabeth Cady Stanton at the World Anti-Slavery Convention when the two women were relegated to the gallery with the other women merely to observe the activities of the Convention.

Instead of sitting quietly in the gallery, Mott and Cady Stanton toured London while discussing "the propriety of holding a womans' convention." Despite the twenty-two-year difference in their ages, the two women had much in common. Cady Stanton looked up to Mott, who was more widely read and was more used to active participation in organizations and to public speaking. Mott became Cady Stanton's mentor. They agreed to have a meeting to address women's issues when they returned to the United States. They didn't realize it at the time, but that meeting would not take place for another eight years.

Elizabeth and Henry Stanton stayed in England and Europe for an extended visit, and when they returned home Henry was busy studying law and Elizabeth was occupied raising their young children. Only after the Stantons moved to Seneca Falls after living in Boston did the planning for the meeting occur. It was facilitated by Lucretia Motts' attendance at a Quaker convention in the area and visiting friends and relatives in nearby Auburn.

Mott and Cady Stanton met at the home of Jane and Richard Hunt in Waterloo. Also present were Mott's sister, Martha Wright, and Mary Ann M'Clintock, a Quaker abolitionist from Waterloo. At this planning meeting for the Convention, the five women discussed their frustration with the limited rights of women and the discrimination they had experienced in the abolition and temperance movements. Cady Stanton was particularly vocal. All five women had attended antislavery and temperance conventions, but Lucretia was the only one with experience as a delegate, orator, and organizer.

The group prepared a notice about the first Women's

Rights Convention to be held on July 19 and 20, 1848, in the Wesleyan Chapel in Seneca Falls. They then agreed to reconvene at the home of Mary Ann and Thomas M'Clintock in Waterloo on July 16 to prepare an agenda for the Convention. At the second meeting, Elizabeth Cady Stanton was the principal author of the *Declaration of Sentiments* modeled on the *Declaration of Independence*. The major difference of opinion among the five women was whether or not to include women's right to vote in the *Declaration of Sentiments*. Cady Stanton prevailed, and it was included.

James Mott called the Convention to order. Lucretia Mott then stated the goals of the Convention and discussed the importance of educating women and of improving the standing of women in society. *The Declaration of Sentiments* was discussed and adopted with minor changes. The resolution about the right of women to vote was the only one that was not adopted unanimously. Some of the attendees were concerned that pushing the elective franchise might reduce the probability of achieving other goals. However, the resolution received enough support to be kept in the document.

Lucretia Mott also spoke at the second Women's Rights Convention two weeks later in Rochester. This was a more intellectual audience, and several conservative clergymen quoted St. Paul on the duty of women to obey their husbands: "Man shall be the head of woman." Mott replied in her eloquent speech, "Many of the opposers of Women's Rights who bid us to obey the bachelor St. Paul, themselves reject his counsel—he advised them not to marry." These clergymen learned to respect Mott's knowledge of the Scriptures.

In 1849, Mott prepared a speech entitled "Discourse on Woman," in which she rebutted many of the male speakers objections to the Women's Rights Movement. She wrote: "Let women then go on—not asking favors, but claiming as a right the removal of all hindrances to her elevation in the scale of being—let her receive encouragement for the proper cultivation of her powers, so that she may enter profitably into the active business of life."

In 1850, Lucretia Mott convinced Quaker businessman William Mullen and his wife to help her raise funds to found the Female College of Pennsylvania in Philadelphia. Lucretia and James Mott were the principal sponsors of the Philadelphia School of Design for Women (now the Moore College of Art). Also, the Motts helped Pennsylvania's first female attorney to gain admission to the Commonwealth of Pennsylvania bar exams. Lucretia Mott believed in doing things, accomplishing things, not just talking about them.

In the fall of 1850, Mott met women's rights leader Lucy Stone at the First National Women's Rights Convention in Worcester, Massachusetts. The two women became close friends and frequent correspondents. By the end of the following year, Lucy Stone had decided to devote her energies to the Women's Rights Movement and not to split her efforts between that activity and the abolitionist movement.

Over her own objections, Mott presided over the National Women's Rights Conventions in 1852 in Syracuse and in 1853 in New York City. The Syracuse Convention proved to be "a stormy and taxing" event at which many verbal attacks were made on Lucretia. Again, her critics at the meeting quoted liberally from the *Bible*. Mott and Antoinette Brown, an ordained minister, countered these critics. Most reviews in the newspapers referred to the Convention leaders' "firm and efficient control of the meetings."

The New York City Convention was also a rowdy one. In fact, a mob broke up the Convention on the evening of September 6. The women retained their composure, and Mott congratulated them for their "self-reliance" at the meeting on the following morning. Attendee Margaret Hope Bacon observed about Mott that "no one else had the poise and authority to keep order nor the leadership to carry the frightened women through such ordeals."

More rowdies entered the convention hall during the day, interrupted the meetings, and became so unruly that in the evening the meeting was adjourned early. At the time of adjournment, "the hall exploded in confusion." Mott observed that some of the women were afraid to leave the hall, so she asked her escort to take them out to the street. Her escort asked how she would get out of the building. She reached for the arm of the nearest troublemaker and said: "This man will see me through." He was surprised, but he saw her safely through the exit door.

In May 1866, the American Equal Rights Association was formed in New York to push for the rights of all citizens without regard for age, class, gender, or race. Mott was elected president. She said that she "would be happy to give her name and influence if she could encourage the young and strong to carry on the good work."

James Mott died on January 26, 1868. Lucretia and James had been so close and so compatible that she was "numbed" by his passing. She told a friend, "Scarcely a day passes that I do not think, of course for the instant only, that I will consult him about this or that." She continued to be active and in 1870 was elected president of the Pennsylvania Peace Society.

On April 14, 1875, Mott was the honored guest at the centennial celebration of the Pennsylvania Abolition Society. Henry Wilson, Vice President of the United States presented her to gathering: "I ... present to you one of the most venerable and noble of American women, whose voice for forty years has been heard and tenderly touched many noble hearts. Age has dimmed her eye and weakened her voice, but her heart, like the heart of a wise man and wise woman, is yet young."

In 1878, Mott attended the thirtieth anniversary celebration of the first Women's Rights Convention in Seneca Falls. She spoke at the celebration; her speech included the observation: "Give women the privilege of cooperating in making the laws, and there will be harmony without severity, justice without oppression." Frederick Douglass and Belva

Lockwood both spoke to the Convention on the topics of equal pay for equal work, improved educational opportunities for women, and women's suffrage. Belva Lockwood was the first woman lawyer admitted to practice before the U.S. Supreme Court and the first woman candidate for President of the U.S. who received electoral votes.

On November 11, 1880, Lucretia Coffin Mott died in her sleep. Several thousand mourners attended her burial at Pairhill Cemetery. A member of the Peace Society made some brief comments on her life and a silence fell over the mourners. Someone asked, "Will no one speak?" Another replied, "Who can speak? The preacher is dead!"

Lucretia Mott's portrait hangs in the National Gallery in Washington, D.C. Adelaide Johnson's sculpture of Lucretia Mott, Susan B. Anthony, and Elizabeth Cady Stanton stands in the U.S. Capitol. In *Century of Struggle*, Eleanor Flexner described the relationship of Lucretia Mott to the other principal leaders of the Women's Rights Movement: "Lucy Stone was its most gifted orator ... Mrs. Stanton was its outstanding philosopher ... Susan Anthony was its incomparable organizer ... Lucretia Mott typified the moral force of the movement." Lucretia Mott was the senior stateswoman of the Women's Rights Movement and the mentor of its younger members.

ALICE PAUL

"She [Alice Paul] has in the first place a devotion to the cause which is absolutely self-sacrificing. She has an indomitable will. She recognizes no obstacles. She has a clear, penetrating, analytic mind which cleaves straight to the heart of things. In examining a situation, she always bares the main fact; she sees all the forces which make for change in that situation. She is a genius for organization, both in the mass and in the detail. She understands perfectly, in achieving the big object, the cumulative effect of multitudes of small

actions and small services. She makes use of all material, whether human or otherwise, that comes along.... Her inventiveness and resourcefulness are endless."

Maud Younger, suffragist

Alice Paul was born in Moorestown, New Jersey, in 1885 to upper-middle-class Quaker parents. Her father was a successful Hicksite farmer and banker. She attended the Friends' elementary and high school in Moorestown and then enrolled in Swarthmore College, which her grandparents had helped to found. She had read English literature and history widely, so she chose to major in biology, a subject about which she knew little.

In her senior year at Swarthmore, Paul's interest shifted to economics and political science. Upon graduation, she was awarded a one-year graduate scholarship at the School of Philanthropy in New York, which later became part of Columbia University. Her fellowship involved work in the College Settlement, which was her first exposure to a heterogeneous group of people. In fact, 1905-6 was a peak of immigration to the United States, and the lower East Side at that time was truly a melting pot.

Paul received a degree in social work and completed a number of assignments in the field, which was one of the few fields other than nursing and teaching that were open to women at the time. The following year, she received a master's degree at the University of Pennsylvania with a major in sociology and a double minor in economics and political science.

In 1907, Paul went to England to study on a fellowship at the Quakers' Woodbrooke Institute. She enrolled in Woodbrooke's combined program of courses at the University of Birmingham, which was principally study in economics and social work. Her fellowship included work at the Summer Lane Settlement. Her lifelong career decision was made, or was thrust upon her, while she was a student at the University of Birmingham.

Paul attended a public meeting sponsored by the head of the University, Sir Oliver Lodge. She described the experience:

> So I went to this public meeting—after school hours, you see. It was Christabel Pankhurst. I don't know that I had ever heard her name before.... She was [militant suffrage leader] Mrs. Pankhurst's daughter.... She was a very young girl and a young lawyer.... Quite an entrancing and delightful person, really very beautiful I thought. So she started to speak. And the students started to yell and shout, and I don't believe anybody heard one single word that Christabel said. So she kept on anyway for her whole speech. She was completely shouted down.

So I just became from that moment very anxious to help in this movement.... I thought, "That's one group now that I want to throw in all the strength I can give to help."

When Paul finished her year at the Woodbrooke Institute, she enrolled at the London School of Economics. She joined the Women's Social and Political Union, did some administrative work for the Pankhursts, and marched in a large suffrage parade through London.

Paul learned how to speak in public, usually on street corners, and how to sell the idea of "votes for women." She also learned how to use the cry "votes for women" to disrupt the speeches of the British political leaders. She was sent to prison three times, where she engaged in a hunger strike and was forcibly fed. She soon became an assistant to Mrs. Pankhurst.

At the London School of Economics, Paul's own social thinking was evolving. She was influenced by Professor

Westermark, a Dutch anthropologist, who wrote the classic book, *The History of Human Marriage*. She concluded that there were certain female traits that were evident in all cultures that distinguished women's personality characteristics and motivations from those of men.

In 1910, Paul rejected a paid position with Mrs. Pankhurst and returned to the United States, where she worked with the Philadelphia suffrage organization. She enrolled in graduate school at the University of Pennsylvania, and, in June 1912, received a Ph.D. degree. Her interests were widening into the field of law, and her doctoral dissertation was "The Legal Position of Women in Pennsylvania."

Later that year, Paul worked with Jane Addams and chaired the Congressional Committee of the National American Woman Suffrage Association (NAWSA). NAWSA's emphasis had been to get suffrage referenda passed in all forty-eight states. Paul's role was to push for a women's suffrage amendment to the Constitution. These were difficult times for the suffrage movement. Referenda had failed to pass in several states, which wasn't surprising because only men could vote.

Paul organized a large suffrage parade whose boisterous crowds caused disorder in the nation's capital. The cavalry was called out to control the rowdy counter-demonstrators. She then mobilized the vote of women in the western states, who had already been granted the right to vote, to hold Woodrow Wilson and the Democrats—the party in power— responsible for their failure to obtain the elective franchise for women.

Paul established a new organization, the Congressional Union, to push for a women's suffrage amendment. NAWSA would not allow it to be an auxiliary of their organization; so she split her organization off from NAWSA. The Congressional Union evolved into the National Woman's Party. In 1917, Paul organized women picketers who carried bright purple, white, and gold anti-Wilson banners outside the grounds of the White House. When mobs attacked the suffragists, the police arrested the women. In prison, Paul and the other suffragists went on hunger strikes and were forcibly fed.

Paul was allowed no visitors in prison, not even her lawyer. Also, she was not permitted to receive mail. Prison psychiatrists interviewed her several times. They asked her questions about her feelings toward President Wilson, and, in particular, if she considered him to be her enemy. They told her that one signature on an admission form was all that was required to commit her to an insane asylum.

Visits from the head physician of the District of Columbia jail were particularly threatening to Paul. She admitted that "I believe I have never in my life before feared anything or any human being. But I confess I was afraid of Dr. Gannon, the jail physician. I dreaded the hour of his visit. [He said:] 'I will show you who rules this place. You think you do. But I will show you that you are wrong.'"

Upon her release from jail, Paul, with the help of a capable staff, directed the fund-raising, lobbying, and publicity efforts of her growing organization. She was good at fund-raising; Mrs. Alva Vanderbilt Belmont was a major contributor. President Wilson's government felt the increasing pressure of their activity. The work of the National Woman's Party was called "militant," but Paul considered them "nonviolent." She counseled her picketers to dress well and not to indulge in conduct unbecoming a lady, such as screaming. Their efforts were probably viewed by the courts as civil disobedience because their picketing was considered to be "obstructing traffic."

Paul focused her organization on women's right to vote. She believed in wider social reform, but, in order to concentrate her effort on obtaining the elective franchise for women, she did not work toward other reform objectives, such as child labor laws, equal pay for equal work for women, or welfare. Although she hoped for the end of World War I, she was not distracted by the peace movement. From 1916 to 1920, NAWSA, the organization from which she had broken off, also pushed forcefully for a women's suffrage amendment.

In August 1920, American women received the right to vote. Paul and her staff were exhausted. However, she continued to work to pay off the debts of the National Woman's Party. She also strived to get discriminating laws replaced in several states. She earned three degrees in jurisprudence by attending classes early in the morning and in the evening.

Paul began to work toward an Equal Rights Amendment, which was submitted to Congress for the first time in 1923. She worked with women attorneys to document the laws affecting the family and women in all states to show the need for a federal Equal Rights Amendment. Not all reformers were in favor of an amendment, partly because of its potential impact on protective labor legislation. They feared hard-fought legislation for women such as maximum hours, minimum wage, restrictions on hours of work at night, and on the weight workers could be required to lift might be lost or reduced.

In the 1920s, Paul and the National Woman's Party pushed to expand the concept of equal rights beyond the United States. In Paris, Mrs. Alva Vanderbilt Belmont corresponded with forty-five feminists in twenty-six countries to form an International Advisory Council of the National Woman's Party.

The international effort's first setback occurred in 1925 when the International Woman Suffrage Alliance, which had been formed by Susan B. Anthony, failed to support them. The National Woman's Party's association with the International Woman Suffrage Alliance was terminated when Carrie Chapman Catt, who was very active in the international women's movement, threatened to pull out of the International Alliance if the advances made in protective labor legislation were threatened by the equal rights activity of the National Woman's Party.

In 1926, the National Woman's Party joined the Open Door Council, a equal rights rights group based in England. Two years later the Party attended the Sixth Pan-American Conference in Havana, at which the Inter-American Commission of Women was established. Paul was appointed to head a committee to prepare a survey of all member nations' laws for nationality requirements. The comprehensive document was called "Alice Paul's Golden Book" by James Brown Scott, an authority on international law.

In 1928, the National Woman's Party participated in a meeting of the Open Door Council in Berlin at which the "Charter of Economic Rights for Working Women" was prepared. The Open Door Council established an Open Door International Office in Geneva to track the activities of the League of Nations and the International Labor Office.

In the 1930s, the International Advisory Committee of the National Woman's Party worked for equal rights in a number of ways, including:

- Working with the Inter-American Commission of Women to submit an Equal Rights Treaty to the Pan-American Conference in 1933, at which the Equal Nationality Treaty was signed and submitted to the Assembly of the League of Nations. Paul led the effort to fight opposition to these treaties that proposed discrimination against women.
- Encouraging League of Nations delegates to sponsor equal nationality rights and equal rights treaties
- Opposing discriminatory resolutions, including no work at night for women, at the International Labor Office in Geneva
- Establishing Equal Rights International to push for an Equal Rights Treaty
- Working with the Women's Consultative Committee on Nationality in the League of Nations to study the national laws' discriminatory impact on women

In 1938, Paul was a driving force in establishing the World Women's Party, which was modeled on the National Woman's Party, to concentrate on equal rights in international rights and treaties. The headquarters, near the League of Nations and the International Red Cross in Geneva, became a refuge for women and their families fleeing the battlefields after World War II began in Europe in 1939. She shifted her efforts to the resettling of the refugees.

After World War II, Paul continued to push for the passage of the Equal Rights Amendment. She ensured that it was introduced in each session of congress until 1972, when it passed from Congress to the states for ratification. Alice Paul died in 1977. That year ratification was three states short of passage. In 1982, another bill using Paul's words was submitted to Congress to continue the effort.

Alice Paul's contributions to the Women's Rights Movement will always be remembered, particularly her work in the trenches leading up to the passage of the Nineteenth Amendment in 1920 that granted women the right to vote. She was the one who organized the picketing and the suffrage parades in Washington, D.C., and who kept the pressure on President Wilson and his administration to support women's suffrage.

Alice Paul was one of the women who because of her firm convictions was sent to jail, where she went on a hunger strike and was forcibly fed—just as she had been in England years previously. Like Susan B. Anthony, Paul never married but devoted her entire career to the Women's Rights Movement.

ANNA SHAW

"There are two things in life which makes its struggle, its pain, its losses, its joys and its victories worthwhile. They are, first, to be so possessed by a fundamental principle of right that it becomes a consuming fire. The other is to have a heart filled with a great love of humanity. Possessed by these two

passions, no struggle can become too severe, no waiting too wearisome, no life useless. In the midst of a multitude or alone with God, at home or abroad, with friends or enemies, life is worthwhile."

Anna Howard Shaw

Anna Howard Shaw, the sixth of seven surviving children of Thomas Shaw and Nicolas Stott Shaw, was born in Newcastle-on-Tyne, England, on February 14, 1847. Thomas Shaw immigrated to the United States when Anna was three years old; the family followed him in 1851. They settled in Lawrence, Massachusetts, where Thomas was active in reform movements, including the antislavery movement. Their home was a station on the Underground Railroad.

In 1859, Thomas Shaw bought 360 acres of wilderness near what became Big Rapids, Michigan. He made a clearing in the woods and built a crude log cabin with a dirt floor and no windows. Anna Shaw, who was twelve at the time, and her younger brother, Henry, cut wood, hauled water, and plowed the land. When her father and her older brothers left to fight in the Civil War, life "degenerated into a treadmill" for Shaw. She decided that she wanted to "to talk to people, to tell them things," and she practiced by preaching sermons in the woods. She provides a lively account of her wilderness experience in her 1915 autobiography, *The Story of a Pioneer*.

Shaw became an voracious reader, and, at the age of thirteen, resumed her formal schooling in a frontier schoolhouse. Two years later, she taught school for two dollars a week and board. After the Civil War, she lived with a married sister and attended high school in Big Rapids. After hearing a woman Universalist minister's sermon, Shaw told the minister of her own desire to preach. Rev. Marianna Thompson encouraged her to continue with her education.

Shaw's high school principal, Lucy Foot, introduced her to the presiding elder of the Methodist Church, which was encouraging women to become licensed ministers. In 1870, she preached her first sermon and then continued to preach in the other thirty-five towns in the district. In 1871, she was licensed as a Methodist preacher. Her family was unhappy with her for leaving the Unitarian church and for becoming a preacher. Her parents offered to pay her tuition at the University of Michigan if she would give up her vocation, but she declined their offer.

In 1873, Shaw entered Albion College in Albion, Michigan, where she supported herself by preaching and by giving lectures on temperance. After two and a half years, she decided that it was time to begin her education for the ministry. In February 1876, she enrolled in the Boston University Divinity School, a decision she later described as "an instance of stepping off a solid plank into space." She was the only woman in her class.

As a woman, Shaw was ineligible for the financial assistance received by the young men who were preparing for ordination. She lived in an attic room with no heat, no light except that coming through a skylight, and no water. She almost starved until she was helped by the Women's Foreign Mission Society. During summers, she earned a small income by substitute preaching on Cape Cod and by serving as a temporary pastor.

In 1878, Shaw graduated with a certificate and became the pastor of the Wesleyan Methodist church in East Dennis, Massachusetts. As a licensed but not an ordained minister, she could perform marriage ceremonies and funeral services, but she could not administer the sacraments or baptize new members of the church. She applied to the Methodist Episcopal church for ordination twice. She was turned down both times, so she applied to the Methodist Protestant church. On October 12, 1880, she was ordained despite considerable opposition.

While in East Dennis, Shaw not only conducted three services on Sunday, did all the necessary parish work, and lectured in Boston, but she also attended the Boston University Medical School. In 1886, she received an M.D. degree. She broadened her horizons in Boston and made many friends, including Louisa May Alcott, Ralph Waldo Emerson, Julia Ward Howe, Mary Livermore, Wendell Phillips, Lucy Stone, and John Greenleaf Whittier. She became interested in both the temperance and the women's rights movements.

Shaw began to realize that both medicine and the ministry were limited in their ability to deal with social problems, particularly the problems of women. In 1885, she became a lecturer for the Massachusetts Woman Suffrage Association, of which Lucy Stone was president. Shaw realized that there was "but one solution for women—the removal of the stigma of disfranchisement." She also served as superintendent of the franchise department of the national Women's Christian Temperance Union from 1886 until 1892.

In 1887, Shaw resigned from her position with the Massachusetts Woman Suffrage Association to pursue a career as a lecturer. On the lecture circuit, she earned a living and had a forum for her two causes, temperance and women's rights—particularly women's suffrage. She was in demand as a speaker and eventually became the premier speaker of the Women's Rights Movement, although Lucy Stone was also known as an excellent speaker.

In 1888, Shaw met Susan B. Anthony at the International Council of Women in Washington, D.C. Although Shaw knew Lucy Stone and the New England leaders of the American Woman Suffrage Association well, she didn't meet the leaders of the National Woman Suffrage Association, including Elizabeth Cady Stanton and Lucretia Mott, until later. Anna Shaw and Susan B. Anthony became close friends as they campaigned together, attended the same conventions, and testified before congressional committees together. Lucy Anthony, Susan B. Anthony's niece, served as Shaw's secretary for thirty years.

Shaw began to work with the National Woman Suffrage Association even before it joined with the American Woman Suffrage Association in 1890. In 1892, Anthony was elected president of the combined National American Woman Suffrage Association and Shaw became the vice president, a position that she held until 1904. Shaw hoped to succeed Anthony when she retired as president of the combined association, but Carrie Chapman Catt was elected to that office. Shaw served Chapman Catt loyally until Mrs. Catt resigned as president in 1904.

In 1904, Anna Shaw became the president of the National American Woman Suffrage Association, a post she held until 1915. Although Shaw was a good public speaker and had the energy for the task, she was not a good administrator. The job required a strong hand, but one that could be flexible with the various factions within the organization. She had difficulty working with others and was suspicious of the motives of those who disagreed with her. She made little effort to cultivate men to work with the Association when their votes were needed.

The Association was a vital, growing organization, but it seemed to lack strategic goals. In particular, the coordinated effort to push for the passage of a federal suffrage amendment seemed to take second priority to the local and state suffrage efforts. In 1914, Alice Paul and Lucy Burns formed the Congressional Union to focus active work on an amendment to the U.S. Constitution that granted women the right to vote. Anna Shaw tried to work with the Congressional Union's young, energetic leaders, but her attempts failed.

This failure and dissatisfaction within the National American Woman Suffrage Association were factors in Shaw's decision to step down as president of the Association at the annual convention in 1915. Carrie Chapman Catt, a strong manager with vision and good judgement, returned as president of the Association.

When the United States entered World War I, Shaw was asked to serve as chair of the Women's Committee of the U.S. Council of National Defense. She concentrated her energies on coordinating women's contributions to the war effort but continued to work part-time on the Women's Rights Movement. In May 1919, she was awarded the Distinguished Service Medal for her services during the war. After the war, she expected to resume work full-time on the women's suffrage effort.

Shaw was asked by ex-President William Howard Taft and president A. Lawrence Lowell of Harvard University to join them on a speaking tour, sponsored by the League to Support Peace, to marshal support for President Woodrow Wilson's League of Nations proposals. In June 1919, she became fatigued by overwork and developed pneumonia on the speaking tour in Springfield, Illinois. She returned to her home in Moylan, Pennsylvania, where she died a few weeks later at the age of seventy-two. However, she lived long enough to hear that the Women's Suffrage Amendment had passed both the U.S. Senate and the House of Representatives and would soon be ratified by the states.

ELIZABETH CADY STANTON

"I suffered with mental hunger, which, like an empty stomach, is very depressing. I had ... no stimulating companionship.... I now fully understood the practical difficulties most women had to contend with in the isolated household, and the impossibility of woman's development if in contact, the chief part of her life, with servants and children."

Elizabeth Cady Stanton

Elizabeth Cady Stanton was born on November 12, 1815, in Johnstown, New York, the fourth of six children of Daniel and Margaret Livingston Cady. Daniel Cady was a lawyer who served as a State Legislator, a U.S. Congressmen, and a judge of the New York Supreme Court. Elizabeth studied Greek, Latin, and mathematics at the Johnstown Academy and in 1832 graduated from Emma Willard's Female Academy in Troy.

Elizabeth first encountered activists when she met antislavery activists at Peterboro, New York, at the home of her cousin, Gerrit Smith, a political reformer and staunch abolitionist. Elizabeth met and fell in love with Henry Stanton, an agent of the American Anti-Slavery Society, on one of her visits to Peterboro. On May 1, 1840, they were married in Johnstown. Despite the resistance of the Presbyterian minister, the word "obey" was omitted from their marriage vows. Instead of being called Mrs. Henry Stanton (she didn't like being called Henry), she combined her family name and her married name. This was not common at the time; it became established practice beginning about 1841.

On their honeymoon, Elizabeth and Henry traveled to London, where they attended the World Anti-slavery Convention. In London, Elizabeth met Lucretia Mott and her husband, James, who were delegates to the Convention. A Quaker minister and a reformer active in both the abolitionist and feminist movements, Lucretia Mott made a strong impression on Elizabeth.

Mott was twenty-two years older than Cady Stanton and became her mentor and role model. She encouraged Cady Stanton to think independently about religion and individual rights: "When I first heard from her lips that I had the same right to think for myself that Luther, Calvin, and John Knox had, and the same right to be guided by my own convictions, I felt a newborn sense of dignity and freedom." Mott and Cady Stanton resolved to convene a women's rights convention as soon as they returned home from London. However, they didn't do so for another eight years.

Upon their return home, Henry Stanton read law with Judge Cady. When he completed his clerkship in 1842, he joined a Boston law firm. Cady Stanton found Boston to be a stimulating city. William Lloyd Garrison and many of the strong-willed abolitionists lived there. It was a home for liberal thinkers. The Stantons entertained frequently; their friends and guests included Ralph Waldo Emerson, Stephen Foster, Nathaniel Hawthorne, James Russell Lowell, and John Greenleaf Whittier. They were happy in Boston, but Henry developed a chronic lung congestion and needed a less humid climate.

In 1847, they moved to Seneca Falls, New York, where Henry resumed the practice of law. Cady Stanton had difficulty settling into the small town atmosphere of Seneca Falls after the stimulating social-political scene in Boston. The demands of her young, growing family weighed upon her. Henry was busy with his career and was frequently out of town on trips to Albany and Washington. Cady Stanton was glad to hear that Lucretia Mott planned to visit her sister in Auburn, just east of Seneca Falls, in July 1848.

On July 9, Cady Stanton met Lucretia Mott at the home of Jane and Richard Hunt in Waterloo. Mott's sister, Martha Wright, and Mary M'Clintock were also at the Hunts' home that day. Cady Stanton was pleased that these four ladies were eager to proceed with the Women's Rights Conference that she and Mott had discussed eight years previously. All but Cady Stanton were Garrison-type antislavery activists. Lucretia Mott was the only one who had experience as a delegate, orator, and organizer. However, they had all attended antislavery and temperance conventions. Cady Stanton remembered that she "poured ... out the torrent of my long accumulating discontent with such violence and indignation that I stirred myself, as well as the rest of the party, to do and dare anything."

The women agreed that it was time to address the conditions that confronted women in the United States; those conditions are difficult to envision today. In the mid-nineteenth century, women were not permitted to vote, to obtain a college education, or to own property, and their wages were turned over to their husbands. In cases of separation and divorce, guardianship of the children was automatically given to the husband. By law, a women's inheritance went to her husband. She was not entitled to the rights given automatically to men of the lowest station, whether they were born in the United States or were immigrants.

The five women called a convention on July 19-20 at the Wesleyan Methodist Chapel in Seneca Falls. A notice appeared in the Seneca County *Courier* announcing a "convention to discuss the social, civil, and religious condition and rights of women." Cady Stanton was the principal author of the *Declaration of Sentiments*, which was based on the *Declaration of Independence*, asserting that "all men and women are created equal." The *Declaration of Sentiments*, which was a declaration of women's rights, was the basis for the resolutions passed at the convention, including:

> Resolved, That all laws which prevent women from occupying such as station in society as her conscience shall dictate, or which place her in a position inferior to that of man, are contrary to the great precept of nature and therefore of no force or validity....

> Resolved, That woman is man's equal and was intended to be so by the Creator, and the highest good of the human race demands that she should be recognized as such....

> Resolved, That it is the duty of the women of this country to secure themselves their sacred right to the elective franchise....

The Convention was the starting point of the Women's Rights Movement in the United States. Most newspaper columnists ridiculed the Convention; however, some editors were sympathetic to the women's cause. Attendee Frederick Douglass, writing in the *North Star*, could see no reason to

deny women the right to vote because "right is of no sex."
The Convention marked the beginning of support for
women's rights from Horace Greeley of the New York
Tribune.

In March 1851, Cady Stanton met Susan B. Anthony while
walking home from an antislavery meeting in Seneca Falls.
Anthony never married and was less of an extrovert than Cady
Stanton. Anthony, with her singleness of purpose, became
totally dedicated to the Women's Rights Movement. Cady
Stanton's and Anthony's abilities complemented each other.
Cady Stanton was the policy formulator, effective writer, and
expressive speechmaker; Anthony's strengths were her
organizational ability, her campaigning skills, and her willingness to make campaign arrangements. In later years, Susan
B. Anthony's reputation as a women's rights leader superced-
ed that of Elizabeth Cady Stanton because Anthony outlived
Cady Stanton and left a strong organization in place that promoted her memory.

In 1854, Cady Stanton spoke to the New York State
Legislature about the need for changes to the Married
Women's Property Law. She reviewed some of the points in
the *Declaration of Sentiments*, discussed the lack of women's
right to vote and to hold office, and cited their inability to earn
wages and to inherit from their family. She argued that
women should be able to own property, to be guardians of
their own children, and to be eligible for higher education. In
1860, when the New York State Legislature passed a law
granting women the right to keep their wages and to be cus-
todians of their own children, she knew that she had contributed significantly to its passage.

In 1869, Cady Stanton and Anthony founded the National
Woman Suffrage Association. Anthony was elected secretary;
Cady Stanton was elected president, a position that she held
for twenty-one years. However, Cady Stanton's strong stands
on women's rights weren't for everyone. In late 1869, a group
of conservative suffragists formed a rival organization, the

American Woman Suffrage Organization. The new organization, comprised mainly of New Englanders, was led by Lucy Stone.

In November 1888, Cady Stanton attempted unsuccessfully to vote in Tenafly, New Jersey; Anthony had tried to vote in 1872 and had also failed. Cady Stanton convinced Senator Aaron Sargent that year to introduce a women's suffrage amendment to supplement the Fifteenth Amendment to the Constitution. It failed passage in 1888 and in every session of Congress until it was adopted in 1920, eighteen years after Cady Stanton's death.

In 1890, the two major women's suffrage organizations were rejoined. Cady Stanton was elected president, Anthony was elected vice president, and Lucy Stone became head of the executive committee of the combined National American Women Suffrage Association. Cady Stanton presided over the new organization for two years and then turned over the reins to Anthony.

Elizabeth Cady Stanton was a dynamic leader who, denied entrance to college because she was a woman, was, to a large extent, self-educated. She never gave up in her quest for the right of women to vote. On October 25, 1902, the day before she died, she wrote a plea to President Theodore Roosevelt for his support in obtaining women's right to vote. Ida Husted Harper, the author and editor, observed that Cady Stanton was the main philosopher, publicist, and politician for the Women's Rights Movement, and that "if the intellect of Elizabeth Cady Stanton had been possessed by a man, he would have had a seat on the Supreme Bench or the Senate of the United States, but our country has no rewards for great women."

LUCY STONE

"Woman will not always be a thing. I see it in the coming events whose shadows are cast before them, and in the steady

growth of those great principles which lie at the foundations of all our relations. I hear it in the inward march of freedom's host and feel it deep in my inner being. Yes, a new and glorious era is about to dawn upon us, an era in which woman taking her place on the same platform with her equal brothers, conscious of her rights, her responsibilities, her duties, will arouse, and apply her long slumbering energies for the redemption of this sin-ruined world. It will take a long time to effect that change; the evil is so deep rooted and universal, but it will come."

Lucy Stone

Lucy Stone, the third daughter of seven surviving children of Francis Stone and Hannah Matthews Stone, was born on August 13, 1818, in West Brookfield, Massachusetts. Francis Stone was a well-to-do farmer and tanner; although he sent his sons to college and could afford to send his daughters to school as well, he refused to pay for the girls' education. When Lucy told him that she wanted to attend college, he asked, "Is the child crazy?" Stone was alone among her peers in the early Woman's Rights Movement in not having a supportive father. Susan B. Anthony, Lucretia Mott, and Elizabeth Cady Stanton all had fathers who believed in education for women, within the limitations of the times.

At the age of sixteen, Stone began to teach district school and then studied at several area seminaries, including Mount Holyoke Female Seminary. In 1843, she enrolled at Oberlin College, which was the first coeducational college in the United States. Stone enrolled at Oberlin College specifically to learn public speaking skills to use in advocating women's rights and the abolition of slavery. She was a follower of William Lloyd Garrison, the New England abolitionist.

The women students at Oberlin discovered early that the College had no intention of training them as public speakers. They learned how to write, but they were "excused" from participation in discussions and debates. Oberlin President Asa

Mahan advocated that women should be taught how to speak as well as how to write, but he was always outvoted by the faculty. The policy was apparently based on the words of St. Paul: "Let a woman learn in silence with all submissiveness."

Stone worked in the kitchen of the women's dormitory and taught in Oberlin's preparatory school to earn living expenses. She also taught remedial courses to adult African Americans. In her third year, her father agreed to loan her the money to stay in college for two more years, if she would sign a note to pay it back.

Stone's opinions about women's rights were formed early. She had observed her mother's lack of self-esteem due to overwork and to being controlled by an autocratic husband. The daughters' legacy in their father's will was $200 each; the sons divided the balance of the family money and property.

As a teacher, Stone was paid half the salary of comparable male teachers. She was not allowed to vote in the Orthodox Congregational Church, even though she was a full member of the church. She built up an inner core of resistance to these inequities. Some women were browbeaten by it; Lucy added another layer to this inner core as each incident occurred.

Stone and Antoinette Brown, who would become the first woman minister in the United States, became close friends and confidants at Oberlin despite their differences of opinion. Stone was more radical than Brown on the subject of abolition. Oberlin was strongly antislavery—it was an active station on the Underground Railroad—but the college and community leaders belonged to the anti-Garrison branch of the movement.

Stone and Brown also had different views on religion. Stone became a Unitarian; she left the Congregational Church because they approved of slavery and opposed women speaking in public. In particular, they condemned the Grimké sisters for speaking to mixed audiences. Brown was disappointed that her friend, Stone, did not support her in her goal to become an ordained minister. However, they both wanted to

57

improve their speaking skills, so they secretly formed a female debating society.

One of Stone's reasons for wanting to become a public speaker was to fight "the principle which takes away from women their equal rights, and denies to them the privilege of being co-laborers with men in any sphere to which their ability makes them adequate." One of her first public speeches was given at a gathering of Oberlin's African Americans to celebrate the ending of slavery in the West Indies.

Stone graduated from Oberlin College with honors in 1847. She was the first woman from Massachusetts to receive a college degree. She refused to write a commencement address, because she was not permitted to present it. It was considered improper for women to participate in public exercises with men at the time; however, thirty-six years later, she was an honored speaker at Oberlin's semi-centennial jubilee.

William Lloyd Garrison attended the commencement exercises in 1847 and described Lucy Stone to his wife: "She is a very superior young woman, and has a soul as free as the air, and is prepared to go forth as a lecturer, particularly in vindication of the rights of women. Her course here has been very firm and independent, and she has caused no small uneasiness to the spirit of secularism in the institution."

In 1847, Stone gave her second speech, the first outside of Oberlin, from the pulpit of the church of her brother William Bowman Stone, who was a minister in Massachusetts. She spoke about women's rights. William and another brother, Frank, were the only members of her family who supported her speaking in public. Her sister, Sarah, told her that public lecturing by a woman was against divine law.

In the following year, Stone was hired by the Massachusetts Anti-Slavery Society as a public speaker. The job required endurance, since she was sent on extensive speaking tours throughout the Northeast over rutty roads using primitive carriages. Her advance posters were torn down, and she was heckled during her talks and jeered by both editors and ministers. One cold winter day, she was drenched when someone thrust a water hose through her carriage window.

Stone interwove the subject of women's rights into her antislavery speeches. The Anti-Slavery Society objected, but they didn't want to lose one of their most effective speakers. She told them, "I was a woman before I was an abolitionist. I must speak for the women." They compromised; she could speak about women's rights during the week if she gave antslavery speeches on the weekends. Before the Women's Rights Convention in Seneca Falls and before she had heard that others were interested in the Movement, she had already considered the pursuit of women's rights to be her major work.

Lucy Stone traveled widely lecturing on women's rights, making trips to Canada, the Midwest, and the South. She was called "the morning star of the Women's Rights Movement." Elizabeth Cady Stanton referred to her as "the first person by whom the heart of the American people was stirred by the woman question."

Later, Stone became one of the best speakers of the Women's Rights Movement. She had a beautiful voice, a sincere delivery, and an aura of authority and self-assurance. She usually spoke extemporaneously. However, she was somewhat dogmatic, intensely earnest, and at times her lack of a sense of humor worked against her.

In the spring of 1850, Stone attended an antislavery convention in Boston at which the attendees were asked if they had any interest in a women's rights convention. Nine women, including Abby Foster and Lucy Stone, met to do the initial planning for the First National Women's Rights Convention that was held in Worcester, Massachusetts, in October 1850.

Many distinguished people signed the call to this Convention, which was organized by Paulina Wright Davis. Signatories included Ralph Waldo Emerson, William Lloyd

Garrison, James and Lucretia Mott, Wendell Phillips, Gerrit Smith, and Elizabeth Cady Stanton. Paulina Davis, who was the editor of one of the first women's rights publications, *The Una,* was nominated as president of the Convention.

Attendees included Antoinette Brown, Abby Foster, Angelina Grimké, Lucretia Mott, Ernestine Rose, and Sojourner Truth. Elizabeth Cady Stanton was unable to attend due to the recent birth of a child, but she prepared a speech that was read. The Convention was Stone's introduction to the formal Women's Rights Movement and gave her the opportunity to meet many of the its policymakers. After making a moving speech that helped to attract Susan B. Anthony to the Movement, Stone left the Convention as one of the leaders of the Women's Rights Movement. She published the proceedings of the Convention at her own expense.

Stone had resolved never to marry, so that she could focus her energies on her two goals, the abolition of slavery and the achievement of women's rights. Her resolve lessened when she met Henry Blackwell, the brother of the pioneer doctor, Elizabeth Blackwell, at an abolitionist meeting. Henry fell in love with Lucy Stone and courted her for two years. When she met Henry's older brother, Samuel, she suggested that he visit her friend, Antoinette Brown, on one of his many business trips. Stone and Brown were to become sisters-in-law.

Henry persuaded Lucy Stone to marry him only after he convinced her that she could be free within their marriage and after he agreed to devote his life to the women's rights cause. They were married on May 1, 1855. Stone did not change her name to Blackwell; from this time onward, women who retained their maiden name after marrying were called "Lucy Stoners."

In 1857, Stone chaired the National Women's Rights Convention in New York. Lucy's and Henry's daughter, Alice Stone Blackwell, was born that year. A son born prematurely died shortly after his birth in 1859. Stone did much of the caring for their daughter herself and was less active in the

Women's Rights Movement during Alice's early years.

In 1858, she let her household goods be sold for taxes in protest against her lack of the vote. She used the incident, which gained the attention of those knowledgeable of the Women's Rights Movement, to write a protest against taxation without representation. In 1863, she supported the Women's Loyal National League. In 1866, she helped to form and served on the executive committee of the American Equal Rights Association and the following year was elected president of the New Jersey Woman Suffrage Association.

The break between the two factions of the Women's Rights Movement occurred in May 1869 at a meeting of the American Equal Rights Association. Susan B. Anthony, Elizabeth Cady Stanton, and the New York faction wanted to push for the elective franchise for women without waiting for African Americans to obtain their right to vote. The New Yorkers also wanted to address divorce laws. The New York faction chose to work actively with the trade unions and generally were more liberal than their counterparts in New England.

The New Englanders, led by Lucy Stone, wanted to wait for African Americans to win the right to vote before striving to obtain the vote for women. Also, the Boston branch wasn't interested in working with the trade unions; they preferred a more conservative approach.

In November 1869, Lucy Stone and the New Englanders formed the American Woman Suffrage Association "to unite those who cannot use the methods, and means, which Mrs. Stanton and Susan use." Lucretia Mott made an unsuccessful attempt to hold the two factions together. The new American Woman Suffrage Association admitted men and women on an equal basis and had many male abolitionists as members; the National Woman Suffrage Association remained principally a women's organization in which men could not hold office.

Stone founded and financed the American Association's weekly newspaper, *Woman's Journal*. Mary A. Livermore served as editor for two years, and then Stone and her husband, Henry, assumed the editorial responsibility. With the help of their daughter, Alice Stone Blackwell, *Woman's Journal* was "the voice of the women's movement" for forty-seven years.

In 1870, Stone and her husband helped to found the Massachusetts Woman Suffrage Association. She devoted much of her time to lecturing, drafting bills, and attending legislative sessions in support of improving women's status.

In 1890, Stone's daughter, Alice Stone Blackwell, was instrumental in bringing together the National and American Woman Suffrage Associations into the National American Woman Suffrage Association. Elizabeth Cady Stanton was elected president, Susan B. Anthony vice president, and Lucy Stone head of the executive committee.

In 1893 at the World's Columbian Exposition in Chicago, Lucy Stone gave what was to be her last speech in support of the Women's Rights Movement. Shortly afterward, her health began to fail. She died in Boston on October 18, 1893, just after urging her daughter, Alice Stone Blackwell, to "make the world better." Over 1,100 mourners attended her funeral.

The Kansas City *Star* observed how "one of the kindest, best-mannered and sweet-voiced of women was met with all sorts of ridicule.... Now all she did is considered right for women.... Lucy Stone will be widely honored and lamented." The Boston *Globe* noted that "it will take generations of coming women to realize the boon bestowed by such a life." The Cleveland *Leader* said that "when Lucy Stone died there passed from the earth one of the noblest women of the century."

CHAPTER 2

Stories of the Pioneers

"The man over there says women need to be helped into carriages and lifted over ditches, and to have the best place everywhere. Nobody ever helps me into carriages or over puddles, or gives me the best place—and ain't I a woman? Look at my arm! I have plowed and planted and gathered into barns, and no man could head me and ain't I a woman? I could work as much and eat as much as a man—when I could get it—and bear the lash as well! And ain't I a woman?"

Sojourner Truth

Margaret Brent—The First Woman to Demand the Vote

"In the new code of laws [the U.S. Constitution] which I suppose it will be necessary for you to make, I desire you would remember the ladies and be more generous and favorable to them than your ancestors. Do not put such unlimited power into the hands of the husbands. Remember, all men would be tyrants if they could. If particular care and attention is not paid to the ladies, we are determined to foment a rebellion, and will not hold ourselves bound by any laws in which we have no voice or representation."

Abigail Adams, 1777

Margaret Brent and her sister immigrated to the colonies from England in 1638 and settled in Maryland. They purchased land, constructed houses, and attracted more settlers from England. Brent bought and sold real estate and became a woman of business and the owner of many properties. She was appointed executrix for the estate of Leonard Calvert upon his death. Calvert was the brother and representative of the colony's founder, Lord Baltimore.

In 1648, which was 129 years before Abigail Adams made her frequently quoted plea to "remember the ladies," Margaret Brent demanded not one vote, but two votes in the proceedings of the House of Burgesses. Brent argued that she should have one because she was a freeholder and another because she was Calvert's attorney and executrix. Her request was denied. Because of the failure of her request, she demanded that all proceedings of that session of the House of Burgesses be declared invalid.

Fanny Wright—America's First Woman Public Speaker

"Examine, enquire ... Know why you believe, understand what you believe."

Fanny Wright

Frances "Fanny" Wright was an attractive, educated Scotswoman and a friend of Mary Godwin Shelley, the daughter of Mary Wollstonecraft—the author of *A Vindication of the Rights of Women*. Fanny Wright was influenced by the progressive ideas of the Godwin circle of friends in London. She espoused education and equal rights for women and believed in many freedoms: freedom of marriage, freedom of politics, freedom from poverty, freedom of religion, and freedom from slavery. Personally, she had freedom from poverty because she inherited money of her own.

In 1824, Fanny Wright visited the United States for the second time. She came as the companion of General LaFayette and stayed after he returned to France. She bought a large number of slaves and 2,000 acres of land near Memphis, Tennessee, and established a colony called Nashoba to prepare the slaves for life as free men and women. However, the goals of the colony were expanded to the point of attempting to achieve too much. Eventually, it failed.

Wright became an editor, a lecturer, and publisher of her own newspaper, the *Free Enquirer*. However, it was as a lecturer that she became known in the United States. She created a stir in this country because of her liberal ideas and because she was the first woman known to have lectured in public. Her wide-ranging interests included birth control, emancipation of slaves, equal treatment for illegitimate children, political rights of workingmen, free public education for everyone, and free religious inquiry.

Wright's lectures drew large audiences, but she became a target of the nation's press and pulpits. She was called a "disgusting exhibition of female impudence," a "fallen and degraded fair one," and a "red harlot." In the early 1800s, it was considered improper as well as unfeminine for a woman to speak in public. To address mixed audiences of men and women was considered to be immoral. For decades to come, any woman who dared to speak in public was accused of "Fanny Wrightism."

The Grimké Sisters—Pioneers in Women's Public Speaking

"We have given great offense on account of our woman-hood, which seems to be as objectionable as our abolition-ism. The whole land seems aroused to discussion on the province of woman, and I am glad of it. We are willing to bear the brunt of the storm, if we can only be the means of making a break in that wall of public opinion which lies right in the way of woman's rights, true dignity, honor, and usefulness."

Angelina Grimké, 1837

Sarah Grimké was born on November 6, 1792, and Angelina Grimké was born February 20, 1805; both were born in Charleston, South Carolina. As a young girl, Sarah, in particular, felt limited by the narrow range of education open to women; subjects for women included art, music, etiquette, and needlework. Sarah used her brothers' books to study geography, history, mathematics, natural history, and Greek. She wanted to become a lawyer, so she studied law books secretly.

Neither sister was comfortable living in an environment that exploited slaves. In 1821, Sarah moved to Philadelphia, and, in 1829, Angelina followed her older sister north. They joined the Philadelphia Female Anti-Slavery Society, became Quakers, and met Lucretia Mott. In 1836, Angelina wrote a pamphlet, "An Appeal to the Christian Women of the Southern States," in which she urged them to work against the institution of slavery. When Angelina and Sarah were invited to work for the Anti-Slavery Society in New York, they became the first two female abolitionist agents in the United States.

Their first speaking assignments were to give talks to women in private homes. When audiences grew too large to be held in parlors, they spoke in public auditoriums—particularly in forums sponsored by churches. The sisters became effective speakers and were in demand by antislavery organizations outside of New York State. In 1837, they made a speaking tour of Massachusetts.

Initially, they spoke to female audiences, but, increasingly, men attended their meetings. The society sponsoring their meetings began to invite both men and women to their sessions. Later, abolition leader Wendell Phillips observed, "No one who remembers 1837 and its lowering clouds will deny that there was hardly any contribution to the antislavery movement greater or more impressive than the crusade of these Grimké sisters through the New England States."

Many New Englanders did not approve of women who spoke before mixed audiences. When the Grimké sisters began to debate with men in their meetings, churches began to withhold permission to hold meetings in their facilities. The New England clergy, who were against the activities of William Lloyd Garrison's abolitionists, came out strongly against the Grimkés.

The clergy distributed a pastoral letter in which they stated... "We invite your attention to the dangers which at present seem to threaten the female character with widespread and permanent injury." They thought that the New Testament instructed women to be "unobtrusive and private." Furthermore, women should confine their activities to "unobtrusive prayers" and "labors of piety and love." "But when she assumes the place and tone of man as a public reformer, her character becomes unnatural." The pastoral letter was followed by two "clerical appeals," which were attacks on Garrison and on female antislavery agents. John Greenleaf Whittier ridiculed this attack on the the Grimkés in his poem, "The Pastoral Letter."

Initially, Angelina and Sarah were concerned by the outcry that they had caused and were worried that it might hurt the antislavery cause. The hostility of the men's sentiments, particularly the clergy, reflected the low regard in which women were held. Angelina became indignant, "I confess my womanhood is insulted, my moral feelings outraged when I reflect on these things ... We are placed very unexpectedly in a very trying situation, in the forefront of an entirely new contest — a contest for the rights of woman as a moral, intelligent, and responsible being."

The better known of the sisters, Angelina was a more effective speaker than writer. In 1837, she wrote a response to Catherine Beecher's *An Essay on Slavery and Abolitionism with Reference to the Duty of American Females*. Catherine Beecher worked to improve educational opportunities for women but was opposed to the Women's Rights Movement and to the women's role in the abolitionist movement. Like many women, she thought that, "men are the proper persons" for organized public action and that women should accept an inferior role. "Heaven has appointed to one sex the superior, and to the other the subordinate station, and this is without any reference to the character or conduct of either."

Angelina's letters in reply were printed in the Garrison's *Liberator* and the *Emancipator* and then published in book form as *Miss Beecher on the Slave Question*. However, it was Sarah who dramatically picked up the gauntlet to defend women's rights in writing. She wrote a series of letters about "The Province of Woman" for the *Spectator*. The letters were reprinted in the *Liberator* and published in a book called *Letters on the Condition of Women and the Equality of the Sexes*. Sarah advocated equal pay for equal work, demanded the same educational opportunities for women as for men, and argued against the legal system that discriminated against women. She counseled women to make the most of their abilities and intelligence.

Sarah disagreed with the position of the clergy on the role of women and cited passages from the Sermon on the Mount, in which Jesus did not distinguish between the sexes. She maintained that "men and women are created equal ... they are both moral and accountable human beings, and whatever is right for man to do, is right for woman to do." Some historians consider Sarah's publication of *Letters on the Condition of Women and the Equality of the Sexes* in 1838 the beginning of the Women's Rights Movement in the United States.

The Grimkés' audiences continued to grow, but they began to hear opposition from friends and associates who thought that efforts on the women's rights question should wait until the antislavery issue was resolved. One of these friends was Theodore Weld, an influential organizer of the abolitionist movement. He was a dynamic speaker and a strongly committed reformer who worked with Angelina to help her prepare more effective talks and to improve her delivery of speeches.

Angelina disagreed with Weld's priorities. With respect to the Women's Rights Movement, she told him, "The time to assert a right is the time when that right is denied ... Can you not see that women could do ... a hundred more times for the slave if she were not fettered." Weld gave in to Angelina's concerns. They fell in love and were married in 1838. They moved to New Jersey, where Sarah lived with them. All three continued with their antislavery activities, although the Welds also devoted energy to raising a family, dealing with financial problems, and struggling with illnesses.

Particularly through their pioneering the establishment of the right of women to speak in public, Angelina and Sarah Grimké made significant contributions to the early phases of the Women's Rights Movement. Also, they were relentless in their efforts for the acceptance of women, as noted by Sarah Grimké, with "the right of all human beings to cultivate the power which God has given us."

The First Women's Rights Convention—Seneca Falls

"A convention to discuss the social, civil, and religious conditions and rights of women will be held at the Wesleyan Chapel at Seneca Falls on Wednesday and Thursday, the 19th and 20th of July, current, commencing at 10 o'clock

a.m. During the first day, the meeting will be exclusively for women, who are earnestly invited to attend. The public generally are invited to be present on the second day, when Lucretia Mott, of Philadelphia, and other ladies and gentlemen will address the convention."

Seneca County Courier, July 14, 1848

The meeting that Lucretia Mott and Elizabeth Cady Stanton had planned in London in 1840 while attending the World Anti-Slavery Convention finally was held eight years later. In early July 1848, Mott visited her sister, Martha Wright, in Auburn and attended the Yearly Meeting of the Friends in Western New York. Mott contacted Cady Stanton in Seneca Falls, and they decided to continue their discussion of women's rights that they had begun in London.

Jane Hunt invited them to tea at her and her husband Richard's home at 401 East Main Street, Waterloo, along with Martha Wright and Mary Ann M'Clintock, a Quaker abolitionist from Waterloo. This meeting at the home of Jane and Richard Hunt in Waterloo was the planning meeting for the first Women's Rights Convention. The five women discussed their frustration with the limited rights of women and the discrimination they had experienced in the abolitionist and temperance movements.

Cady Stanton was pleased that these four ladies were eager to proceed with a women's rights convention as she and Mott had discussed eight years previously. All but Cady Stanton were Garrison-type antislavery activists. Mott was the only one who had experience as a delegate, orator, and organizer. However, they had all attended antislavery and temperance conventions. Cady Stanton remembered that she "poured ... out the torrent of my long accumulating discontent with such violence and indignation that I stirred myself, as well as the rest of the party, to do and dare anything."

The women prepared a notice about the Convention that

appeared in the Seneca County *Courier* on July 14th. They agreed to reconvene at the home of Mary Ann and Thomas M'Clintock at 16 East William Street, Waterloo, on July 16 to prepare an agenda for the first Women's Rights Convention on the nineteenth and twentieth.

At their meeting on July 16, the women decided to list their grievances and to propose resolutions to address them. Initially, they planned to model the document listing their grievances and resolutions on documents that they had seen at abolitionist and temperance conventions. They soon realized that they should take a more radical approach. Cady Stanton was the principal author of the *Declaration of Sentiments* patterned on the *Declaration of Independence*. The *Declaration of Sentiments* began with the lines "We hold these truths to be self-evident; that all men and women are created equal." The mahogany table around which they sat to prepare their agenda is now in the Smithsonian Institution.

Elizabeth Cady Stanton wanted the right to vote to be one of the resolutions. The other women wanted to emphasize other women's rights first and defer the right to vote issue as being too controversial. Cady Stanton prevailed, and the right of women to vote became one of the resolutions.

On July 19, the first people to arrive at the Wesleyan Chapel, the site of the Convention, found the doors locked. Cady Stanton's nephew was lifted through an open window to unbar the front door. The church filled up quickly with men and women. Men had been invited to the second day of the Convention but not the first day. The women organizing the Convention decided that since men were already there, they might as well stay.

James Mott—tall, dignified, and conservatively dressed—called the Convention to order. Mary Ann M'Clintock was appointed secretary. Lucretia Mott stated the goals of the Convention and discussed the importance of educating women and elevating the standing of women in society. Mary Ann M'Clintock and Elizabeth Cady Stanton read prepared speeches and Martha Wright read newspaper articles that she had written about the plight of women.

Ansel Bascom, a member of a recent New York State Constitutional Convention, spoke about a property bill for married women that had just been passed by the State Legislature. Samuel Tillman, a young law student, read a series of statutes for women prepared by both American and British jurists that provided examples of conditions that women must overcome. E. W. Capron, Frederick Douglass, and Thomas M'Clintock participated in the discussions.

After the *Declaration of Sentiments* was discussed, Elizabeth Cady Stanton read it to the audience, who adopted it with some minor amendments. The only resolution that was not unanimously adopted was the ninth, which concerned the right of women to vote. Some attendees of the Convention thought that advancing the elective franchise of women at this time might reduce the probability of achieving other women's rights. Frederick Douglass and Cady Stanton pointed out that the ability to chose representatives and to make laws were rights upon which all other rights were based. Douglass and Cady Stanton persisted, and, eventually, the resolution passed with a slight majority.

The proceedings of the Convention were widely published. They were ridiculed by newspaper editors and denounced by ministers. The organizers were surprised at the amount of mocking and taunting that occurred. Some of the men and women who signed the *Declaration of Sentiments* withdrew their names as the volume of ridicule increased.

The women who organized this first Women's Rights Convention were true pioneers. They addressed issues that cried out to be addressed, and they had the courage to endure public criticism and continue to seek redress for decades to come. Soon after the first Women's Rights Convention in Seneca Falls, women's rights conventions were held else-where in New York and in Indiana, Massachusetts, Ohio, and Pennsylvania.

The First Woman Physician in the United States

"The idea of winning a doctor's degree gradually assumed an immense attraction for me... This work has taken deep root in my soul and become an all-absorbing duty. I must accomplish my end. I consider it the noblest and most useful path I can tread."

Elizabeth Blackwell

Elizabeth Blackwell was the first woman graduate of a medical school in modern times. Although she was happy with her social and family life in Cincinnati, she did not feel challenged. She knew from an early age that she wanted to study to become a medical doctor. However, before she could begin her medical studies, Blackwell had to earn the money to pay for them. Her father, Samuel Blackwell, had died at the age of forty-eight leaving the family in debt. Blackwell, her mother, and her brothers and sisters all worked to pay off the family debts.

Blackwell taught school in Asheville, North Carolina, and then in Charleston, South Carolina, to earn money for medical school. She sent out applications to medical schools while teaching at Charleston. She was particularly interested in Philadelphia. With its four highly regarded medical schools, she considered it the medical center of the U.S.

Blackwell sent one of her first inquiries to Dr. Joseph Warrington in Philadelphia. His response was not encouraging; he viewed men as doctors and women as nurses and recommended that she pursue a career in nursing. However, he added that "if the project be of divine origin and appointment, it will sooner or later be accomplished." She applied to twenty-nine medical schools and received twenty-eight rejections.

In late October 1847, Blackwell received an acceptance from the medical school of Geneva College, Geneva, New York. Dr. Benjamin Hale, the president of Geneva College and a very open-minded individual, had recruited an extremely capable dean for the medical school, Dr. Charles Lee. The medical school later became part of Syracuse University, and Geneva College was renamed Hobart College. The medical school was thriving when she became student no. 130.

The circumstances surrounding Blackwell's acceptance were unusual. Dr. Warrington wrote a letter to Dr. Lee on her behalf. The faculty was unanimously against the admission of a woman to their medical school; however, they didn't want to be responsible for rejecting the highly regarded Philadelphia doctor's request. The faculty turned the decision over to the medical students. They were confident that the students would vote against her admission.

Dr. Lee read Dr. Warrington's letter to the students and informed them that the faculty had decided to let them decide the issue. He instructed them that one negative vote would prevent Blackwell's admission. The students were enthusiastic about her acceptance, and the one dissenting voice was browbeaten into submission. She received a document composed by the students and signed by class chairman Francis Joel Stratton:

- Resolved—That one of the principles of a Republican government is the universal education of both sexes; that to every branch of scientific education the door should be open equally to all; that the application of Elizabeth Blackwell to become a member of our class meets our entire approbation; and in extending our unanimous invitation we pledge ourselves that no conduct of ours shall cause her to regret her attendance at this institution.

- Resolved—That a copy of these proceedings be signed by the chairman and transmitted to Elizabeth Blackwell.

Blackwell was overjoyed to receive the acceptance, and she immediately packed and traveled to Geneva. She arrived there on November 6th, five weeks into the session. She had grown up with brothers and was not an overly sensitive young woman; however, she wasn't sure what to expect from her fellow medical students. She dressed conservatively in Quaker style and was well-mannered.

The Geneva community wasn't ready for a female medical student, and, initially, Blackwell had trouble finding a place to live. She moved into a drafty attic room in a boarding house, where she fed wood into a wood-burning stove to keep warm. She quickly realized that she was the subject of ostracism. The other boarders were unfriendly at mealtime, the women she passed on the street held their skirts to one side and didn't speak, and one doctor's wife snubbed her openly. Her feelings were hurt by this treatment; she retreated to her room to study.

Dr. James Webster, professor of anatomy, was friendly and sincerely glad to have Blackwell in his class. However, he soon tried to prevent her from attending a dissection. He wrote her a note explaining that he was about to lecture on the reproductive organs, and he could not discuss the material satisfactorily in the presence of a lady. He offered her the opportunity to study of this part of the course in private.

Blackwell was unaware that Dr. Webster had a reputation for being coarse in covering this material; he sprinkled his lecture with humorous anecdotes. The students enjoyed this approach and responded rowdily.

Blackwell wrote to Dr. Webster to remind him that she was there as a student with a serious purpose; she was aware of the awkward position in which he found himself, particularly "when viewed from the low standpoint of impure and unchaste sentiments." She asked why a student of science would have his mind diverted from such an absorbing subject by the presence of a student in feminine attire. She offered to remove her bonnet and sit in the back row of benches. If the other students desired it, she would not attend the class at all.

Dr. Webster acquiesced and, with Blackwell in attendance, conducted the class without the usual anecdotes. To her, the class was "just about as much as I could bear." She made an entry in her diary: "My delicacy was certainly shocked, and yet the exhibition was in some sense ludicrous. I had to pinch my hand until the blood nearly came, and call upon Christ to keep from smiling, for that would have ruined everything; but I sat in grave indifference, though the effort made my heart palpitate most painfully."

One of the few places open to Blackwell for summer work was the Blockley Almshouse in Philadelphia, which cared for 2,000 lower-class unfortunates. Again, she had to pay for being a pioneer. The resident doctors openly snubbed her and made a point of leaving a ward when she entered it. They made her life difficult by not entering diagnoses and medication prescribed on the patients' charts. She had to make many of her own diagnoses. However, her preparation of a thesis on typhus was a major accomplishment; she received many compliments on the thesis from the senior staff physicians.

Blackwell studied hard in medical school. She was a disciplined student who maintained a friendly but impersonal relationship with her classmates. Although she had always received good grades, she approached her final examinations with trepidation. When the results were compiled, she had the best academic record in her class. However, the administration of Geneva College vacillated on the question of becoming the first in the United States to award a medical degree to a woman.

Dr. Webster defended Blackwell, saying, "She paid her tuition, didn't she? She passed every course, each and every one with honors! And let me tell you, gentlemen, if you hold back, I'll take up the campaign in every medical journal." She received her medical degree on January 23, 1849. Her brother, Henry, who later married Lucy Stone, traveled to Geneva to share the experience with her.

Blackwell was the last to be called to receive a diploma from Dr. Hale. In presenting her diploma, he used the feminine word Domina in place of Domine. She replied, "Sir, I thank you. By the help of the Most High, it shall be the effort of my life to shed honor on your diploma."

Henry Blackwell documented his recollections of the ceremony:

> ... He [Dr. Lee, who gave the valedictory address] pronounced her the leader of the class; stated that she had passed through a thorough course in every department, slighting none; that she had profited to the utmost by all the advantages of the institution, and by her ladylike and dignified deportment had proved that the strongest intellect and nerve, and the most untiring perseverance were compatible with the softest attributes of feminine delicacy and grace, to all which the students manifested, by decided attempts at applause, their entire concurrence.

As Blackwell left the ceremony, the women of Geneva displayed their smiles and friendly faces to her. She was pleased to see this change of attitude, but she recorded her true feelings in her diary: "For the next few hours, until I left by train, my room was thronged by visitors. I was glad of the sudden conversion thus shown, but my past experience had given me a useful and permanent lesson at the outset of life as to the very shallow nature of popularity."

Blackwell returned to Philadelphia to find the same coolness that she had previously experienced. It was clear that she was not going to be given the opportunity to gain the practical medical experience that she needed. She obtained that experience at St. Bartholomew's Hospital in London and at La Maternite in Paris. Again, she encountered bias. She was not given access to all departments at St. Bartholomew's, and at La Maternite she was considered an aide, not a doctor.

Upon her return to New York, Blackwell was unable to find a position at the city dispensaries and hospitals. She opened her own dispensary in Washington Square, lectured on women's health subjects, and published two books.

On May 12, 1857, Blackwell opened the New York Infirmary for Women and Children. Charles A. Dana, Cyrus W. Field, and Horace Greeley were trustees for the Infirmary. In 1868, she opened a medical college for women. Her medical college provided medical education for women until 1899, when it was incorporated into the Cornell Medical Center. The New York Infirmary founded by Blackwell still exists in lower Manhattan as part of the New York Downtown Hospital.

In 1899, Hobart College, the successor to Geneva College, named its first residence hall for women Blackwell House. Elizabeth Blackwell overcame many obstacles and made significant contributions to the medical profession.

The First Woman Ordained Minister in the United States

"The prophet Joel is quoted as saying, 'And it shall come to pass in the last days, saith God, I will pour out my spirit upon all flesh; and your daughters shall prophesy, and your young men shall see visions, and your old men shall dream dreams, and on my handmaidens I will pour out in those days of my spirit; and they shall prophesy ...' In the eleventh chapter of First Corinthians we learn that females were accustomed to act as prophetesses in those days under direct sanction of the apostles. We have no reason to think it was therefore unlawful for women of that time to speak in church ... Again, when St. Paul says, 'I suffer not a woman to teach,' if we are to take this admonition literally, we should not even feel free to teach our own children."

Antoinette Brown Blackwell

Antoinette Louisa Brown, the seventh of ten children of Joseph Brown and Abigail Morse Brown, was born in Henrietta, New York, in May 1825. Antoinette indicated her interest in religion at an early age, when she gave a spontaneous prayer to conclude a family prayer meeting at the age of eight. In the following year, she spoke up about joining the village Congregational Church at a time when joining the church so young was rare.

The small Henrietta church was a member of the liberal branch of the Congregational Church, which emphasized God's mercy and forgiveness in addition to human goodness and initiative. The orthodox branch of the church believed that humans were morally corrupt, sinful, and dependent upon an all-powerful God, who would condemn them to hell if they did not obey His word.

As a teenager, Brown decided that she wanted to be a minister. No woman had been ordained as a minister; however, in the 1820s a Methodist woman had attempted to preach in New York State, but gave in to public opposition. The Quakers, who considered all members to be ministers, permitted all women to speak at worship services, but women were not usually considered leaders in the church.

Brown was active in her Henrietta church and spoke frequently at prayer meetings, where any church member was permitted to speak. She decided to attend the Oberlin Collegiate Institute in Ohio, where her brother William studied theology. Oberlin was the first U.S. college to admit women to take college courses with men. In the spring of 1846, she began her studies at Oberlin.

Oberlin had been founded in 1833 by ministers from New England and New York. By the time that Brown arrived, the College had developed its own ideology, which was a combination of liberal religion, practical training, and the politics of reform. The spiritual leader of the Oberlin community was professor of theology Charles Grandison Finney, who had impressed Brown's parents at a series of revival meetings in Rochester during the winter of 1831. He was a captivating speaker who advocated the individual's dual responsibility of commitment to God and of work to create a better society. He suggested that this dual responsibility should be fulfilled by applying one's intellect and education to saving individual souls and to improving society. He became Antoinette's mentor.

In the winter of 1846-47, during Oberlin's lengthy vacation, Brown taught at a large private academy in Rochester, Michigan. The experience verified what she already knew: "God never made me for a school teacher." The headmaster encouraged her to give her first public speech. She spoke in the village church and was pleased that "it was fairly well received by the students and by the community."

Brown met Lucy Stone, who later became a leader of the Women's Rights Movement, at Oberlin. Brown and Stone became close friends and confidants despite their philosophical differences. Stone was more radical on the subject of abolition, and she had left the Congregational Church because it approved of slavery and was against women speaking in public. Brown was disappointed that her closest friend did not agree with her goals:

> I told her of my intention to become a minister. Her protest was most emphatic. She said, "You will never be allowed to do this. You will never be allowed to stand in a public pulpit nor to preach in a church, and certainly you can never be ordained." It was a long talk but we were no nearer to an agreement at the end than at the beginning. My final answer could only be, "I am going to do it."

Brown completed her undergraduate studies at Oberlin in the summer of 1847. She returned home to Henrietta and practiced her public speaking: "I go out into the barn and make the walls echo with my voice occasionally but the church stands on the green in such a way that I have too many auditors when I attempt to practice there. The barn is a good large one however, and the sounds ring out merrily, or did before father filled it full of hay."

Brown returned to Oberlin in the fall to study theology. She felt that she was called to this vocation, and she was motivated to use her intellect, her ability as a public speaker, and her interest in public reform. However, although Oberlin was committed to providing women with a general education, the only profession that it prepared women for was teaching. In the Theology Department, women were welcome to sit in on classes if their goal was only self-improvement.

Brown was assigned to write essays on the passages in the Bible stating that women should not preach: "Let your women keep silence in the churches, for it is not permitted unto them to speak.... Let the women learn in silence with all subjection. I suffer not a woman to teach, nor to usurp authority over the man, but to be in silence." She found confirmation of her choice of a profession in the words of the prophet Joel: "And it shall come to pass in the last days, saith God, I will pour out my spirit upon all flesh; and your sons and daughters shall prophesy."

In her assigned essay, Brown observed that St. Paul's suggestion that women should learn in silence had been misinterpreted. She suggested that St. Paul only intended to caution against "excesses, irregularities, and unwarranted liberties" in public worship. Professor Asa Mahan selected her essay for publication in the *Oberlin Quarterly Review.*

In the last year of their studies, Oberlin theology students were allowed to preach in area churches, but not to perform any of the sacraments. Brown said: "They were willing to have me preach, but not to themselves endorse this as a principle.... They decided, after much discussion, that I must preach if I chose to do so on my own responsibility." Although she was not given official recognition, she spoke in small churches nearby, usually on the popular subject of temperance.

Upon completion of her theology studies, Brown chose not

to be ordained at Oberlin. Not only did she think that it would be "a delicate thing" with Oberlin's difference of opinion on women ministers, but also she preferred the usual path of ordination by a local parish that wanted her as a pastor. She cited "an instinctive desire to be ordained in my own church, and a belief that I could one day in the future be ordained by my own denomination which was then the Orthodox Congregational."

Brown did not participate in the graduation exercises. In later years, she observed: "We were not supposed to graduate, as at that time to have regularly graduated women from a theological school would have been an endorsement of their probable future careers." Her name did not appear in the roll of the theological school class of 1850 until 1908.

In 1850, Brown attended the First National Women's Rights Convention in Worcester, Massachusetts, where she spoke to disprove the Biblical argument that women should not speak in public. She met Lucretia Mott and Elizabeth Cady Stanton, the organizers of the Seneca Falls Convention two years earlier, and was introduced to many men and women who were active in social reform. She maintained her contacts with those whom she met, although she thought that her cause would probably not be best served by working with organized groups.

Brown decided to earn her living as a public speaker as her friend, Lucy Stone, was doing. Before radio and television, the lecture circuit or lyceum was an important means of informing and entertaining people. Women speakers were usually paid less than men. She told the lyceum organizers that "my terms, from principle, are never less that the best prices received by the gentlemen of the particular association where I speak." She found the work to be satisfying, and she consistently received favorable reviews in the local newspapers where she spoke.

Liberal ministers such as William Henry Channing and Samuel J. May invited Brown to preach in their churches. Her oldest brother, William, who had initially opposed her desire to preach, invited her to speak in his church in Massachusetts. She decided that the time had come to pursue her calling in earnest, and she began to actively seek a church in need of a pastor.

During one of her speaking tours across New York State, Brown visited South Butler, in Wayne County. The small Congregational Church listened to her speak, and then invited her to become their pastor at an annual salary of $300. In the late spring of 1853, she moved to South Butler and began to give two sermons every Sunday, one prepared and the other extemporaneous.

Brown's responsibilities included pastoral duties such as visiting the sick, and she felt suited to her role as minister. She observed, "My little parish was a miniature world in good and evil. To get humanity condensed into so small a compass that you can study each individual member opens a new chapter of experience. It makes one thoughtful and rolls upon the spirit a burden of deep responsibility."

Brown's friend, Lucy Stone, met Henry Blackwell, the brother of the pioneer doctor, Elizabeth Blackwell, at an abolitionist meeting. Henry Blackwell fell in love with Lucy Stone and immediately began to court her. Stone met Blackwell's older brother, Samuel, and suggested that he visit her friend Antoinette Brown while on his travels. The Blackwell brothers were business partners in Cincinnati. Samuel called on Brown while en route to Boston. Samuel "enjoyed the visit exceedingly." She observed that "he stayed perhaps a half a day and had a pleasant visit.... He was not handsome." She was preoccupied with her church duties.

Brown's church appreciated her work, and the governing body decided to proceed with her ordination. She already administered the sacraments, but the ceremony would provide public recognition of her ministry. Reverend Luther Lee, a minister from nearby Syracuse whom she knew from abolitionist meetings, agreed to preach the ordination sermon.

Reverend Lee based his sermon on the text, "There is neither male nor female; for ye are all one in Christ Jesus." He said, "... in the Church, of which Christ is the only head, males and females possess equal rights and privileges; here there is no difference.... I cannot see how the test can be explained so as to exclude females from any right, office, work, privilege, or immunity which males enjoy, hold or perform." He concluded with: "All we are here to do, and all we expect to do, is, in due form, and by a solemn and impressive service, to subscribe our testimony to the fact that in our belief, our sister in Christ, Antoinette L. Brown, is one of the ministers of the New Covenant, authorized, qualified, and called of God to preach the Gospel of His Son Jesus Christ."

During the winter of 1854, Brown's duties began to weigh heavily upon her. Her job was a difficult one, and her responsibilities began to cause her emotional strain. A minister's functions were many and varied. He or she was expected to be tolerant and understanding, but at times authoritative and judgmental. It was difficult for her to be a "father" figure. Her role would have been easier if she had the support of her friends and associates. However, Susan B. Antony, Elizabeth Cady Stanton, and Lucy Stone all disapproved of her church affiliation. They did not perceive her ministerial duties as a contribution to the effort of effecting change in women's status. She felt isolated:

> It was practically ten years after my ordination
> before any other woman known to the public
> was ordained. It was therefore doubly hard for
> me—a young woman still in her twenties—to
> adapt myself to the rather curious relationship
> I must sustain either to home conditions or to
> those of a pastorate. Personally this was more
> of an emotional strain than the enduring of any
> opposition that ever came to me as a public
> speaker or teacher.

This isolation began to affect her in a very serious way. Brown began to question her faith, particularly the belief that the individual was condemned to eternal damnation unless saved by a stern God. She was more motivated by Charles Grandison Finney's teachings that stressed human goodness and striving to approach moral perfection. In July 1854, overcome by mental conflict and nervous exhaustion, she returned home to rest.

One of the individuals who helped Brown find herself during this difficult time was Samuel Blackwell. She had stayed with the Blackwell family when she visited Cincinnati on the lecture circuit. Samuel's five sisters were all achievers: Elizabeth and Emily became doctors, Ellen and Marian were active in the Women's Rights Movement and other reform efforts, and Anna, who lived at the Transcendentalist commune at Brook Farm for awhile, was a newspaper reporter in Paris. Samuel Blackwell was used to activist women.

At the end of 1854, Lucy Stone agreed to marry Henry Blackwell if he would agree to devote his efforts to women's rights. Perhaps motivated by his brother's action, Samuel Blackwell proposed to Brown at about the same time. She hesitated, but she considered some of the women that she knew—Lucretia Mott was an example—who had children, husbands, and homes, in addition to careers.

Later, Brown observed, "When the early faith seemed wholly lost and the new and stronger belief not yet obtained, there seemed no good reason for not accepting the love and help of a good man and the woman's appreciation of all else that this implied." After their marriage, she was known as Reverend Antoinette L. B. Blackwell.

At the end of the 1860s, Brown devoted herself to writing. Her first large published work was *Studies in General Science*, a collection of essays. In 1875, she published *The Sexes Throughout Nature*, a compilation of essays first published in periodicals. In 1876, she published *The Physical Basis of Immortality*, which was a synthesis of her philosophy. *The Philosophy of Individuality, or the One and the Many*, was published in 1893. Her last two books, *The Making of the Universe* and *The Social Side of Mind and Action* were published in 1914 and 1915.

Brown was drawn to the Unitarian Church. Samuel Blackwell and three of his sisters had already joined the Unitarians. In the spring of 1878, she joined the Unitarian Fellowship and asked to be recognized as a minister. In the fall of 1878, the Committee on Fellowship of the American Unitarian Association acknowledged her as a minister.

Oberlin College finally recognized Brown's status in 1879 awarding her an "honorary" master of arts degree, the degree that she had earned during three years of study in the Theological Department. One change from her studies thirty years previously was that she no longer stood alone as woman minister. In 1864, Olympia Brown, motivated by Brown's talk to her class at Antioch College, was ordained as a Universalist minister. By 1880, almost 200 women were recognized as ministers, and many held full-time pastoral jobs.

In addition to her participation in the Women's Rights Movement, Brown was active in the Association for the Advancement of Women and the American Association for the Advancement of Science. Although she hadn't had the responsibility of a parish for decades, she considered herself to be a "minister emeritus" during her later years.

In June 1908, Brown was invited to Oberlin College to receive an honorary Doctor of Divinity degree. In introducing her to Oberlin President Henry Churchill King at the commencement ceremony, Dr. Charles Wager spoke to the audience:

> It is appropriate for the institution that was the first to provide for higher education of women to honor, at its seventy-fifth anniversary, a woman who has eminently justified that daring innovation, a woman who was one of the

first two in America to complete a course in divinity, who as preacher, as pastor, as writer, as the champion of more than one good cause, has in the past conferred honor upon her Alma Mater, and who today confers upon it no less honor by an old age as lovely as it is venerable.

Her health began to slip during the spring and summer of 1921. She was at peace with herself. She was ready for death and looked upon it as a reunion with Samuel and all of her loved ones who had predeceased her. In late November, 1921, at the age of ninety-seven, Reverend Antoinette L. B. Blackwell, the first woman minister, died in her sleep.

The First U.S. Woman Appointed Justice of the Peace

"Women have exercised their elective franchise ... with such good judgment and modesty as to recommend it to the men of all parties who hold the good of the Territory in high esteem ... women are benefited and improved by the ballot.... The fact is, Wyoming has the noblest and best women in the world because they have more privileges and know better how to use them.... Woman suffrage is a settled fact here, and will endure as long as the Territory. It has accomplished much good; it has harmed no one; therefore we are all in favor, and none can be found to raise a voice against it."

U.S. District Attorney Melville C. Brown,
Wyoming Territory, 1884

Esther McQuigg Slack Morris, Wyoming Justice of the Peace and suffragist, was born on August 8, 1814, in Spencer, Tioga County, New York. She was the eighth child of Daniel and Charlotte Hobart McQuigg, who had emigrated from England and Scotland before the Revolutionary War. Orphaned at the age of eleven, Esther was apprenticed to a seamstress in Owego.

In 1841, Esther McQuigg married Artemus Slack, a civil engineer with the Erie Railroad. Their son, Edward Archibald, was born the following year. In 1845, Slack died, leaving property in Peru, Illinois, to his young widow. She moved to Illinois where she met and married John Morris, a prosperous merchant and storekeeper. Their twin sons, Edward and Robert, were born in 1851. In 1869, the family moved to South Pass City in Wyoming Territory, where John Morris opened a saloon and then worked in the mines.

H. G. Nickerson, who was a candidate for the legislature of the Territory of Wyoming in the fall elections of 1869, credited Esther Morris with a key role in the introduction of women's suffrage to the legislature late that year. Nickerson recalled that both he and the other candidate, William H. Bright, were invited to a tea at the Morris home prior to the election. Esther Morris obtained a promise from both candidates to introduce a women's suffrage bill to the legislature if they were elected.

Bright, the winning candidate, introduced a suffrage bill that included the right of women to hold office. It passed the legislature on December 10, 1869, and shortly afterward was signed into law by Governor John A. Campbell. Bright was obviously influenced by his wife, who was a strong advocate of women's suffrage. Bright stated his viewpoint clearly to his wife:

> Betty, it's a shame that I should be a member of the Legislature and make laws for such a woman as you. You are a great deal better than I am; you know a great deal more, and you would make a better member of the Assembly than I, and you know it. I have been thinking about it and have made up my mind that I will go to work and do everything in my power to

give you the ballot, then you may work out the
rest in your own way.

Governor Campbell was visited in Cheyenne by a group of
women led by Amalia Post, the wife of Wyoming Territory
delegate to Congress Morton E. Post, who threatened to stay
until he signed the bill into law. Campbell signed the bill willingly.

In February 1870, Esther Morris was appointed Justice of
the Peace of South Pass City after Governor Campbell was
petitioned by the county attorney and the county commis-
sioners of Sweetwater County. Just under six feet tall, she
weighed 180 pounds and was a forceful speaker. Historian
Grace Raymond Hebard described her as "heroic in size, mas-
culine in mind." She was considered a tough-skinned, no-non-
sense purveyor of frontier justice. She tried thirty to forty
cases in her eight and a half months in office; none was
referred to a higher office. She performed her duties
admirably, and, in her opinion, passed "the test of woman's
ability to hold office."

In late 1879, Morris separated from her husband after a
domestic altercation and moved to Laramie, where she was
nominated for State Representative from Albany County but
chose not to run. She emphasized, however, that her withdrawal from the race was not a withdrawal from the
"woman's cause."

In 1874, Morris left Wyoming and lived for a while in New
York State. By 1890, she was back in Wyoming living with
her son, Edward, who was editor of the *Daily Leader* in
Cheyenne. In a celebration of Wyoming's statehood that year,
she was honored as a pioneer of women's suffrage.

In 1895, Morris attended a dinner in Cheyenne for Susan
B. Anthony and was elected as a delegate from Wyoming to
the National American Woman Suffrage Association
Convention in Cleveland. Esther Morris died in Cheyenne in
1902 at the age of eighty-seven.

In 1955, Esther Morris was chosen as Wyoming's outstanding deceased citizen. Statues of her were placed in Statuary Hall in the U.S. Capitol in Washington, D.C., and in front of the State House in Cheyenne.

The First Woman Admitted to Practice Law Before the U.S. Supreme Court

"I never stopped fighting. My cause was the cause of thousands of women."

Belva Lockwood

Belva Ann Bennett, the second child of Lewis Bennett and Hannah Green Bennett, was born on October 24, 1830, on a farm in Royalton, Niagara County, New York. She attended local schools and became a teacher at the age of fifteen. In 1848, she married Uriah McNall, a sawmill operator. They had one daughter, Lura. McNall died in an accident in 1853. Belva went back to teaching school until she realized that women were paid half the salary of men.

Belva attended Genesee Wesleyan Seminary and Genesee College (later incorporated into Syracuse University) at Lima, New York, and graduated with honors in 1857. She returned to teaching at Lockport and Oswego, New York. In 1860, Belva became interested in women's rights after meeting Susan B. Anthony at a teachers' institute. In 1866, she moved to Washington, D.C., where she opened a private coeducational school. Two years later, she married Ezekiel Lockwood, a dentist and former Baptist minister. In 1867, she was a founder of the Universal Franchise Association, one of the first suffrage groups in Washington.

Belva Lockwood applied for admission to Columbian College (later George Washington University) Law School but was denied admission because "her presence would distract the attention of the young men." She was also denied admission to the law schools of Georgetown and Howard universities before being accepted at National University Law

90

School. She successfully completed law school in 1873, but her diploma was withheld. She received her degree after she wrote to President Grant, the ex-officio president of National University.

Lockwood was admitted to the District of Columbia bar and specialized in cases of claims against the government. When one of her cases reached the federal Court of Claims, she was denied, because she was a woman, the right to plead the case. In 1876, her petition for admission to plead cases before the Supreme Court was denied "on the grounds of custom." She lobbied vigorously and obtained the support of pro-suffrage Senators Aaron Sargent of California and George Hoar of Massachusetts. On March 3, 1879, she became the first woman admitted to practice law before the U.S. Supreme Court.

In the 1870s and early 1880s, Lockwood participated in the Washington conventions of the National Woman's Suffrage Association. She addressed Congressional committees and prepared bills and resolutions. In 1870, she circulated a petition at the New York conventions of the American and National Woman Suffrage Associations that prepared the way for the passage two years later of legislation giving women government employees equal pay for equal work.

In 1872, Victoria Woodhull announced her candidacy for President of the United States by writing a letter to the New York *Tribune*. Belva Lockwood spoke at the Cooper Union in New York in support of Victoria Woodhull's candidacy, although later that year Lockwood spoke throughout the South in support of the Republican candidate, Horace Greeley.

In 1884, the National Equal Rights Party nominated Belva Lockwood as their candidate for President of the United States. Lockwood supported equal rights for everyone, without distinction of color, sex, or nationality; curtailment of the traffic in liquor; uniform marriage and divorce laws; and universal peace. She was against monopoly. She received 4,149 votes in the following six states and the entire electoral vote of Indiana:

New Hampshire	379 votes
New York	1,336 votes
Michigan	374 votes
Illinois	1,008 votes
Maryland	318 votes
California	734 votes

In 1888, Lockwood ran again, but received less support than she had received four years earlier. Although Victoria Woodhull announced her candidacy for President in 1872, Belva Lockwood was the first woman to receive electoral votes for the office of President.

In the 1880s and 1890s, Lockwood served as vice president, corresponding secretary, and lobbyist for the Universal Peace Union. She also served on the Union's executive committee and on the editorial board of the *Peacemaker*, the organization's newspaper. She was the Union's delegate to International Peace Congress in 1889 and the American secretary of the International Bureau of Peace founded in Bern in 1891. In 1893, she was active in the International Council of Women and served on the nominating committee for the Nobel Peace Prize.

In 1903, Lockwood prepared amendments to the statehood bills for Arizona, New Mexico, and Oklahoma that would grant suffrage to women. She received an honorary LL.D. degree from Syracuse University in 1909.

Belva Lockwood died in Washington in 1917. Dr. Anna Howard Shaw assisted at her funeral services at the Wesleyan Methodist Episcopal Church. She was buried in the Congressional Cemetery in Washington.

Belva Lockwood was a life-long pioneer in the Women's Rights Movement. Her home and her law office served as meeting places for national leaders of the struggle for women's rights. She was an eloquent advocate and speechmaker who lived up to her statement, "I never stopped fighting. My cause was the cause of thousands of women."

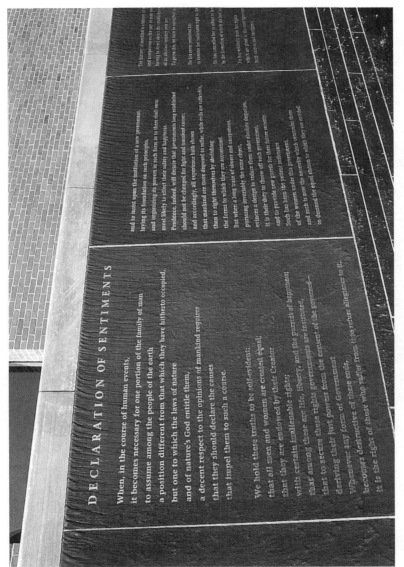

Waterwall at the Wesleyan Chapel, Seneca Falls

CHAPTER 3

Stories of the Struggle

"They [the women of America] cut a path through the
tangled underwood of old traditions, out to broader ways.
They lived to hear their work called brave and good,
But oh! the thorns before the crown of bays.
The world gives lashes to its Pioneers
Until the goal is reached—and then deafening cheers."

Anna Howard Shaw

Mary Wollstonecraft's Influence on the Women's Rights Movement

"Those who are bold enough to advance before the age they live in, and to throw off, by the force of their own minds, the prejudices which the maturing reason of the world will in time disavow, must learn to brave censure. We ought not to be too anxious respecting the opinion of others."

Mary Wollstonecraft

Mary Wollstonecraft, who was born in London in 1759, helped shape the Women's Rights Movement even though she was born a century before the first organized actions of the Movement in the United States. Her book, *A Vindication of the Rights of Women*, which was published in 1792, provided a source for the principal themes of the Movement. In the dedication of the book, she wrote, "the main argument of the work is built on this simple principle that if woman is not prepared by education to become the companion of man, she will stop the progress of knowledge, for truth must be common to all, or it will be ineffective with respect to its influence or general practice."

Mary Wollstonecraft thought that young women should be educated, not to serve men but for women's own purposes, as reasoning creatures "who, in common with men, are placed on this earth to unfold their faculties." Women's principal goal should be to develop their character "as a human being, regardless of the distinction of sex." Wollstonecraft thought that independence was the "grand blessing" of life, and that a young woman's education should develop her mind and body to yield a self-reliant, thinking individual who could earn her own living.

Those who spoke out against the book were more disturbed by the personal life of the author than the material that she included in the book. Mary Wollstonecraft, an independent woman who supported herself, had lived with two men without being married and had an illegitimate daughter. She was a professional writer of anthologies, children's stories, essays, reviews, and translations. She was part of a group of writers that included William Blake, Thomas Paine, and William Godwin, the author of works on political science.

Mary Wollstonecraft and William Godwin fell in love and married. She died at the age of thirty-eight after giving birth to their daughter, Mary. Mary Godwin grew up to become Mary Godwin Shelley, the second wife of the poet Percy Bysshe Shelley. Her book, *Frankenstein*, established an international reputation for her when it was published in 1818.

A Vindication of the Rights of Woman created waves as soon as it was published. Boston and Philadelphia editions followed the London edition, and it was translated into French. The book and its author were widely praised by progressive thinkers. In 1840, Lucretia Mott and Elizabeth Cady Stanton discussed the book when they met at the World Anti-Slavery Convention in London.

Decades later, Mary Wollstonecraft's thoughts were incorporated into the writings and speeches of the U.S. Women's Rights Movement. In 1881, the first volume of the *History of Woman Suffrage* was dedicated to nineteen women "Whose Earnest Lives and Fearless Words were a Constant Inspiration." Mary Wollstonecraft's name led the list.

Margaret Fuller's Early Thoughts on Feminism

"We would have every path laid open to women as freely as to man.... Inward and outward freedom for woman as much as for man shall be acknowledged as a right, not yielded as a concession.... Man cannot by right lay even well-meant restrictions on woman.... What woman needs is not as a woman to act or to rule, but as a nature to grow, as an intellect to discern, as a soul to live freely and unimpeded, to unfold such powers as were given her."

Margaret Fuller

Margaret Fuller was born in Cambridge, Massachusetts, on May 23, 1810. Her father, Timothy Fuller, a lawyer, was a member of the Senate of the Commonwealth of Massachusetts and of the U.S. Congress. He had received a classical education at Harvard College and was determined to pass his learning on to his oldest child. Margaret Fuller began reading Latin at the age of six and learned French, Greek, and Italian within a few years; she added German in her late teens. She read extensively in all of these languages. She began as a "youthful prodigy" and became one of the most learned American women.

In 1835, Fuller began to teach languages in Alcott's school, and, in 1837, was the principal teacher at the Green Street School in Providence. Teaching was not challenging enough for her, however. She said, "I must die if I do not burst forth in genius or heroism." She was concerned that women had so few opportunities to use their intellect. She wanted to teach women to think analytically, "to systemize thought and give a precision and clearness in which our sex are so deficient ... because they have so few inducements to test and classify what they receive."

In 1839, Fuller began her famous "conversations," a series of meetings for the educated women of Boston at which they discussed a wide range of topics and read papers that they had prepared. She guided the discussion, but all attendees were required to speak to improve their ability to organize ideas and present them effectively. Women did not speak in public at this time; these "conversations" were another step along the way to prepare women for speechmaking.

In 1840, Fuller was appointed chief editor of the Transcendentalist magazine, the *Dial*. The Transcendentalists were an informal group of scholars, writers, and ministers who met to discuss the new idealistic philosophies that had originated in Germany and taken root in England and France. These philosophies were called "transcendental" because they went beyond, or transcended, the limitations of logic and material concerns. In addition to Fuller, the group included Bronson Alcott, Ralph Waldo Emerson, Sophia and Elizabeth Peabody, George and Sarah Ripley, and Henry David Thoreau. Sophia Peabody later married Nathaniel Hawthorne.

The Transcendentalists emphasized freedom and tolerance and believed in the individual worth of men and women. They accepted women as the intellectual equals of men and later supported the Women's Rights Movement. George and Sarah Ripley founded Brook Farm, a Utopian colony.

In 1842, Fuller turned over her duties as editor the *Dial* to Ralph Waldo Emerson, although she continued as associate editor and contributor. One of the articles that she wrote for the *Dial* was "The Great Lawsuit: Man versus Woman, Woman versus Man," which dealt with feminist issues. She expanded the periodical article into *Woman in the Nineteenth Century*, the first full-length feminist book in the U.S.

In that book, Fuller affirmed that, "Earth knows no fairer, holier relation than that of a mother," but she stressed the need for "a complete life" for women as well as for men. Every opportunity open to men, she argued, should also be open to women. She concludes her book with a plea for self-reliance for women: "Women must take the responsibility for their own lot ... women are the best helpers of one another. Let them think, let them act, 'til they know what they need...." The book, along with Mary Wollstonecraft's *A Vindication of the Rights of Women*, became a source of doctrine for the Women's Rights Movement.

From 1844 to 1846, Fuller was the literary editor, and the first woman staff writer, of the New York *Tribune*. Horace Greeley called her "the best instructed woman in America." Considered one of the most capable literary critics in the United States, she introduced many French and German authors, including Goethe, to America. She visited hospitals and prisons and wrote a series of articles alerting the public to the inhumane conditions that existed in these institutions.

Fuller visited England and France in 1846 and settled in

Italy, where she married the Marquis Giovanni Ossoli and had a son. Her husband was a follower of Mazzini, the great liberal patriot. During the three-month siege of Rome, she took charge of a hospital while her husband fought on the walls. During this difficult time, she wrote a book on the struggle for Italian freedom and continued to contribute to the New York *Tribune*.

In May 1850, the Ossoli family sailed for the United States. On June 16, their ship went aground on a sandbar about fifty yards off Long Island in a heavy gale. The lifeboats were swept away before the passengers could board them. The Marchioness Ossoli and her husband and child drowned in the storm.

Fuller died just as the Women's Rights Movement was beginning. Plans had been made to invite her to become a leader in the Movement upon her return to the United States. Cady Stanton said that she had influenced "the thought of American women more that any other woman previous to her time." By her life, Margaret Fuller showed what a woman could accomplish and provided an example of the complete person that she advocated. She would have been a strong contributor to the Women's Rights Movement had she lived.

Amelia Bloomer's Role in the Women's Rights Movement

"The Lily was the first paper devoted to the interests of woman and, so far as I know, the first one owned, edited, and published by a woman, It was a novel thing for me to do in those days and I was little fitted for it, but the force of circumstances led me into it and strength was given me to carry it through. It was a needed instrumentality to spread abroad the truth of new gospel to woman, and I could not withhold my hand to stay the work I had begun. I saw not the end from the beginning and little dreamed whereto my proposition for society would lead me."

Amelia Bloomer

Amelia Jenks Bloomer, for whom bloomers were named, was born on May 27, 1818, in the village of Homer, New York. She was the youngest of four daughters of Ananias Jenks, clothier, and Lucy Webb Jenks. She attended Homer schools and, after graduating at the age of seventeen, accepted a teaching position in the village of Clyde in Wayne County.

In 1836, the Jenks family moved to Waterloo, which was the home of their daughter, Elvira. In 1837, Amelia became the governess and tutor for the children of a Waterloo family. She met Dexter Bloomer, who was an owner and editor of the Seneca County *Courier* that was printed weekly in Seneca Falls. They fell in love and were married on April 15, 1840. She agreed with her husband to leave out the word "obey" in their wedding vows.

The temperance movement was very active in the first half of the nineteenth century, and speaking out against "demon drink" was a popular cause. Bloomer helped to establish the local temperance society and contributed to its newsletter, the *Water Bucket*. She became an officer of the Ladies Temperance Society and published its newsletter, the *Lily*.

Temperance society activity was her principal interest until 1847, when Elizabeth Cady Stanton moved to Seneca Falls. Cady Stanton, Lucretia Mott, and three other women called the first Women's Rights Convention in Seneca Falls on July 19-20, 1848. Bloomer attended the Convention and was impressed with the speakers, particularly with Cady Stanton.

In the spring of 1849, Dexter Bloomer was appointed Postmaster of Seneca Falls, and Amelia accepted the position of Assistant Postmaster. The new Assistant Postmaster considered herself as an example "of a woman's right to fill any place for which she had the capacity." She performed well in the position for the next four years, while continuing to edit and publish the *Lily*. Elizabeth Cady Stanton wrote articles for the *Lily* using the pseudonym "Sun Flower." The newsletter became more militant with the addition of the letterhead, "The Emancipation of Woman from Intemperance, Injustice,

Prejudice, and Bigotry."

In 1851, Bloomer introduced two people who were to have a significant impact on life in the United States. She wrote in her journal:

> It was in the spring of 1851 that I introduced Susan B. Anthony to Mrs. Stanton. Miss Anthony had come to attend an antislavery meeting in Seneca Falls, held by George Thompson and William Lloyd Garrison, and was my guest. Returning from the meeting we stopped at the street corner and waited for Mrs. Stanton, and I gave the introduction which resulted in a life-long friendship. Afterwards, we called together at Mrs. Stanton's house and the way was opened for future intercourse between them. It was, as Mrs. Stanton says in her history, an eventful meeting that henceforth in a measure shaped their lives. Neither would have done what she did without the other. Mrs. Stanton had the intellectual, and Susan the executive, ability to carry forward the movement then recently inaugurated. Without the push of Miss Anthony, Mrs. Stanton would never have gone abroad into active life, or achieved half she has done; and without the brains of Mrs. Stanton, Miss Anthony would never have been so large-ly known to the world by name and deeds. They helped and strengthened each other, and together they have accomplished great things for women and humanity. The writer is glad for the part she had in bringing two such char-acters together.

One of the many conditions that women had to tolerate in

the mid-1800s was a lack of freedom in their style of dress. A woman's dress was complicated in the 1850s. Under her long skirts, she wore a cambric petticoat, a plain longcloth petticoat, two flannel petticoats with scalloped hems, a lined petticoat with a hem that stood out, and lace-trimmed drawers. Three starched muslin petticoats usually replaced the flannel petticoats in hot weather.

In January, 1851, Dexter Bloomer's successor as editor of the Seneca County *Courier* wrote an article about women's clothing in London in which he mentioned that "improvement in the attire of females was being agitated." He suggested that women's dress should be less cumbersome and recommended that women wear Turkish pantaloons with a skirt that reached below the knee.

Amelia Bloomer responded in the *Lily*: "now that our cautious editor of the *Courier* recommends it [wearing pantaloons], we suppose that there will be no harm in our doing so. Small waists and whalebones can be dispensed with, and we will be allowed breathing room; and our forms shall be what nature made them. We are so thankful that men are beginning to undo some of the mischief they have done us."

In February, 1851, the issue of women's clothing was raised when Elizabeth Cady Stanton's cousin, Libby Smith Miller, visited her in Seneca Falls. Miller had just returned from a honeymoon grand tour of Europe. In Switzerland, she had seen women in sanatoriums wearing long, full Turkish trousers made of broadcloth with a short skirt that reached just below the knee. She made a traveling costume for herself in this style. Her cousin immediately adopted the style of dress. The two cousins visited Bloomer at the Post Office, and, within a few days, she had donned the new costume too.

Bloomer wrote an article about the new style of dress and provided a sketch of it in the next issue of the *Lily*. She had no thoughts of completely adopting the style, of establishing fashion, or of attracting national attention. The New York *Tribune* was the first city newspaper to refer to her article;

that reference was followed by many others. Some praised the costume, but many ridiculed it. Finally, one of the journalists referred to the "Bloomer costume," and the word entered the English lexicon. Bloomer tried to give credit to Libby Smith Miller for introducing the style to the United States, but newspaper publicity had established the word "bloomers" forever.

Soon, half of the mail handled by the Seneca Falls Post Office was addressed to Amelia Bloomer. Women from all over the country wrote for more information on how to make the costume. The dress became popular among supporters of the Women's Rights Movement, and Bloomer was invited to England to speak about the costume.

Eventually, wearing the bloomer costume became controversial. When it began to detract attention from the issues of the Women's Rights Movement, supporters of the movement, including Elizabeth Cady Stanton, stopped wearing it.

In the spring of 1852, Bloomer was elected corresponding secretary of the Women's Temperance Society for the State of New York. In 1853, she lectured at Metropolitan Hall in New York City. Three thousand people bought tickets; many were turned away. She had become a national figure.

In 1855, Dexter Bloomer purchased the *Western Home Visitor*, and the Bloomer family moved to Council Bluffs, Iowa. Amelia Bloomer edited the newspaper; when she caught the typesetters drinking on the job, she replaced them with female typesetters. She crusaded for the temperance movement and the Women's Rights Movement all her life. She died on December 30, 1894.

Susan B. Anthony's Trial

"Abraham Lincoln said: 'No man is good enough to govern another man without his consent.' Now I say to you, 'No man is good enough to govern any woman without her consent.'"

Susan B. Anthony, 1895

On November 1, 1872, Susan B. Anthony and her sisters Guelma, Hannah, and Mary decided to register to vote. The election inspectors told them that, according to New York State law, they would not be permitted to register. Susan quoted to them from the Amendments to the Constitution and insisted that she, as a citizen, had a right to vote. They were permitted to register. Anthony and her sisters then voted in the general election on November 5th. She received wide newspaper coverage, including articles in the Chicago *Tribune* and the New York *Times*. She realized that she may have broken the law and might be liable for a $500 fine. On November 18th, a marshal came to the Anthony home and arrested them.

Anthony and her sisters were arraigned and their bond set at $500 each. Her sisters each posted the $500 bail, but Anthony refused to pay it. Her lawyer, Henry Selden, who did not want to see his client go to jail, paid her bail. Unfortunately, by posting her bail he had inadvertently prevented her from appealing to higher courts—potentially as far as the U.S. Supreme Court. Posting bail indicated that she was not contesting the lawfulness of her arrest. Susan made many speeches describing what was happening to her, including speeches in Monroe County, where her case was to be tried. Because of the intense public interest in her case in Monroe County, the trial was moved to Ontario County, south of Rochester.

On June 17, 1873, Anthony's trial began in Canandaigua. Judge Ward Hunt, who had only recently been appointed to the bench, was selected to try her case. Selden conducted a skillful defense, pointing out that Anthony sincerely believed that she had been given the right to vote by the Fourteenth and Fifteenth Amendments. Judge Hunt refused to let her speak in her own defense.

Judge Hunt stated that it didn't matter what Susan's beliefs were; she had broken the law. He took a note from his pocket, turned toward the jury, and read from it. The note concluded with the statement, "If I am right in this, the result

Susan B. Anthony House, Rochester

must be a verdict ... of guilty, and I therefore direct that you find a verdict of guilty." An incensed Selden reminded the judge that he did not have the right to instruct the jury in that way and demanded that the jury be asked for their verdict. Hunt ignored Selden, instructed the court clerk to record the verdict, and dismissed the jury.

This miscarriage of justice was widely covered by the press. Even people who disapproved of Anthony's voting sided with her because of this unjust treatment in the court-room. Judge Hunt's actions were politically motivated. His mentor was Roscoe Conkling, U.S. Senator from New York and a professed foe of the Women's Rights Movement. Selden requested a new trial on the basis that Anthony had been denied a fair trial by jury. Judge Hunt denied the request and stated her sentence—a $100 fine. She responded: "I shall never pay a dollar of your unjust penalty." The fine was never paid.

The Support of George Francis Train

"Mr. Train is a pure, high-toned man, without a vice. He has some extravagances and idiosyncrasies, but he is willing to devote energy and money to our cause when no other man is. It seems to me it would be right and wise to accept aid even from the devil himself, provided he did not attempt to lower our standard."

Elizabeth Cady Stanton

In 1867, a referendum was held in Kansas on propositions to eliminate the words "male" and "white" for the requirements for voters in the State Constitution. Lucy Stone and her husband, Henry Blackwell, spent the spring of 1867 touring the state advocating the acceptance of both propositions. In the late summer and early fall, Susan B. Anthony and Elizabeth Cady Stanton traveled around Kansas promoting the propositions.

They contended with bad food and primitive living conditions, including prairie insects and bedbugs. Their efforts were unsuccessful; both propositions failed. Susan B. Anthony and Elizabeth Cady Stanton were undeterred, however. They stayed in Kansas for an additional month on the lecture circuit.

Their male friends were increasingly backing away from the Women's Rights Movement to concentrate on obtaining the vote for African Americans. For example, Gerrit Smith, who had supported the rights of women strongly in the past, told them that addressing "the political disabilities of race is my first desire—of sex, my second." Women began to realize that they were going to have to rely upon members of their own sex to make the changes that they sought.

Their Republican friends in Kansas had not supported them actively, and the women felt that they had been let down. The Republicans were concerned about failing to secure the vote for African Americans and the accompanying loss of potential new voters. They began not only to reduce their support of women's suffrage but also to openly oppose it due to their own political priorities.

At the peak of Anthony's and Cady Stanton's disappointment with the weak Republican support, the St. Louis Suffrage Association offered to send a Democratic speaker to Kansas to encourage votes for women's suffrage. They considered the Democratic party a supporter of slavery, but they were willing to accept help from any source that offered it.

The Democratic speaker was George Francis Train, a wealthy, eccentric Irish-American financier who made his fortune building clipper ships, constructing street railways in England, and developing the Union Pacific Railroad. He saw himself as the "Champion Crank," because of the scrapes with the law and scandals in which he had been involved.

Train's radical views disturbed both abolitionists and conservative women. He espoused ideas that were ahead of their time, such as the eight-hour workday, organized labor, paper currency, Irish independence, and women's suffrage. Train also wrote articles about open immigration and the abolition of standing armies. He offered to pay his own expenses and Anthony made the travel arrangements for him. Train, who dressed well and had a romantic image, was a dynamic speaker who proved to be an effective agent for women's suffrage.

Helen Elkin Starret, one of Anthony's coworkers in Kansas, commented upon Train's efforts for women's suffrage in Kansas:

> The work of George Francis Train has been much and variously commented upon. Certainly when he was in Kansas he was at the height of his prosperity and popularity, and in appearance, manners, and conversation, was a perfect, though somewhat unique specimen of a courtly, elegant gentleman. He was full of enthusiasm and confident he would be the next President. He drew immense and enthusiastic audiences everywhere, and was a special favorite with the laboring classes on account of the reforms he promised to bring about when he should be President. Well do I remember one woman, a frantic advocate of Women's Suffrage, who buttonholed everybody who spoke a word against Train to beg them to desist; assuring them that he was the special instrument of Providence to gain for us the Irish vote.

Susan B. Anthony was sufficiently impressed with Train to pay him this tribute:

> At this auspicious moment George Francis Train appeared in the State. He appealed most effectively to the chivalry of the intelligent

Irishman, and the prejudices of the ignorant; conjuring them not to take the word "white" out of their Constitution unless they did the word "male" also; not to lift the Negroes above the heads of their own mothers, sisters, and daughters. The result was a respectable Democratic vote in favor of women's suffrage.

Upon completion of their speaking tour in Kansas, Train made Susan B. Anthony and Elizabeth Cady Stanton two offers: to finance a women's suffrage newspaper and to pay all expenses if they would accompany him on a lecture tour on their return trip to the East. They accepted and stayed at the best hotels. Train paid for the printing costs of their hand-bills and pamphlets. They spoke before packed houses in fifteen cities. The return trip cost him over $3,000. Upon their arrival in New York, Train gave them $600 to start their news-paper.

In January 1868, Train and his friend, Thomas Clark Durant, an associate with the Union Pacific Railroad, arrived in Queenstown, Ireland, on the steamship *Scotia*. Ireland, at the time, was tense from insurrections in the southern and western parts of the country during the previous summer and fall. Martial law had been imposed upon Dublin. Train was arrested and sent to the county jail in Cork.

Train was known as a supporter of the Fenian Brotherhood, and he had a reputation as an England-baiter. He immediate-ly appealed for release via the U.S. Consul, E. G. Eastman. Later, he was moved to a prison in Dublin. He was kept in prison for almost ten months without being convicted of any offense. Train contributed articles to the women's rights newspaper that he helped to finance, the *Revolution*, until Susan B. Anthony and Elizabeth Cady Stanton decided that his association with them was a negative influence.

Train announced his candidacy for the Presidency in 1869 and made campaign speeches for the next three years. He had no further direct association with the Women's Rights Movement. He was the author of many books, including his autobiography, *My Life in Many States and Foreign Lands*, which was published in 1902. George Francis Train died in New York City on January 19, 1904.

The *Revolution*

"The establishing of woman on her rightful throne is the greatest revolution the world has ever known or will know. To bring it about is no child's play. You and I have not forgotten the conflict of the last twenty years—the unmixed bitterness of our cup. A journal called the Rosebud might answer for those who come with kid gloves and perfumes to lay immortal wreaths on monuments which in sweat and tears others have hewn and built; but for us there is no name like the Revolution."

Elizabeth Cady Stanton

The newspaper that George Francis Train offered to finance for the Women's Rights Movement was called the *Revolution*. Its motto was "Men, their rights, and nothing more; women, their rights, and nothing less." Susan B. Anthony and Elizabeth Cady Stanton wanted a forum for Cady Stanton's use in putting forward their ideas about the Women's Rights Movement. Train gave them $600 to pay for the publication of the first issue of the *Revolution*, which was published on January 8, 1868.

The newspaper began as a six-page weekly. Elizabeth Cady Stanton and Parker Pillsbury, an experienced journalist and antislavery activist, were the editors, and Susan B. Anthony was the business manager and publisher. Train acquired David Melliss, financial editor of the New York *World*, as a partner. Train and Melliss agreed to finance the publication of the paper until it became self-sufficient in return for the use of the back pages to discuss their opinions about financial and

111

political issues, such as President Johnson's impeachment trial and the 1868 party conventions. Melliss provided a folksy column about Wall Street. Cady Stanton contributed articles on a variety of subjects beyond universal suffrage, including:

- additional occupations for women
- revision of the divorce laws
- equal pay for equal work
- role of the church on women's rights
- health care for women
- training for women to be self-supporting
- problems of poverty

Anthony was doing what she wanted to do. She observed that her time as editor of the *Revolution* was "one the happiest of my life, and the most useful."

The *Revolution* filled a real need in the Women's Rights Movement because it contained information on subjects of interest to women that no other newspaper carried. It served as a clearinghouse for such news about women as their movement into new occupations. Harriet Beecher Stowe, the author of *Uncle Tom's Cabin*, refused to write an article for the *Revolution* unless its name was changed to a less aggressive title, such as the *True Republic*. The editors were not willing to change the name.

Many supporters of the newspaper questioned linking up with George Francis Train, whom William Lloyd Garrison considered to be a "crack-brained harlequin and semi-lunatic" who was "as destitute of principle as he is of sense." Garrison also observed, "He may be of use in drawing an audience, but so would a kangaroo, a gorilla, or a hippopotamus."

Lucy Stone, who chaired the executive committee of the Equal Rights Association, thought that Train's "presence as an advocate of women's suffrage was enough to condemn it in the minds of all persons not already convinced." He was considered to be against seeking the vote for African Americans before women, a viewpoint he advanced with statements such as "Woman first, and Negro last is my program."

The Women's Rights Movement began to move in two different directions, one sponsored by the "New York" contingent of Susan B. Anthony, Lucretia Mott, Ernestine Rose, and Elizabeth Cady Stanton, and the "Boston" group lead by Lucy Stone and her husband, Henry Blackwell. The New Yorkers wanted to discuss divorce at the women's rights conventions; the New Englanders disagreed.

The principal difference between the two groups was that the Boston group wanted to push African-American suffrage first, holding off the effort to obtain women's suffrage until that goal was reached. The New Yorkers favored moving ahead with both African-American and Women's suffrage. In particular, the New Englanders objected to the *Revolution*, with its articles on divorce and criminal cases involving women.

One of the first actions of the Boston group after splitting off from the National Woman Suffrage Association was to establish their own conservative newspaper, the *Woman's Journal*. Its first issue was published in January 1870. The editors were Mary Livermore, Lucy Stone, and Julia Ward Howe. In 1869, Mary Livermore, the editor-in-chief, had founded a suffrage newspaper, the *Agitator*, which merged with the *Woman's Journal* the following year. Julia Ward Howe, an activist in the antislavery and woman right's movements, is remembered for composing "The Battle Hymn of the Republic" in 1861.

Mary Livermore had considered merging with the *Revolution*, but she decided against it because she was "repelled by some of the idiosyncrasies of our New York friends ... their opposition to the Fifteenth Amendment, the buffoonery of George F. Train, and the loose utterances of the *Revolution* on the marriage and dress questions."

The new newspaper had a profound impact on the *Revolution*. Already in financial trouble, the *Revolution* began to fail when the *Woman's Journal* took part of its readership. George Francis Train had left for Ireland shortly after giving Anthony $600 to pay for the first issue. He told her that Melliss would pay to publish further issues. When Train spent the following year in jail in Ireland, he sent articles to be printed in the *Revolution* but no money. Melliss provided some money to publish the newspaper, but it wasn't enough.

Train suggested that the newspaper might have wider acceptance if his name was disassociated with it, and articles written by him were discontinued in May 1869. However, the *Revolution* lasted only one more year. Anthony worked hard to expand the circulation and did everything she could to save the newspaper, including borrowing from relatives and friends. In May 1870, she sold the newspaper for one dollar to Laura Curtis Bullard, who initially published it as a literary and society journal and then merged it with the New York *Christian Enquirer*.

Susan B. Anthony assumed the unpaid debts of more than $10,000, which she personally paid—primarily by speaking on the lecture circuit and by scrimping on personal expenditures. Her family and friends counseled her to declare the *Revolution* bankrupt, which would have absolved her from the newspaper's financial obligations. However, she told Elizabeth Cady Stanton, "My pride for women, to say nothing of my conscience, says no." In May 1876, after working on the Lyceum lecture circuit for six years, she made the last payment on the debt.

The Schism within the Women's Rights Movement

"For over thirty years some people have said from time to time that I have injured the suffrage movement beyond redemption; but it still lives. Train killed it, Victoria Woodhull killed it, the Revolution killed it. But with each death it put on

a new life.... Reforms are not made of blown glass to be broken to pieces with the first adverse wind."

Elizabeth Cady Stanton, 1880

By 1867-68, many of the leaders of the Women's Rights Movement disagreed with the actions taken by Susan B. Anthony and Elizabeth Cady Stanton. In particular, they disagreed with their association with George Francis Train and with the tone of the *Revolution*. Many members of the movement blamed Anthony for these activities and disagreed with her "dictatorial" methods. They thought that she was a bad influence on Cady Stanton, whose friends tried to persuade her to distance herself from Anthony and from the *Revolution*.

However, Cady Stanton remembered that early in the Civil War, Anthony had counseled to continue with the Women's Rights Movement during the war. Most of the other leaders of the Movement recommended that they renew their effort after the war. They convinced Cady Stanton to go along with them. After the war, she realized that Anthony had been right; the loss of four years merely delayed further the achievement of their goals. Cady Stanton said, "ever since, I have taken my beloved Susan's judgment against the world."

The movement began to split into two wings. The "New York" wing included Susan B. Anthony, Lucretia Mott, Ernestine Rose, Elizabeth Cady Stanton, and Martha Wright. The "Boston" contingent lead by Lucy Stone and her husband, Henry Blackwell, included many of the male antislavery activists.

One of the personal factors in the schism was the coolness that had developed between Susan B. Anthony and Lucy Stone. Anthony had warned Stone that her marriage and childbearing would reduce her commitment to the Women's Rights Movement. Stone felt that her family decisions were personal ones and looked upon Anthony's comments as interference in her personal life.

Another difference of opinion between the two groups was whether or not divorce should be a topic at women's rights conventions. The New York wing wanted divorce included in the agendas and the Boston group did not. The Boston group was unhappy that the articles on divorce in the *Revolution* were perceived as speaking for the entire Women's Rights Movement. Some members of the public who read the articles considered the Movement to be against marriage. Generally, the New Englanders viewed the New Yorkers as outspoken extremists.

The greatest difference of opinion between the two wings of the Movement was their positions on whether to push for the vote for women and for African Americans simultaneously or to work for winning the vote for African Americans first. The New Yorkers worked to obtain the vote for both women and African Americans at the same time; the New Englanders wanted to concentrate on African-American suffrage first. The inclusion in the Boston group of many men who had been antislavery activists was an influence on their approach.

Elizabeth Cady Stanton's viewpoint on the effort to obtain the vote for African Americans prior to women represented the New Yorkers. "If we love the Black man as well as ourselves, we shall fulfill the Bible injunction. The ... requirement to love him better is a little too much for human nature." When the New York contingent was asked to choose between women and Negroes, they began to move away from advocating universal suffrage and toward supporting suffrage for the educated because it favored the women's cause.

The New Yorkers argued that if African-American men were given the right to vote first, the number of men who might vote against suffrage for women would be increased. However, if women were given the vote first, African-American suffrage would not be affected negatively, because most of those in the Women's Rights Movement advocated the Negro vote.

In 1868, the division between the two factions widened

with the active discussion of the Fifteenth Amendment to the Constitution. The New Yorkers wanted the word "sex" included with the phrase "on account of race, color, or previous condition of servitude" in reference to withholding rights to citizens. Elizabeth Cady Stanton wrote an editorial, "That Infamous Fifteenth Amendment" in the *Revolution* and began to push for a Sixteenth Amendment to address the vote for women. Lucy Stone and her New Englanders wanted to wait until the Fifteenth Amendment granting the vote to African Americans was ratified.

Also in 1868, Susan B. Anthony began to organize workingwomen's organizations to further support the Women's Rights Movement. The first labor organization that she formed was the Workingwomen's Association, which was principally for members of the printing trades. Her second effort, appropriately called Workingwomen's Association No. 2, was for members of the seamstress trades.

Stone was interested in the rights of women to control their own earnings and their own property, but she had no interest in the trade union movement. Also, she disliked some of the techniques used by labor organizations, such as strikes.

Anthony's search for support for the Women's Rights Movement in the trade union movement was not entirely successful. Workingwomen wanted the eight-hour workday, equal pay for equal work, and the equivalent opportunities for advancement as men. She tried to convince workingwomen to increase their political rights first and then to use these increased rights to pursue improved economic rights. Workingwomen were concerned that agitating for the vote would delay reaching their goal of improved working conditions. The Women's Rights Movement continued to be mainly an activity of middle-class women. Working-class women had other priorities.

In May 1869, a dramatic break between the two factions of the Women's Rights Movement occurred at a meeting of the Equal Rights Association. Many of the attendees opposed

Susan B. Anthony and Elizabeth Cady Stanton because of their association with George Francis Train and the opinions the *Revolution*. However, differences in opinions about the Fifteenth Amendment were in the forefront at this convention.

Frederick Douglass, a former slave who had been a strong supporter of the Women's Rights Movement since the first Women's Rights Convention in Seneca Falls, spoke passionately in support of the Fifteenth Amendment:

> Black men first and white women afterwards ... I must say that I do not see how anyone can pretend that there is the same urgency in giving the ballot to women as to the Negro. With us, it is a question of life and death ... When women, because they are women ... are objects of insult and outrage at every turn; when they are in danger of of having their homes burnt down over their heads; when their children are not allowed to enter schools; then they will have an urgency to obtain the ballot equal to our own.

Immediately after the meeting of the Equal Rights Association, the women who agreed with Susan B. Anthony and Elizabeth Cady Stanton met to organize the National Woman Suffrage Association to work for the passage of an amendment to the Constitution granting the vote to women. Lucy Stone and the New England wing of the Movement were offended by not being included in the planning session for the new organization. Furthermore, they were upset that the new organization called themselves a "national" organization, which implied that it represented a broader group than it did.

In November 1869, Stone and the New Englanders formed the American Woman Suffrage Association "to unite those who cannot use the methods, and means, which Mrs. Stanton and Susan use." The American Woman Suffrage Association admitted men and women on a equal basis; the National Woman Suffrage Association was principally a women's organization in which men could not hold office.

Henry Ward Beecher, the abolitionist minister and editor, was elected president of the American Association, and Henry Blackwell was a secretary. The American Association focused on a narrower set of issues, specifically local and state suffrage, and avoided controversial issues. The National Association concentrated on obtaining a woman suffrage amendment to the Constitution and on issues affecting women's role in society.

Initially, Lucretia Mott tried to bring the two organizations together, but their viewpoints were too far apart. She and Martha Wright were active members of the National Association. Most of the women of the West were allied with Susan B. Anthony and Elizabeth Cady Stanton of the National Association. The westerners had always looked to Anthony and Cady Stanton for leadership, and they were less concerned than the conservative New Englanders about discussions about birth control, divorce, and sex.

The American Woman Suffrage Association and the National Woman Suffrage Association both worked toward the same general goals. Both organizations had a place in the scheme of pursuing additional rights for women. Women who wanted the vote, but who didn't want to be involved in the more controversial issues found a home in the American Association.

After twenty years of operating two separate organizations, the leaders of the Women's Rights Movement realized that their effort would be more efficient if the two associations were merged into one. Alice Stone Blackwell, Lucy Stone's daughter, played a key role in the union of the two organizations. In 1890, after two years of negotiations, the National American Woman Suffrage Association was established. Elizabeth Cady Stanton was elected president, Susan B.

Anthony became the vice president, and Lucy Stone was head of the executive committee.

Victoria Woodhull's Campaign

"When the men who make laws for us in Washington can stand forth and declare themselves pure and unspotted from all the sins mentioned in the Decalogue, then we will demand that every woman who makes a Constitutional argument on our platform shall be as chaste as Diana.... We have crucified the Mary Wollstonecrafts, the Fanny Wrights, the George Sands, the Fanny Kembles, of all ages.... If Victoria Woodhull must be crucified, let men drive the spikes and plait the crown of thorns."

Elizabeth Cady Stanton

Victoria Claflin Woodhull contributed one of the most unusual chapters to the Women's Rights Movement. She married "Dr." Canning Woodhull, who had some limited medical training, when she was sixteen. Dr. Woodhull joined the Claflin family, who were known in Ohio for their beliefs in spiritualism and faith healing, and in selling patent medicine called "the elixir of life." The Woodhulls and Victoria's sister, Tennessee (Tennie C.) Claflin, moved to Pittsburgh were they met Cornelius Vanderbilt.

Vanderbilt was attracted to Tennessee by her youth, her liveliness, and her reputation as a faith healer. He established the sisters in a brokerage business in New York and gave them financial advice with which they made a small fortune. They began to publish *Woodhull and Claflin's Weekly*, a newspaper devoted to political and social reform. The masthead declared "PROGRESS! FREE THOUGHT! UNTRAMMELED LIVES! / Breaking the Way for Future Generations."

The weekly contained financial information, but it also included articles on a wide variety of subjects, including birth control, free love, sex, and spiritualism. It supported the

Women's Rights Movement with articles on vocational training for young women and on women's suffrage.

Victoria Woodhull's personal life was considered scandalous. She divorced Dr. Woodhull and married a Colonel Blood. However, Dr. Woodhull continued to live in her house; she explained that her ex-husband was required to correct grammar in the weekly newspaper that she and her sister published. The Claflin sisters believed that they should have the same sexual freedom as men. Woodhull was quoted as saying that it was her "unalienable right" to have as many lovers as she wanted.

Woodhull also had strong feelings about women's suffrage. In some of her articles, she attempted to make a case for the Fourteenth and Fifteenth Amendments giving women the right to vote. The Fourteenth Amendment includes the sentence, "All persons born or naturalized in the United States and subject to the jurisdiction thereof, are citizens of the United States and of the State wherein they reside." Section 1 of the Fifteenth Amendment states that "the right of citizens of the United States to vote shall not be denied or abridged by the United States or by any State on account of race, color, or previous condition of servitude."

In 1871, Woodhull was granted permission to present a petition to the judiciary committee of the House of Representatives. She referred to the rights that these two Amendments granted to U.S. citizens. She argued that since women were citizens, these rights were granted to them also. She addressed the judiciary committee on the same morning on which the annual convention of the National Woman Suffrage Association was scheduled to open in Washington, D.C. When Susan B. Anthony heard about Woodhull's address, she postponed the opening of the Convention and attended the meeting of the judiciary committee.

Anthony and her associates were impressed by the modest and sincere manner in which the attractive, well-dressed Victoria Woodhull presented her speech. They invited her to repeat her address to the National Association's annual convention the following day. In May 1871, Elizabeth Cady Stanton invited Woodhull to speak at the anniversary convention of the National Woman Suffrage Association in New York City.

Woodhull wasn't well known in Washington, D.C., but in New York City her lifestyle was trumpeted by the press. The newspapers published articles linking the Women's Rights Movement with free love and the destruction of the institution of marriage. Some officers of the National Association refused to sit on the same stage with the notorious Victoria Woodhull.

Susan B. Anthony began to question the help that Woodhull was offering the Women's Rights Movement. Elizabeth Cady Stanton had no such doubts about that "grand, brave woman." In January 1872 at the next annual convention of the National Association when Woodhull proposed the creation of a new political party, the Equal Rights Party, with herself as candidate for President, Anthony's doubts grew stronger. She squelched Victoria's proposal at the Convention and then left on a lecture tour of the West.

Anthony was alarmed to read in *Woodhull and Claflin's Weekly* that the National Woman Suffrage Association would hold a convention the following month in New York City to form a new political party and to nominate candidates for President and Vice President. Furthermore, she was mortified to note that the list of signatures on the announcement included not only Elizabeth Cady Stanton's but also her own. She sent a telegram to Cady Stanton demanding that the proposal to form a new party be withdrawn and that her name be disassociated with the activity.

Cady Stanton was so upset by Anthony's telegram that she resigned as president of the National Woman Suffrage Association. Anthony was elected to replace her as president. The new president defeated all attempts to use the Convention as a forum to establish a new political party. On the following day, without the benefit of the support of a national association, Victoria Woodhull announced the formation of the Equal Rights Party with her as the nominee for President and Frederick Douglass as Vice President. This came as a surprise to Douglass, who hadn't been consulted in the matter. He declined the nomination.

Elizabeth Cady Stanton was more of a visionary than Susan B. Anthony and tended to be more imaginative and impulsive. However, she respected Anthony's judgment and her tendency to consider the practical viewpoints of an issue. Eventually, Cady Stanton realized that Anthony had been right on this difference of opinion.

Ultimate Success—Obtaining the Right to Vote in the United States

"To get the word, male, out of the Constitution, cost the women of this country fifty-two years of pauseless campaign; 56 state referendum campaigns; 480 legislative campaigns to get state suffrage amendments submitted; 47 state constitutional convention campaigns; 277 state party convention campaigns; 30 national party convention campaigns to get suffrage planks in party platforms; 19 campaigns with 19 successive Congresses to get the federal amendments submitted, and the final ratification campaign. Millions of dollars were raised, mostly in small sums, and spent with economic care. Hundreds of women gave the accumulated possibilities of an entire lifetime, thousands gave years of their lives, hundreds of thousands gave constant interest and such aid as they could."

Carrie Chapman Catt

By the early 1900s, the Women's Rights Movement in the United States had lost momentum. Suffragists considered the years from 1896 to 1910 "the doldrums." During that time, no states passed woman suffrage laws and all of the referendums were lost, in New Hampshire, Oregon, South Dakota, and Washington. The effort to place an amendment to the Constitution before Congress was moribund.

In 1900, Susan B. Anthony stepped down as president of the National American Woman Suffrage Association and turned the reins over to Carrie Chapman Catt. The only time the Movement had a national headquarters was a brief period when Carrie Chapman Catt had a functioning national center in New York. The default headquarters was Warren, Ohio, the home of the treasurer, Harriet Taylor Upton. Catt served ably for four years, but she was worn out from ten exhausting years in the Movement and her husband was seriously ill. Also, she was becoming increasingly involved in the international suffrage movement.

In 1904, Dr. Anna Howard Shaw became the president of the National American Suffrage Association. She served as president for the next eleven years. Anna Shaw was Susan B. Anthony's closest friend and had the best interests of the Suffrage Association at heart. Although she was an intelligent person, management was not one of her strengths, and she was not a visionary. At a time when the Women's Rights Movement in the United States needed its batteries recharged, that recharge came from England.

In 1902, Harriot Stanton Blatch, Elizabeth Cady Stanton's daughter, returned to the United States with her family after living twenty years in England. She had followed closely the efforts of the Pankhurst family in England. She knew that the American suffrage movement could learn from the experience in England, particularly in obtaining the support of working-class women.

Susan B. Anthony had courted working-class women through her activity with the union movement, but she was distracted by having to provide the overall direction of the Suffrage Association. Neither Carrie Chapman Catt nor Anna Shaw promoted the interests of the working woman. Most of the Suffrage Association's members were middle-class women.

Harriot Stanton Blatch observed:

> The suffrage movement was completely in a rut in New York State at the opening of the twentieth century. It bored its adherents and repelled its opponents. Most of the ammunition was being wasted on its supporters in private drawing rooms and in public halls where friends, drummed up and harried by the ardent, listlessly heard the same old arguments....

> The only method suggested for furthering the cause was the slow process of education. We were told to organize, organize, organize, to the end of educating, educating, educating public opinion.... There did not seem to be a grain of political knowledge in the movement....

In 1907, Harriot Stanton Blatch founded the Women's Political Union in New York with three goals:

- to generate dramatic propaganda for the suffrage movement
- to bring professional and working-class women into the movement
- to educate its members to be more politically minded

The scene was being set for the final drive for the vote.

In 1912, one of the key players in that drive joined the suffrage movement in Washington, D.C. Alice Paul, who earned a Ph.D. in social studies from the University of Pennsylvania, returned from England where she had participated in the Women's Rights Movement with the Pankhursts. Like a younger version of Susan B. Anthony, Paul was totally dedicated to the Movement. She had experienced both jail and forcible feeding in England. She became the Movement's leader in the trenches; she was not afraid of being cursed and pummeled. One of her strengths was her ability to get people to work for the Movement.

Within two months, Alice Paul and her lieutenant, Lucy Burns, organized a parade of 5,000 women on the day before the inauguration of Woodrow Wilson. President-elect Wilson arrived in Washington to find bare streets and no welcoming crowd. He asked where all the people were and was told that they were all over at Pennsylvania Avenue watching the women's suffrage parade.

A rowdy crowd attempted to prevent the women from marching. It took the women an hour to fight their way through the first ten blocks. Ruffians greeted the marchers with obscene language and tried to trip them. The rowdies slapped them in the face, spit on them, and threw lit cigar stubs at them. Cavalry from Ft. Myers, members of the Massachusetts and Pennsylvania National Guard, and troops from Ft. Knox were required to restore order. The Chief of Police of Washington lost his job over the incident.

Alice Paul mobilized the vote of women in the western states that had already been granted the right to vote, including Wyoming, Utah, Colorado, Idaho, and California, to hold responsible Woodrow Wilson and the Democrats—the party in power—for their failure to obtain the elective franchise for women. Alice established a new organization, the Congressional Union, to push for a women's suffrage amendment. The National American Woman Suffrage Association (NAWSA) would not allow Paul's Union to be an auxiliary of their organization; The Congressional Union was too much of an activist organization for them. Alice split off from NAWSA, and the Congressional Union evolved into the National Woman's Party.

In 1916, Carrie Chapman Catt reassumed the presidency of

the NAWSA. She chose a board of dedicated, full-time members to work with her. The suffrage movement now had two organizations with trained and experienced staffs to work toward its goals. Paul concentrated on getting a women's suffrage amendment through Congress, and Chapman Catt dedicated her organization to obtaining the elective franchise for women state by state. Amateur activists had been replaced by professional organizers, and the Women's Rights Movement was now in position to accomplish its goals.

Chapman Catt knew that the suffrage issue was a political issue, one that could only be resolved by political action. She was able to devise a plan of action and to effectively implement that program. She was an outstanding manager who developed an effective organization to carry out the plan to achieve her vision.

Chapman Catt continued to work to win the support of President Wilson. She invited him to speak at the NAWSA Convention in Atlantic City, where she proposed to unveil "the Winning Plan" for obtaining the vote for women. The President agreed to speak at Atlantic City, where he said, "I come not to fight for you, but with you."

Paul sent a continual stream of delegations of women to the White House demanding the vote. In December 1916, the President's message to Congress contained no reference to women's suffrage. She sent a delegation to the Capitol gallery to drape over the railing a banner containing the question, "Mr. President, what will you do for women's suffrage?" Guards moved toward the holders of the banner, and a page jumped up and pulled the banner down.

Paul began to send pickets to the White House gates. A mediator asked her to stop sending the pickets for reasons concerning the President's security. She refused. Next, the Chief of Police of Washington, D.C., requested that the picketing be stopped. Again, she refused. She sent a delegation to the White House to display a banner at the east gate. The police were about to arrest the contingent when they realized that the banner contained President Wilson's own words.

The police began to arrest the picketers for obstructing the roadways. They were taken to rat-infested cells at the District of Columbia jail. The thirty-day sentences were extended to sixty days. The women were transferred to the Occoquam Workhouse, which, although it was in the country, imposed worse conditions than the jail—including worms in the food.

Alice Paul was taken to jail with the others, including an elderly woman who had a heart attack but received no medical treatment and a woman who was thrown down, hit her head on a bed frame, and was knocked unconscious. Paul asked for some ventilation for their foul-smelling cell. The guards refused so the resourceful Paul threw a volume of Elizabeth Barrett Browning's poetry through the windowpane high on the wall of the cell. Then they had ventilation.

Paul began a hunger strike, but was forcibly fed and taken to the prison hospital. A nurse was instructed to flash a light in her face every hour throughout the night. On December 3, 1917, Paul and the other women prisoners were released. By the time of their release from jail, women had been granted full suffrage in New York and partial suffrage in seven other states.

The House of Representatives scheduled a vote on the suffrage Amendment for January 10, 1918. The 65th Congress had the first woman Representative in the history of that legislative body—Jeanette Rankin of Montana, who had led the State's successful fight for women's suffrage in 1914. The Amendment was forty-five votes short of approval by two-thirds majority, with forty-seven members undecided.

Congressman Ireland of Illinois was delayed by a train accident from returning to Washington. An attempt was made to pair his vote with an absent member of the opposition, but no opponent was found in time. Four members of Congress got out of their sick beds to vote: Representative Sims of Tennessee with a broken arm and shoulder that had not yet been set; Republican House minority leader Mann of Illinois, who had been in a Baltimore hospital for six months and was barely able to stand; Representative Crosser of Ohio; and Representative Barnhart of Indiana, who was brought in on a stretcher for the last roll call.

The wife of Congressman Hicks of New York had just died. He delayed making arrangements for her funeral so that he could be in Washington for the vote. The vote passed 274 to 136, which was exactly the two-thirds majority required to pass an amendment to the Constitution. The women outside the gallery began to sing "Praise God From Whom All Blessings Flow."

Most of the "nay" votes came from the South and from the industrial states of Massachusetts, New Jersey, Ohio, and Pennsylvania. The Amendment had passed the house, but it still required a majority in the Senate and ratification by the States. A poll of the Senate indicated fifty-four in favor, which was ten votes short of a two-thirds majority. By April, eight more votes had been added to the "yeas."

The suffragists began to target Senators who where up for re-election in November who were against their cause. Suffragists' opposition was decisive in causing the defeat of Senator Weeks of Massachusetts and Senator Saulsbury of Delaware.

President Wilson was by now in favor of granting the vote to women. He told one delegation, "I am, as I think you know, heartily in sympathy with you. I have endeavored to assist you in every way in my power, and I shall continue to do so. I shall do all that I can do to assist the passage of the Amendment by an early vote."

Tennessee was the scene of the last great battle; it was the thirty-sixth state to ratify the suffrage Amendment. On August 18, 1919, ninety-six out of ninety-nine Tennessee representatives were present at the vote. Two legislators in favor to granting suffrage to women were ill. One representative supporting suffrage had gotten out of bed recovering from an operation, and one had hurried back from California. The "nays" thought that they had the vote by forty-nine to forty-seven; however, representative Banks Turner switched sides from "nay" to "yea," causing a forty-eight to forty-eight tie.

One of the youngest representatives, twenty-four-year-old Harry Burn, had followed the wishes of his rural electors and had voted against the Amendment. However, Harry had recently received a letter from his mother strongly urging him to vote for women's suffrage. He decided that if a single vote was required for the Amendment to pass, he would give it. He did, and the vote stood at forty-nine for and forty-seven against. Attempts were made to overturn the vote, but they were unsuccessful and the Amendment became law.

Ratification of the Nineteenth Amendment, the "Susan B. Anthony" Amendment, finally occurred in 1920. It had taken fifty-three years from the first state suffrage referendum held in Kansas in 1867 and seventy-two years from the first Women's Rights Convention held in Seneca Falls in 1848, but the goal had finally been reached. Over half of the population was given a right that should have been theirs all along. As Susan B. Anthony had predicted, "Failure is impossible."

The hard work and dedication of Carrie Chapman Catt and Alice Paul have not received the recognition from historians that they deserve. The efforts of the women who were the driving forces early in the Women's Rights Movement, such as Susan B. Anthony, Lucretia Mott, Elizabeth Cady Stanton, and Lucy Stone cannot be overestimated. However, the women who took the Movement the last mile deserve more recognition for their contribution to the ultimate success.

CHAPTER 4

The Pankhurst Family and the Women's Rights Movement in England

"My childhood was protected by love and a comfortable home. Yet, while I was still a very young child, I began to instinctively feel that there was something lacking, even in my own home, some incomplete ideal. This vague feeling began to shape itself into conviction about the time my brothers and I were sent to school ... My parents, especially my father, discussed the importance of my brothers' education as a matter of real importance. My education and that of my sister were scarcely discussed at all ... A girl's education at that time seemed to have for its prime object the art of 'making the home attractive'—presumably to migratory male relatives. It used to puzzle me why I was under such a particular obligation to make home attractive for my brothers.... "

Emmeline Pankhurst

The women's suffrage movement in England was much more militant than in the United States, and the right of women to vote in England was granted in stages. In February 1917, a bill was proposed to give the vote to women over thirty who were either college graduates, local government electors (owner or tenant householders), or wives of men in the first two categories. The bill was extended to the wives of all voters when it passed in January 1918; it enfranchised 8,500,000 women. In 1928, the vote was extended to all women of voting age.

Emmeline Pankhurst and her three daughters played a major role in the Women's Suffrage Movement. Emmeline, who was born in 1858, was the handsome, delicate eldest daughter of Robert Goulden, a wealthy Manchester cotton manufacturer. She was sent to finishing school in Paris where her best friend was Noémie de Rochefort, the daughter of the Marquis de Rochefort, a hero of the Paris Commune of 1871.

After returning from Paris in 1878, Emmeline met Richard Pankhurst, a radical advocate who had been called to the Bar in 1867 after receiving the highest law degrees at London University. In 1865, when Emmeline was only seven years old, Pankhurst had helped found the Woman's Suffrage Society in Manchester. In 1870, he drafted the Married Women's Property Bill that gave women the right to own property and to keep the wages they earned. Also that year, he drafted the first of many parliamentary bills to give women the vote.

Emmeline and Richard fell in love at first sight. She was captivated by his eloquence, his idealism, and his "beautiful white hands." He was a forty-year-old bachelor who lived at home with his mother. When his mother died in 1879, he proposed to Emmeline. Theirs was a happy marriage, partly because they saw each other as kindred spirits ("Every struggling cause shall be ours"). Although she offered to dispense with the legal formalities of marriage to demonstrate their disregard for convention, he was unwilling to expose her to the public response that it would invite.

Four children were born during the first six years of their marriage: Christabel in 1880, Sylvia in 1882, Adela in 1885, and a son who died in childhood. Pankhurst thought of his four children as the four pillars of his house. He told them: "If you do not grow up to help other people, you will not have been worth the upbringing." He continually counseled them that drudgery and drill are important components of life, but that "life is nothing without enthusiasms."

In 1883, Emmeline supported her husband's political campaign when he resigned from the Liberal Association and ran unsuccessfully as an Independent in the Manchester by-election. He advocated the abolition of the House of Lords, establishment of an international court, nationalization of the land and of the mines, reduction in the size of the army and navy, suffrage for adults of both sexes, and the founding of an United States of Europe.

Two years later, Pankhurst ran for office as a Radical candidate in Rotherhithe. This losing effort was Emmeline's first exposure to the heckling and disorder of a brawling campaign. She thought that her husband was able but misunderstood, and that his talent needed a new venue. Emmeline suggested that they move to London, where she would open a shop to support their sagging finances.

At 8 Russell Square, a large double drawing room, which she painted her favorite color (yellow), was the site of her musical afternoons, poetry readings, and suffrage meetings. She invited agitators, anarchists, Fabians, free thinkers, political thinkers, and radicals, including Annie Besant, the brilliant pamphleteer; Tom Mann, the union leader; and William Morris, the artist, craftsman, and poet. Her visitors also included Elizabeth Cady Stanton and her daughter, Harriot Stanton Blatch.

Emmeline didn't believe in sending her daughters to school. Their education was provided by instruction from governesses, by reading, and by visiting museums. The three girls developed very different personalities. Christabel, who inherited her mother's charm and social graces, was an extrovert. Sylvia was introverted and shy; she was also obedient and subject to bouts of depression. Sylvia developed an interest in drawing and sketching. When they finally were entered into schools, Christabel was happy in her new environment; Sylvia was miserable.

Sylvia was devoted to her mother but was influenced more by her father whom she called "splendid father." In her autobiography, Sylvia wrote, "Our father, vilified and boycotted yet beloved by a multitude of people in all walks of life, was a standard bearer of every forlorn hope, every popular yet unworthy cause then conceived for the uplifting of oppressed and suffering humanity." She considered her mother his most fervent disciple.

The subject of women's rights was Pankhurst's most zealous activity and was the one in which he was a strong influence on his wife and daughters. As one who opposed exploitation of all kinds, he couldn't tolerate half of the population being held back economically and politically. In 1890, when Christabel was ten and Sylvia was eight, the usually calm Pankhurst erupted after a meeting of the Women's Franchise League at their home. He burst out, "Why don't you force us to give you the vote? Why don't you scratch our eyes out?" Christabel and Sylvia were startled by his outburst; Emmeline was astonished at the vehemence of his feelings.

Emmeline's career as a shopkeeper was not successful. Financial problems continued to plague the family. Years of overwork caught up with Pankhurst, and he began to be bothered by gastric ulcers. In order to reduce expenses, the family moved back to Manchester, where the Pankhursts remained politically active. They asserted themselves as Socialists as well as feminists.

Few politicians of the time supported women's rights. The earliest to support the women's cause was Keir Hardie, the first independent working-class Member of Parliament (MP).

A former miner, Hardie joined the trade union movement and ran unsuccessfully for office in 1888. In 1892, he was elected as the Radical Association candidate from West Ham. In 1893, he helped to found the Scottish Labour Party and the Independent Labour Party (ILP), which evolved into the Labour Party of today.

In 1894, married women were given the right to vote in local elections and became eligible for election as district councilors and Poor Law Guardians. The following year, Emmeline was elected to the Chorlton Board of Guardians. When she was told that the Guardians couldn't provide relief to the "able bodied poor," she organized food kitchens with the help of the ILP. She was horrified by conditions in the workhouses and incensed by the treatment of young women with illegitimate babies. Years later, she wrote, "though I had been a suffragist before, I now begin to think about the vote in women's hands not only as a right, but as a desperate necessity."

In 1895, Pankhurst ran unsuccessfully again for Parliament as the ILP candidate from Gorton. The Pankhurst daughters watched helplessly as toughs threw stones at their mother while they celebrated the Tory victory. In 1896, the Manchester Parks Committee ruled that the ILP could no longer use Boggart Clough, a large, municipally-owned field, for their meetings as they had for several years. Speakers were fined and were sent to jail unless they paid the fines. Emmeline, as the wife of a senior member of the Bar, surprised the magistrates when she told them she would pay no fine and would continue to attend the ILP meetings there. Eventually, the ban was retracted; controlled agitation, courage, and persistence had won the cause.

In 1898, Richard Pankhurst died suddenly of a perforated ulcer. He had no money to leave the family. The ILP offered to establish an education fund for the Pankhurst children, but Emmeline was too proud to permit it. Pankhurst had frequently asked his children what they wanted to be when they grew up. He advised them, "Get something to work at that you like and can do." However, at the time of his death, none of the children were educated or trained to help their mother support the family. Christabel had considered both ballet dancing and dressmaking, but she wasn't encouraged to do either.

Sylvia had taken art lessons from a well-known artist and had displayed a definite talent. When her mother sold their furniture before moving to a smaller house, their old paintings were assessed and the assessor sent some of Sylvia's drawings to the Manchester School of Art. Sylvia was offered a full scholarship to the School. Later, her artwork was frequently used by the suffragists.

Emmeline was offered a position as registrar of births and deaths by the Chorlton Board of Guardians. She also opened another shop, even though she had been unsuccessful with the shop in London. Christabel worked in the shop, but was unhappy with the role of shopkeeper. She enrolled in courses at the University of Manchester, where she participated in discussions. Her perceptive responses brought her to the attention of the Vice Chancellor of the University and of Eva Gore-Booth and Esther Roper of the suffragist movement.

After the death of Lydia Decker, their dynamic leader, the suffragists in England became divided on the amount of political involvement that they should have. Lydia's successor was Millicent Fawcett, a capable leader but one without Lydia's drive. Eva and Esther, who were looking for dynamic women to work in the movement, asked Christabel if she would join their cause. Christabel was flattered and pursued her new duties with vigor. Emmeline's interest in the suffrage movement was increased by her daughter's participation. She gave up her shop and began to work actively for the Women's Rights Movement, thereby establishing an extraordinary mother-daughter partnership.

Christabel discovered that she was a natural leader and speaker. Her intelligence, pleasant appearance, and forceful personality impressed her audiences. Christabel had an internal need to dominate her environment. Sylvia described her sister as being "tenacious of her position." The suffrage movement provided Christabel with a forum to display her strengths.

Sylvia, who had been studying in Venice to further develop her painting, was asked on her return to decorate a hall that the ILP had built in Salford as a memorial to her father. She worked without pay morning, afternoon, and evening for three months to complete the work on schedule, only to find that women could not use Pankhurst Hall because it had a men-only club attached to it. The Pankhurst women were outraged by this rule; they concluded that men were never going to liberate women, and that women must liberate themselves.

In 1903, Emmeline invited ILP women to a meeting at her home and founded the Women's Social and Political Union (WSPU), a name suggested by Christabel. Their motto was "Deeds, not words"; their slogan was "Votes for women." For the next eleven years, it disseminated the views of this remarkable mother-daughter partnership.

Sylvia won a scholarship to the Royal College of Art and studied in London. Her friendship with Keir Hardie was deepening, and they spent every other Sunday together at his sparsely furnished lodgings in Neville Court. Sylvia joined the Fulham branch of the ILP and worked in the women's suffrage campaign at the request of her mother. Sylvia's apartment in Chelsea became a center of WSPU activity.

In 1905, Emmeline and Sylvia heavily lobbied the Members of Parliament to provide a place in their ballot in support of the women's cause. Again, Keir Hardie was their only supporter. Finally, when MP Branford Slack, "at the request of his wife," agreed to introduce a women's suffrage bill, it was scheduled for debate on May 12. Many women attended the debate; some came from as far away as Australia. Unfortunately, filibusters took up most of the available time, and MP Slack was allowed only a half hour. Women's suf-

frage had not been defeated; debate on it had merely been cir-
cumvented.

The women were upset with the Government. They realized that relying on private members' bills wasn't the path to
success; the government must legislate. Two months later,
Keir Hardie led an effort to pass a bill to help the unemployed
in an economy in which unemployment was increasing.
Prime Minister Balfour's government attempted to postpone
the bill. Several thousand destitute workers marched from the
East End to Westminster in protest. In Manchester, mobs of
enraged unemployed men marched in the streets, and four
men were arrested. Ten days later, Arthur Balfour backed
down, and the bill became law.

This success was not lost on the women of the WSPU.
They had noticed that the threat of violence had caused the
Government to act. If a threat of violence was required to get
bills passed into law, then they would become increasingly
militant. Sylvia observed, "It was only a question of how militant tactics would begin." The Pankhursts were thrust into a
nationwide militant movement operating out of Manchester
and led by Christabel.

Esther Roper, who was impressed with Christabel's skill in
arguing issues, suggested to Emmeline that her oldest daughter should study law. Emmeline asked Lord Haldane to sponsor Christabel as a student at Lincoln's Inn, where her father
had studied. Lord Haldane agreed, but her application was
rejected because women weren't allowed to practice at the
Bar. She enrolled at Manchester University's law school
instead, while continuing to participate in suffrage work.

Christabel's coworker, Annie Kenney, wondered, "Where
she studied, how she studied is a mystery. She was working
for the movement the whole of the day and practically every
night." However, as her final examination approached,
Christabel said, "panic prompted concentration, and I withdrew from human society to that of my books." In June 1906,
she graduated with honors and used her new skills to support

the women's cause. Christabel focused on one overriding cause—obtaining the vote for women. All other causes, including social reform issues, were going to have to wait.

Christabel's first unladylike step occurred in 1904 at a Liberal Party meeting at the Free Trade Hall in Manchester at which Winston Churchill launched the campaign for the general election. When a resolution supporting free trade was agreed upon and the speeches were over, Christabel rose from her chair on the platform and asked the chairman if she could propose an amendment on women's suffrage. The chairman denied her request amid cries from the audience, and Christabel backed down.

Later, she recalled, "This was the first militant step—the hardest for me because it was the first. To move from my place on the platform to the speaker's table in the teeth of the astonishment and opposition of will of that immense throng, those civic and county leaders and those Members of Parliament, was the most difficult thing I have ever done." However, it was "a protest of which little was heard and nothing remembered—because it did not result in imprisonment!" She formed the opinion that she must go to prison to arouse public opinion; she must become a martyr.

In 1905, Cristabel and her friend, Annie Kenney, attended a Liberal Party rally in the Free Trade Hall in Manchester. Christabel had told her mother, "We shall sleep in prison tonight." They carried a banner that asked "Will you [the Liberal Party] give votes for women?" Both Annie and Christabel asked the question on their banner. The Chief Constable of Manchester told them that their question would be answered later. It was ignored, so they asked it again. The crowd responded, "Throw them out!"

Stewards bruised and scratched them while attempting to remove them from the hall. Christabel realized that they hadn't done enough to be taken to prison. She knew that she was going to have to do more to be arrested; however, she wasn't sure how to do that with her arms held behind her back.

Finally, she was arrested and charged with "spitting at a policeman."

Her account of the incident was, "It was not a real spit, but only, shall we call it, a 'pout,' a perfectly dry purse of the mouth. I could not really have done it, even to get the vote, I think." Christabel was kept in jail for seven days; Annie was jailed for three days. Christabel received the publicity that she sought. Unfortunately, it was not clear that it helped the suffrage cause.

Sylvia and Annie interrupted a speech in Sheffield by Herbert Asquith, Chancellor of the Exchequer, and were jostled by the stewards. Men in the crowd hit them with fists and umbrellas as the women were roughly forced from the hall. The Pankhursts decided to spread their activities to London. Unfortunately, they didn't have the finances to do it. They were eternal optimists; they thought, "That, too, will come." Annie Kenney was sent to London to spread their version of militant suffrage activity with £2 in her pocketbook. Emmeline Pankhurst instructed her "Go and rouse London."

The necessary financing did come to them. Frederick and Emmeline ("the other Emmeline") Pethick-Lawrence were visiting South Africa when they heard of the suffragist activities in England. They hurried home to see what they could do to help. The Pethick-Lawrences were philanthropists who had contributed to university settlements and women's hospitals and had founded boys' clubs. They expanded the scope of their monthly newspaper, the *Labour Record*, from supporting the Labour cause to supporting the suffragist movement.

Initially, Emmeline Pethick-Lawrence hesitated before backing the Pankhursts. In her autobiography, she observed, "I had no fancy to be drawn into a small group of brave and reckless and quite helpless people who were prepared to dash themselves against the oldest tradition of human civilization as well as one of the strongest Governments of modern times." She was moved by Annie Kenney's willingness to "rouse London" with £2 in her pocketbook. "I was amused by

Annie's ignorance of what the talk of rousing London would involve and yet thrilled by her courage."

The "other Emmeline" attended a suffragist meeting at Sylvia's lodgings and was impressed with the audacity of the six women who were there. She said, "I found there was no office, no organization, no money—no postage stamps even ... It was not without dismay that it was borne on me that somebody had to come to the help of this brave little group and that the finger of fate pointed to me." Emmeline helped to establish the Central Committee of the WSPU and became its honorary treasurer.

Not only was Emmeline Pethick-Lawrence an effective treasurer, she was also a source of many good ideas. Money began to flow in to the Movement, including generous contributions from Pethick-Lawrence's husband. Collections were taken at WSPU gatherings, and Keir Hardie raised £300 from supporters of the Independent Labour Party. The Pethick-Lawrences allowed the Pankhursts to use their house at Clements Inn as their base of operations, retaining only the upstairs apartment for their own use in addition to one room as an office for the *Labour Record*. They treated Christabel as a favored daughter.

The *Daily Mail* called the militant suffragists "suffragettes," a name that Christabel liked. In her opinion, the suffragists merely desired the vote, but, if you pronounce the hard g, the suffragettes "mean to get it." Membership in the WSPU grew rapidly. Middle class women joined because they were looking for "wider and more important activities and interests." Women of the upper class were drawn to the WSPU for other reasons.

Sylvia noted that "daughters of rich families were often without personal means, or permitted a meager dress allowance, and when their parents died, they were often reduced to genteel penury, or unwelcome dependence on relatives." Sylvia decided that with workers of the lower class, the middle class, and the upper class all joining the suffragettes, she was going to have to become a more active participant herself and spend less time on her artistic pursuits.

Sylvia and Christabel began to have different views on the movement. Sylvia advocated social reform along with women's suffrage; Christabel was exclusively focused on the suffragettes' activity. Christabel began to move away from the Labour Party, including Keir Hardie. Sylvia didn't think they should separate themselves from Labour Party support, particularly when Keir Hardie was elected chairman of the group of twenty-nine Labour MPs.

The command of the Movement became a triumvirate: Christabel and the two Emmelines. There was no question as to who was in charge; it was Christabel. Some women were surprised how willingly Emmeline Pankhurst followed the direction of her oldest daughter.

In early 1906, thirty women carrying banners marched in front of the residence of the Chancellor of the Exchequer, Herbert Asquith. The marchers were punched and kicked by police, who attempted to break up the march. Annie Kenney and two other suffragettes were sent to jail for six weeks, and Emmeline Pankhurst was handled roughly for asking a question at one of Asquith's meetings. In October 1906, ten women were arrested for making speeches in the lobby of Parliament.

Sylvia went to their aid at the Cannon Row Police Court and was thrown into the street and arrested for obstruction and abusive language. She spent fourteen days in the Third Division of Holloway Prison. In the Third Division, the lowest division, the women were considered common criminals. They ate prison food, were subjected to coarse treatment, and wore prison clothing. Treatment in the Second Division was marginally better. Prisoners in the First Division enjoyed many privileges, including the right to have friends visit, to wear their own clothing, and to have food, writing materials, and other amenities from the outside world.

In 1907, the triumvirate called a Women's Parliament near

Westminster to coincide with the opening of Parliament. When they heard that there had been no mention of women's suffrage in the King's Speech, 400 women stormed Parliament. Sylvia described the activities of the constables:

> Mounted men scattered the marchers; foot police seized them by the back of the neck and rushed them along at arm's length, thumping them in the back, and bumping them with their knees in approved police fashion. Women, by the hundred, returned again and again with painful persistence, enduring this treatment by the hour. Those who took refuge in doorways were dragged down by the steps and hurled in front of the horses, then pounced on by the constables and beaten again.

Fifty women were arrested, including Christabel and Sylvia. Sentences ranged from one to three weeks. This time, the women were placed in the First Division.

Emmeline Pankhurst was asked by the Registrar-General of the Guardians to give up her suffrage activities. She resigned her position as registrar, giving up her job and the income and pension that accompanied it. She said that she was willing to give up her life, if necessary.

In 1908 at the by-election in mid-Devon, Emmeline Pankhurst and a fellow suffragist were attacked by a gang of young Liberal toughs, who were unhappy that their candidate had lost to the Tory candidate. Mrs. Pankhurst was knocked unconscious into the mud and injured her ankle. The young toughs were about to stuff her into a barrel and roll her down main street, when she was rescued by mounted police. The effects of the ankle injury persisted for months and motivated her to work harder for the vote.

Christabel decided that the next step was for her mother to go to jail. From a small cart, the injured Emmeline led a delegation of thirteen women who marched on Parliament. All thirteen women were sent to prison for six months in the Second Division. In her first visit to prison Emmeline tolerated the stripping, the body search, the bath in filthy water, and the patched and stained prison clothing made of coarse material.

She knew that the cold cells and the plank bed would be uncomfortable, but she was unprepared for the sobbing and foul language of the other prisoners. In particular, she was affected by the claustrophobic living conditions of many women in a small cell. Within two days, dyspepsia, migraine headaches, and neuralgia caused her to be moved to the prison hospital.

Emmeline Pethick-Lawrence proposed that the WSPU should have their own colors and their own flag. Purple, white, and green were selected, and Sylvia designed banners, borders, emblems, and flags displaying these colors. Many of the women wore clothing of the three colors when they marched.

Another march on Parliament was planned. They weren't sure which verb to use. They considered "besiege," "invade," "raid," and "storm," and finally settled on "rush, " which was enough of an action word to provoke the government. They circulated a leaflet with the message, "Men and Women— Help the Suffragettes to Rush the House of Commons," and Christabel, Emmeline, and Flora Drummond (called "the General" because of her efficient methods) spoke in Trafalgar Square. Their call to action was heard by Lloyd George, Chancellor of the Exchequer, and they were charged with "inciting the public to a certain wrongful and illegal act—to rush the House of Commons.... "

Christabel conducted her own defense and that of the other two women in their trial at Bow Street. The magistrate rejected her request for a trial by jury, but she managed to call Lloyd George and Herbert Gladstone, the Home Secretary, as witnesses. The public was captivated by a young woman lawyer cross-examining cabinet ministers. The suffrage movement received much publicity, but, after two days, Emmeline and Flora were sentenced to three months in the Second Division and Christabel to ten weeks.

During the trial, Max Beerbohm was impressed with Christabel. He wrote in the *Saturday Review*: "She has all the qualities which an actress needs and of which so few actresses have.... Her whole being is alive with her every meaning, and if you can imagine a very graceful rhythmic dance done by a dancer who uses not her feet, you will have some idea of Miss Pankhurst's method." Furthermore, he noted "the contrast between the buoyancy of the girl and the depression of the statesman [Lloyd George]."

While her mother and her sister were in jail, Sylvia planned a rally at Albert Hall, where Lloyd George was to speak. She stayed at suffrage headquarters and waited for women to return from the speech. They were bruised and their clothing was in disarray. Some had their corsets ripped off and their false teeth knocked out. One woman had been whipped with a dog whip, and another had a wrist burned by a man using it to put out his cigar while other men struck her in the chest. The Manchester *Guardian* reported that the women had been treated "with a brutality that was almost nauseating."

Muriel Matters of the Women's Freedom League could not be thrown out of Parliament when she rose to speak because she had chained herself to the grille behind which women were required to stand. From then on, only relatives of Members of Parliament were permitted in the gallery.

The more activist members of the movement began to become impatient with the government's delays. They threw stones wrapped in WSPU literature through the windows of government buildings. When they were arrested, they went on hunger strikes. Women who were prevented from attending public meetings climbed onto the roof of the hall and used axes to chop off slates. One woman was imprisoned for throwing an iron bar through the window of an empty railroad car on the train carrying the Prime Minister back to London.

The women were given sentences ranging from two weeks to four months. Many of them went on hunger strikes. The Home Secretary ordered that they be forcibly fed using rubber tubes through their mouth or nose. In one case, the feeding tube was accidentally passed into the trachea instead of the esophagus, and the woman developed pneumonia from broth forced into her lung.

Sylvia described being forcibly fed in graphic terms. She experienced shivering and heart palpitations when told that she was going to be forcibly fed. Six big, strong wardresses pushed her down on her back in bed and held her by her ankles, knees, hips, elbows, and shoulders.

A doctor entered her room and attempted unsuccessfully to open her mouth. He then tried to push a steel gag through a gap between her teeth, making her gums bleed. Next two doctors thrusted a pointed steel instrument between her jaws, which were forced open by the turn of a screw, and forced a tube down her throat. While Sylvia panted and heaved, she tried to move her head away. She was almost unconscious when they poured the broth into her throat. As soon as the tube was withdrawn, she vomited. She said: "They left me on the bed exhausted, gasping for breath, and sobbing convulsively." The women were subjected to this treatment twice a day.

Women began to die for their beliefs in the women's cause. In December 1910, Celia Haig, a sturdy, healthy woman, died of a painful illness from injuries incurred when she was assaulted at a public gathering. Mary Clarke, Emmeline Pankhurst's sister, died of a stroke after being released from prison "too frail to weather this rude tide of militant struggle." Henria Williams, who had a weak heart, died in January 1911 from injuries suffered during a rally.

Early in 1912, Emmeline Pankhurst broke several windows at the Prime Minister's residence at 10 Downing Street. She went to jail for two months with 218 other women. In March

1912, the police raided WSPU headquarters and arrested Emmeline and Frederick Pethick-Lawrence. Christabel had recently moved into an apartment and wasn't at Clements Inn when the police arrived. It was obvious to Christabel that the "ringleaders" were being rounded up. She fled to France to ensure that the movement's leaders weren't all in jail. Annie Kenney became her link with Clements Inn.

Frederick and the two Emmelines were sent to prison for seven months in the Second Division. Emmeline Pankhurst refused to be treated as she had been on her first trip to prison. Sylvia described the scene: "Mrs. Pankhurst, ill from fasting and suspense, grasped the earthen toilet ewer and threatened to fling it at the doctors and wardresses, who appeared with the feeding tube. They withdrew and the order for her release was issued the next day." Emmeline Pethick-Lawrence was forcibly fed once, and her husband for five days; they, too, were released early.

The militant wing of the Movement began to set fire to buildings. Sylvia suspected that Christabel was behind this phase of their effort. They burned down churches, historic places, and empty buildings. They tried to set fire to Nuneham House, the home of Lewis Harcourt, an anti-suffragist Minister. Mary Leigh and Gladys Evans attempted to burn down the Royal Theatre in Dublin, where Herbert Asquith was scheduled to speak.

Christabel's mother convinced her that increased militancy was the direction in which they should move. This caused a rift with the Pethick-Lawrences, who preferred a more moderate approach. When they returned from a trip to Canada, the couple who had contributed so much effort and money to the campaign found that they had been frozen out of the leadership.

Frederick Pethick-Lawrence commented on their falling out in unselfish terms. "Thus ended our personal association with two of the most remarkable women I have ever known.... They cannot be judged by ordinary standards of conduct; and those who run up against them must not complain of the treatment they receive." He realized that the Pankhursts shared a common characteristic: "their absolute refusal to be deflected by criticism or appeal one hair's breath from the course they had determined to pursue."

Emmeline Pethick-Lawrence didn't accept the split with the Pankhursts as easily as her husband did. She observed "There was something quite ruthless about Mrs. Pankhurst and Christabel where human relationships were concerned.... Men and women of destiny are like that." The couple recognized Christabel's intelligence and political acumen as well her appeal to young men and young women. They also appreciated Mrs. Pankhurst's ability to move an audience with her appeals to their emotions by modulating her voice.

The level of destruction caused by the suffragettes stepped up as they became increasingly frustrated with the delay in obtaining the vote. It included:

- widespread burning with acid of the message "votes for women" on golf greens
- cutting telephone wires
- burning of boathouses and sports pavilions, including the grandstand at Ayr racecourse
- slashing of thirteen paintings at the Manchester Art Gallery and the Rokeby "Venus" at the National Gallery
- destroying with a bomb a home being built for Lloyd George
- smashing the glass orchid house at Kew Gardens
- breaking a jewel case in the Tower of London
- burning of three Scottish castles and the Carnegie Library in Birmingham
- flooding the organ in Albert Hall
- exploding a bomb in Westminster Abbey

Emmeline Pankhurst was charged with "counseling and

procuring" the blowing up of the house being constructed for Lloyd George at Walton-on-the-Hill. That bombing was done by Emily Wilding Davison, one of the most impulsive suffragettes. To protest not being granted the vote, Davison waited at the turn at Tattenham Corner and committed suicide by throwing herself under the King's horse at the Derby.

During her imprisonment, Emmeline Pankhurst experienced a new government tactic, implementation of the Prisoners Temporary Discharge Bill—the "Cat and Mouse Act." Prisoners who refused to eat would be released when their health began to be affected, and then imprisoned again when they were at least partially recovered. Mrs. Pankhurst was released nine times after hunger and thirst strikes, only to be returned to prison.

In 1914, Adela Pankhurst, who had not been as active in the suffrage movement as her mother and her sisters, sailed for Australia. She became a leader of the Socialist women's movement there. Adela converted to Catholicism late in life and died in Sydney, Australia in May 1961.

The militancy of the movement in England ceased with the outbreak of World War I. Christabel moved back to England, confident that the government would have more on its mind than pursuing her. She announced, "This was national militancy. As suffragettes we could not be pacifists at any price. We offered our service to the country and called upon all our members to do likewise." Christabel supported Asquith in the war effort as fervently as she had opposed him prior to the war.

In August 1916, Asquith surprised the House of Commons by declaring that if the voting franchise were expanded, women had an "unanswerable" case for being offered the vote. He observed that "during this war the women of this country have rendered as effective a service in the prosecution of the war as any other class of the community."

In February 1917, a committee recommended that the vote be granted to all men over twenty-one and women over thirty who were university graduates or local government electors (owners or tenant householders), or the wives of both. Sylvia was upset by this discrimination. The bill was extended to the wives of all voters and became law in January 1918. Eight and a half million women were enfranchised. Ten years later, the remaining political limitations on women were removed.

Emmeline Pankhurst died in June 1928, a month before her seventieth birthday. Christabel wrote, "The House of Lords passed the final measure of Votes for Women in the hour her body, which had suffered so much for that cause, was laid in the grave. She, who had come to them in their need, had stayed with the women as long as they might still need her, and then she went away."

Christabel became a Second Adventist and in 1936 was made a Dame Commander of the British Empire for "public and social services." She moved to the United States and died in Santa Monica, California, in 1958. Sylvia was involved in the Bolshevik Revolution after World War I and later moved to Ethiopia. She died in Addis Ababa in 1960. The Emperor attended her funeral.

The Pankhursts were a family of achievers. Perhaps the characteristic that led to their many accomplishments was best summarized by Frederick and Emmeline Pethick-Lawrence: "Their absolute refusal to be deflected by criticism or appeal one hair's breadth from the course they had determined to pursue... Men and women of destiny are like that."

CHAPTER 5

Seneca Falls

"The first Women's Rights Convention to discuss the social, civil, and religious conditions and rights of women will be held at the Wesleyan Chapel at Seneca Falls on Wednesday and Thursday [July 19-20] current, commencing at ten a.m. During the first day, the meeting will be exclusively for women, who are earnestly invited to attend. The public generally are invited to be present on the second day when Lucretia Mott of Philadelphia will address the convention."

Seneca County Courier, July 14, 1848

Brief Description and History

Seneca Falls is known as the birthplace of women's rights in the United States. The first Women's Rights Convention was held there in 1848, when Elizabeth Cady Stanton, of Seneca Falls, presented her *Declaration of Sentiments* modeled on the *Declaration of Independence* written by Thomas Jefferson. The Convention was called by Cady Stanton and her mentor, Lucretia Mott, a visiting Quaker from Philadelphia, and three other area women. Elizabeth Cady Stanton became the policymaker and spokeswoman for the Women's Rights Movement.

The first Women's Rights Convention was held in the Wesleyan Chapel. The Chapel subsequently became Johnson's Opera House, a Ford dealership, and then a laundromat. The east and west walls and the roof have been restored.

The Women's Rights National Historic Park, established in 1980, maintains a Visitor Center at 136 Fall Street and the Stanton home at 32 Washington Street. The National Women's Hall of Fame is located at 76 Fall Street but plans to move to a larger facility. It was established in 1969 to "provide a permanent place of honor for America's most outstanding women, a place for people to visit and learn about the significant contributions—often against tremendous odds—that these women have made to our country," according to a Hall of Fame brochure.

Amelia Jenks Bloomer, for whom bloomers are named, is another well-known Seneca Falls resident. She wrote about the loose trouser outfit worn by members of the Women's Rights Movement in her temperance newspaper, the *Lily*, but she didn't invent bloomers. She published a drawing of them that was widely copied. Elizabeth Smith Miller, daughter of abolitionist Gerrit Smith, wore the costume, consisting of Turkish trousers and short skirts, when visiting Elizabeth Cady Stanton in 1849. Miller had seen a similar costume worn by Swiss nurses.

Waterfalls that no longer exist provided Seneca Falls with its name; the fifty-foot drop in elevation of the Seneca River is now accommodated by Locks 2 and 3 on the Cayuga-Seneca Canal. Lawrence Van Cleef, an early settler, first visited the region as a member of General Sullivan's expedition during the Revolutionary War. Early in the life of the village, the Bayard Company, a monopolistic land syndicate, obtained the water rights to the Seneca River and set high fees for its use.

Colonel Wilhelmus Mynderse was an early agent for the syndicate that owned a grist mill and a store at the falls. The syndicate's high rates hindered development of the settlement until the State took over the water rights in 1827 to build the Cayuga-Seneca Canal parallel to the river. Most of the mills were concentrated along the river and on the islands between the canal and the river.

In 1915, the present configuration of the Cayuga-Seneca Canal was completed by joining the Canal and the River, replacing the falls with the two locks and submerging the industrial islands, thus creating Van Cleef Lake. Trinity Episcopal Church on the lake, built in 1885-86 in early Gothic style, is one of the most photographed scenes in New York State. A park is also named for Van Cleef. The name Mynderse has also survived; the high school in Seneca Falls is called Mynderse Academy, and the village library is Mynderse Library.

Wooden pumps were made in Seneca Falls beginning in 1840. In 1850, Seabury Gould began the manufacture of iron pumps at what became the Gould Pump Company, which was known worldwide for quality products. In 1997, it was purchased by the ITT Corporation.

The Montezuma Wildlife Refuge, maintained by the U.S. Fish and Wildlife Service of the Department of the Interior, is located a few miles northeast of Seneca Falls. Cayuga Lake State Park is several miles southeast of the village, along the

153

west shoreline of the Lake.

The New York Chiropractic College is located on Route 89 on what was originally the Eisenhower College campus, just east of Seneca Falls. Approximately 650 students attend the college. Sauder's Mennonite Farmers' Market is located in several buildings on River Road near the intersection with Route 414.

Seneca Falls received a grant from the New York State Canal Corporation to install information kiosks and wayside exhibits throughout its Urban Cultural Park and to construct a lighted overlook of the "lost village" beneath the Cayuga-Seneca Canal in Van Cleef Lake. Seneca Falls is a harbor in the Canal Recreationway Plan and was granted funds including $4 million in Canal Corporation funds and $2.6 million in other grants to become a "Gateway to the Finger Lakes." Plans for the harbor include a boats-for-hire terminal, amenities for visitors, and links from the Canal to the Women's Rights National Historic Park, the National Women's Hall of Fame, and other historic sites in the village. The harbor is expected to help attract over 200,000 tourists annually to Seneca Falls.

The Seneca Falls Connection with the movie *It's a Wonderful Life*

Speculation has persisted for years that Seneca Falls is the Bedford Falls of the 1946 movie that starred Jimmy Stewart, Donna Reed, and Lionel Barrymore and was produced and directed by Frank Capra. The classic movie depicts the life of George Bailey, a family man who feels trapped by his home town and by the responsibility of managing the building and loan association that he inherited from his father. On Christmas Eve, his uncle Billy loses $8,000 that is vital to the business, and Bailey is faced with going to jail. He becomes despondent and wonders if the world of Bedford Falls would be a better place if he had never been born.

Bailey contemplates committing suicide by jumping off a bridge. He is saved by an elderly guardian angel who has come down from heaven to earn his wings. The angel shows Bailey what Bedford Falls would have been like if he hadn't been born. Bailey realizes that he has influenced the lives of many others, and that no one who has friends should consider himself a failure.

In the December 19, 1996, Rochester *Democrat and Chronicle*, Doris Wolf listed the many similarities between Seneca Falls and Bedford Falls:

- Both are mill towns on a river.
- Both have Victorian streetscapes with iron-front stores.
- Both communities had large immigrant Italian communities struggling to make a new life in an industrial society.
- A grassy median that was down the center of the main street in Bedford Falls is similar to one that was in the center of Lower Falls Street.
- Both have streets with large Victorian mansions, including one at 54 Cayuga Street that looks like the Granville mansion in which George and Mary Bailey lived.

155

- The Bridge Street bridge in Seneca Falls looks remarkably like the bridge Bailey jumped from to save his angel, Clarence. A plaque on the bridge honors Antonio Varacalli, who leaped from the bridge in 1917 to save a woman's life. Unlike Bailey, Varacalli drowned.
- John Rumsey, a Seneca Falls Pump Manufacturer, built low-cost housing for his employees in a place called Rumseyville. Bailey, head of a building and loan association, also sponsored a low-cost housing project in an area called Bailey Park. The wrought-iron archway gate to Bailey Park is similar to the arched gate with the words "Seneca Falls" that originally stood at the village cemetery and is now on Water Street.
- Frank Capra, the director of the movie, had an aunt in Auburn and is believed to have visited Seneca Falls. A local barber [Tommy Bellissima] says that he cut Capra's hair at least twice in 1945, when Capra was preparing to film the movie.

Central and western New York locations are mentioned in the dialogue of the movie. When George Bailey's brother, Harry, returns to Bedford Falls with his new bride, Ruth, she talks about a job for Harry. George asks about the job, and Ruth replies, "Oh, well, my father owns a glass factory in Buffalo. He wants to get Harry started in the research business."

George Bailey talks on the telephone with his friend, Sam Wainwright, who reminds George of a discussion that they had about making plastics out of soybeans. Sam says: "Well, dad snapped up the idea. He's going to build a factory outside of Rochester. How do you like that?"

Mr. Carter, the bank examiner, is waiting for George Bailey at the Bailey Building and Loan Association. He says to George: "Now, if you'll cooperate, I'd like to finish with you tonight. I want to spent Christmas in Elmira with my family."

The original screenplay for *It's a Wonderful Life* included a reference to Cornell University in Ithaca. However, the RKO film company's lawyers suggested that the reference should be cut from the script. Frank Capra took their advice.

It can't be proved that Seneca Falls is Bedford Falls, but the similarities are striking. Initially the movie, which critics called a simplistic fairy tale, was unsuccessful. However, the upbeat plot has made it the favorite movie of many people. One Seneca Falls resident observed, "If Seneca Falls isn't Bedford Falls, it should be."

Seneca
Falls

PLACES TO SEE / THINGS TO DO

1) Elizabeth Cady Stanton House

Elizabeth Cady Stanton was one of the organizers of the first Women's Rights Convention on July 19-20, 1848, and was the principal author of the *Declaration of Sentiments* read at the Convention. She became the major author, policymaker, and speechwriter for the Women's Rights Movement. Her friend, Susan B. Anthony, became the Movement's main organizer.

In 1847, the Stantons moved from Boston to 32 Washington Street, Seneca Falls. They lived there with their seven children until 1862. Commenting on the lack of intellectual and cultural pursuits she enjoyed in Boston and feeling burdened with housework and child care, Elizabeth Cady Stanton wrote in her autobiography *Eighty Years and More*:

> The general discontent I felt with women's portion as wife, mother, housekeeper, physician, and spiritual guide, the chaotic conditions into which every thing fell without my constant supervision, the wearied anxious look of the majority of women, impressed me with a strong feeling that some active measures should be taken to remedy the wrongs ... [done to] women....

The Elizabeth Cady Stanton House is owned by the National Park Service. The existing portion of the house has been restored to its 1848 appearance and is open to the public.

2) National Women's Hall of Fame

The National Women's Hall of Fame is located at 76 Fall Street, but plans to move to a larger facility. Its goal is "to honor in perpetuity those women, citizens of the United States of America, whose contribution to the arts, athletics,

Elizabeth Cady Stanton House, Seneca Falls

business, education, government, humanities, philanthropy and science, have been of the greatest value for the development of their country."

The permanent exhibits of the National Women's Hall of Fame focus on the lives of women inducted through public nomination. Each year two more women are nominated.

At least seven of the Hall of Fame honorees have Finger Lakes ties: Susan B. Anthony, Rochester; Clara Barton, Dansville; Antoinette Brown Blackwell, Henrietta; Elizabeth Blackwell, Geneva; Margaret Sanger, Corning; Elizabeth Cady Stanton, Seneca Falls; and Harriet Tubman, Auburn. Other inductees include Jane Addams, Dorothea Dix, Helen Keller, Margaret Mead, Alice Paul, Eleanor Roosevelt, and Sojourner Truth.

In addition to permanent exhibits, changing exhibits use portraits, photographs, letters, and memorabilia to interpret women's role in society. Tours are available.

3) Women's Rights National Historic Park Visitor Center

The Women's Rights National Historic Park operates a Visitor Center at 136 Fall Street. A schedule of activities is posted in the center, which houses many exhibits. An orientation video and a 25-minute movie, "Dreams of Equality," are available for viewing.

Twenty bronze statues of organizers of the first Women's Rights Convention, men who supported the organizers, and other Convention attendees face visitors as they enter the Visitor Center. The statues are likenesses of Elizabeth Cady Stanton, Frederick Douglass, Martha Wright, Lucretia and James Mott, Mary Ann and Thomas M'Clintock, Jane and Richard Hunt, and eleven unidentified convention attendees.

The second floor of the Visitor Center has displays about the *Declaration of Sentiments*, plus displays such as "Inauguration of a Rebellion," "True Womanhood," "School Matters," "Campaigning Women Fashioning an Image," and "Women at Work." The second floor also contains temporary

Women's Rights National Historic Park Visitors Center

exhibits and a classroom.

The Visitor Center, which includes a bookstore, is open daily year-round except for Thanksgiving Day, Christmas Day, and New Year's Day. The Center is fully accessible to the mobility-impaired. Declaration Park, adjacent to the Visitor Center, features a commemorative waterwall engraved with the words of the *Declaration of Sentiments* and the names of the 100 women and men who signed the document.

4) Wesleyan Chapel

The Wesleyan Chapel, adjacent to Women's Rights National Historic Park Visitor Center, was the site of the first Women's Rights Convention on July 19-20, 1848. The roof and side walls of the Chapel have been restored.

5) Urban Cultural Park — Village of Seneca Falls

The Village of Seneca Falls Urban Cultural Park operates a Visitor Center in the historic Partridge Building at 115 Fall Street. The Urban Cultural Park focuses on the themes of industrialization, reform movements, and transportation. It highlights the village's role in the development of the Women's Rights Movement.

The village's history as a center of water-powered industry and transportation is depicted in exhibits and audiovisual programs. On display are locally manufactured goods such as bells, pumps, and tools. Fiber-optics maps illuminate the systems of canals, highways, railroads, and turnpikes that contributed to the development of industry and the spread of ideas of social reform. The history of the mills is displayed along with the contributions of the Irish and Italian men and women who built and operated the canals and factories.

6) Seneca Falls Historical Society Museum

The Victorian mansion at 55 Cayuga Street is the home of the Seneca Falls Historical Society. The twenty-three-room home was built in Italianate style in 1855 by Edward Mynderse, son

Seneca Falls Historical Society Museum

of an early settler. In 1880, Ellen Partridge bought the house and contracted the prominent Rochester architect, James D. Cutler, to enlarge and redesign the home in the popular Queen Anne style. Many of the furnishings and art pieces are from the Becker family, who lived in the house for over fifty years.

The mansion is decorated with the original chandeliers and light fixtures, intricately carved golden oak woodwork, ornate door hinges, carpet loomed in France, and mid-nineteenth-century wallpaper. The stained glass windows in the stairwell were designed by W. J. McPherson of Boston. A sunflower motif, which was the symbol of the Aesthetic Movement, is displayed in the doors, glass, and woodwork. In the butler's pantry and kitchen, visitors can see reminders of the long-vanished era of the coal cook stove, ice box, and water pump.

A tea set used by President James Monroe during his administration is displayed in a special exhibit in the front parlor. Mary Lincoln purchased new china when she and President Lincoln moved into the White House. She gave the tea set in the exhibit to William Seward, who was Lincoln's Secretary of State. The tea set was later acquired by the Seneca Falls Historical Society. Both Eleanor Roosevelt and Jacqueline Kennedy asked for it to be returned to the White House, but the Historical Society voted to keep it on display.

The Museum's extensive archives, photographic collection, and library are used by researchers throughout the United States. The library and archives are open for scholarly and genealogical research; assistance is available. The collections are particularly rich in the areas of the Civil War, local history, and women's history. The Museum sponsors lectures, classes and workshops for children and activities during Convention Days and Empire State Farm Days. It is open from 9 a.m. to 5 p.m. on Mondays through Fridays, and from noon until 4 p.m. on Saturdays. During the summer, the Museum is also open Sunday afternoons from noon until 4 p.m.

7) Convention Days

The first Convention Days Celebration was held in Seneca Falls in mid-July 1979 to commemorate the First Women's Rights Convention held July 19 and 20, 1848. Convention Days Celebrations include a street parade and reenactment of the 1848 Women's Rights Convention. Other events are concerts, historical tours, five- and ten-kilometer races, children's activities, dancing in the park, speeches, tournaments, and a fireworks display.

CHAPTER 6

Seneca Falls' Neighboring Municipalities along Routes 5 and 20 Brief Description and History

"Western New York's road to the past and to the future, Routes 5 & 20, is a 70-mile stretch of the nation's only remaining transcontinental highway. Built on what was an Iroquois path 1,000 years ago, it became a frontier road for westward pioneers and continues to tell the story of how we live.

Avon ... anchors 5 & 20's western end.... Auburn ... is the [eastern] end of the road for Routes 5 & 20. Inauspiciously, in the midst of a commercial-residential area, it forks into Route 5—the stop-and-go route to Syracuse—and Route 20—the scenic route to Skaneateles, Cazenovia, and beyond."

Mary Hedglon, "Along the way: Routes 5 & 20 Offer Slice of Finger Lakes Life." Rochester Democrat and Chronicle.

CANANDAIGUA

I've seen "The Chosen City"
    On Canandaigua Lake.
Here's [Kershaw] Park where people
    Find joys and merrymake.
....

It was a fair-sized village
    When Syracuse was young;
Rochester was a marshland
    Where dread disease germs sprung....

Historic Canandaigua
    Had notables galore.
Upon its roll are statesmen
    Who shined in legal lore.

This lake town is a showplace
    With large majestic trees,
And many fine old buildings
    That boast rich histories.

Canandaigua, New York by Edwin Becker

Canandaigua, the county seat of Ontario County, is a city of over 12,000 at the northern end of Canandaigua Lake. It is the home of Sonnenberg Gardens, a beautiful garden estate with a 1887 Victorian mansion surrounded by nine gardens; the Finger Lakes Performing Arts Center, the summer home of the Rochester Philharmonic Orchestra on the campus of the Finger Lakes Community College; and the Finger Lakes Race Track, the only thoroughbred race track in central New York.

Other Canandaigua attractions include the Granger Homestead and Carriage Museum and the Ontario County Historical Society Museum. Canandaigua is the headquarters of the Canandaigua Brands Company, the second-largest winery in the United States. Only E. and J. Gallo of Modesto, California, is larger. The winetasting room of the Canandaigua Brands Company is located on the grounds of Sonnenberg Gardens.

With its wide main street and stately homes, the city was chosen as the location of the land office of Nathaniel Gorham and Oliver Phelps in the 1700s. It was the most important municipality in the region before the Erie Canal and the New York Central Railroad shifted the economic expansion to the north, along a line from Syracuse to Rochester to Buffalo.

The present location of the Ontario County Courthouse in Canandaigua was the site of the signing of the the 1794 Treaty of Canandaigua (the Pickering Treaty), which established peace between the Six Nations of the Iroquois Confederacy and the young United States of America. The treaty defined Iroquois property rights, including the placement of a western boundary on their land, and reserved land for a military road along the Niagara River. Goods and a higher annuity were granted to the Indians, cementing the relationship so that the Iroquois fought against Great Britain in the War of 1812. Timothy Pickering signed the Treaty for the United States; Cornplanter, Farmer's Brother, Fish Carrier, Handsome Lake, Little Beard, Red Jacket, and forty-four others signed with crosses for the Iroquois.

At least two famous trials have been held in Canandaigua: that of Jemima Wilkinson, the leader of a religious sect, in 1799 for blasphemy, and that of Susan B. Anthony, the Women's Rights Movement leader, in 1873 for attempting to register to vote. Anthony's trial was held at the Ontario County Courthouse.

The charge of blasphemy was leveled at Jemima Wilkinson by James Parker, a magistrate of Ontario County, who had previously been a member of her religious sect. During the first attempt to serve her a warrant, she outrode the servers and escaped. At the second attempt, she and the women in her household workshop physically threw out the two servers, tearing their clothing. The third attempt was made by a posse of thirty men who surrounded her house at midnight; however, Dr. Fargo, who came with the posse, warned them that Jemima's health wouldn't permit her to be taken into custody.

She agreed to appear before the next session of the Ontario County Circuit Court in Canandaigua. The case was presented to a grand jury, but, when the presiding judge ruled that blasphemy was not an indictable offense, her case was dismissed.

Two individuals who spent their youth, or at least part of it, in Canandaigua were Stephen A. Douglas and John Willys. Douglas was known for his participation in the Lincoln-Douglas debates when he and Abraham Lincoln were campaigning against each other for the U.S. Senate. Douglas attended the Canandaigua Academy in the early 1830s, before he moved to the Midwest and became a U.S. Senator from Illinois. He was active in the debating society at the Canandaigua Academy, polishing the skills with which he defeated Lincoln for the Senate seat.

John North Willys was born in Canandaigua in 1873 and became an entrepreneur at an early age. He was half-owner of a laundry at sixteen and made his early money in the bicycle business, grossing a half million a year by the time he was twenty-seven. He went into the automobile business in 1900 and eventually owned and ran the Willys-Overland Company, which later was the original manufacturer of the Jeep.

In 1914, he turned down an offer of $80 million for his share of Willys-Overland, but he hung on and added to his fortune in World War I. His fortunes waned in the recession after World War I, and he sold his share of the company for $20 million in 1929. President Hoover appointed him Ambassador to Poland.

Willys died in New York City in 1935. His automobile company became a part of American Motors and then part of Chrysler Corporation, when American Motors was bought out by the third largest automobile manufacturer in the U.S.

GENEVA

Beside the peerless Seneca our charming city lies,
Bewitching as a fiery gem beneath the northern skies.
The fairest of the fair is she that dwells beside a lake,
And fitting is the show of pomp her lovely outlines make.
A queen enthroned mid hills of green, maiden of our love,
With steeples towering aloft to greet the clouds above.

....

Below and clear is that renowned and ancient azure lake,
Adorned with all the loveliness Nature's hand can make.

....

Beneath the waters of the lake reside those famous "drums,"
Resounding with a hollow roar from gloomy adytums.
The Indian of ancient lore then dropped upon his knees,
With history and story old her annals gleam and glow,
Like sparkling waters of a rill reflecting as they flow.

....

Geneva, New York by Edwin Becker

Geneva, a city of over 14,000 at the northern end of Seneca
Lake at the junction of Route 14 and Routes 5 and 20, is six
miles south of New York State Thruway exit 42. South Main
Street is a street of stately homes and centuries-old trees; it
was the center of the aristocracy of early Geneva. Pulteney
Square and Trinity Episcopal Church, the oldest Episcopal
church in western New York, give the street an old-world
look. Hobart College extends along the street. Many of the
multiple-level homes back up to Seneca Lake.

In addition to Hobart College, the oldest college in western
New York, Geneva is the home of William Smith College and
the New York State Agricultural Experiment Station. Two
nearby state parks are Seneca Lake State Park in Geneva and

Sampson State Park, twelve miles south of the city on the east side of Seneca Lake. Some additional Geneva attractions include the Prouty-Chew Museum, Rose Hill Mansion, and the Smith Opera House for the Performing Arts.

Geneva is on the general site of the Seneca Indian village called Kanadesaga. It was a village of fifty homes, with cultivated fields and orchards, centered on the grounds of the present location of the New York State Agricultural Experiment Station. In 1756, Sir William Johnson, the British Superintendent of Indian Affairs, had an oak and pine stockade constructed at the site. With the exception of Jemima Wilkinson's religious colony, originally located south of Geneva near Dresden, Geneva is the oldest non-Native American settlement in western New York.

A surveyor's error prevented Geneva from playing an even more important role in the development of western New York. The original Royal Charter of Massachusetts provided that state with a claim to the lands of western New York. To settle the claim dispute between the two states, both states agreed to a Pre-emption Line from Sodus Bay on Lake Ontario south along Seneca Lake to the Pennsylvania line.

The first survey of the Pre-emption Line, which defined the border of Massachusetts' preemptive rights (to sell the land), placed the line slightly to the west of Geneva. This caused Oliver Phelps, who with Nathaniel Gorham purchased the land from Massachusetts, to build his land office at Canandaigua instead of Geneva, his original choice.

The first medical degree awarded to a woman in modern times was awarded to Elizabeth Blackwell in 1849 by Geneva College, which became Hobart College in 1851. The Medical School of Geneva College was founded in 1834 and was located in Geneva until it was moved and became part of Syracuse University in 1872. Elizabeth had been rejected by twenty-eight medical schools before being accepted by the Medical School of Geneva College. She graduated first in her class on January 23, 1849.

Elizabeth founded both a medical college that was incorporated into Cornell Medical Center and an infirmary in New York, which is now the New York Downtown Hospital. The first women's residence hall at Hobart / William Smith Colleges was named Blackwell House in her honor, when it was built in 1899.

Geneva is developing its lakefront on Seneca Lake, including a hotel and biking and hiking trails. The Finger Lakes Interpretive Center, which is expected to attract 50,000 visitors annually, will be built near the entrance to Seneca Lake State Park. It will include an auditorium, computerized interpretive displays, video presentations, and exhibits about science, technology, and agriculture.

WATERLOO

"Official recognition was given Waterloo, New York, as the birthplace of Memorial Day when both Houses of Congress passed House Concurrent Resolution 587 which reads in part as follows:

> *'Resolved that the Congress of the United States, in recognition of the patriotic tradition set in motion one hundred years ago in the village of Waterloo, New York, does hereby officially recognize Waterloo, New York, as the birthplace of Memorial Day ...'*

This resolution introduced by Congressman Samuel S. Stratton unanimously passed the House of Representatives May 17, 1966 and received the same approval in the Senate two days later."

From The History and Origin of Memorial day in Waterloo, New York, Waterloo Memorial Day Centennial Committee, 1966.

Waterloo is west of and virtually contiguous with its neighbor, Seneca Falls. Waterloo is recognized as the birthplace of Memorial Day by the sanction of the U.S. Congress, and by the presidential proclamation of President Lyndon Johnson in 1966. The village had the first community-wide observance of Memorial Day on May 5, 1866, when businesses closed and black-draped flags were flown at half-staff. Community leaders and veterans marched to three local cemeteries, where ceremonies were held and graves were decorated with evergreen boughs, floral crosses, and wreaths.

The Memorial Day Museum, a twenty-room brick mansion built in the 1830s, is located at 35 E. Main Street. The museum displays items pertinent to Memorial Day, the Civil War, World Wars I and II, and the Korean Conflict.

Credit for the origination of Memorial Day is sometimes given to southern women, who placed flowers on the graves of both Confederate and Union soldiers. However, this was an uncoordinated activity that was not done on one particular day. On May 5, 1868, General John A. Logan, Commander-in-Chief of the Grand Army of the Republic, designated May 30, 1868, as the day for decorating the graves of those who died for their country during the Civil War. Thus, May 30th became known as "Decoration Day." The name was changed to Memorial Day in 1882, but people continued to use both names.

The idea of setting aside a day as "Memorial Day" was originally conceived by Henry C. E. Wells, a Waterloo merchant, and was supported by General John B. Murray of Waterloo, county clerk of Seneca County. Murray became known as the "father of Memorial Day." In fairness, the two men should be called "the fathers of Memorial Day."

The Hunt House, located at 401 East Main Street, Waterloo, was the site of the first planning meeting for the Women's Rights Convention in Seneca Falls on July 19-20, 1848. The house, which was built in 1829, was the home of Jane and Richard Hunt. On July 9, 1848, Jane Hunt invited four women to tea: Mary Ann M'Clintock, a Waterloo Quaker and abolitionist; Lucretia Mott, Quaker minister and abolitionist; Elizabeth Cady Stanton of Seneca Falls, and Martha Wright, Lucretia Motts' sister.

All five women were frustrated with the inferior status of women in society and with the discrimination that they had encountered in the abolitionist and temperance movements. The decided to convene a women's rights convention to provide a forum to discuss their grievances. They placed a notice in the Seneca County *Courier* on July 14th to announce the Convention to the public.

On July 16, 1848, the organizers of the Women's Rights Convention planned for July 19-20 in Seneca Falls met at the home of Mary Ann and Thomas M'Clintock at 16 East William Street, Waterloo, to prepare an agenda for the Convention. The women decided to prepare a document to list their grievances and to propose resolution of the grievances.

They chose to pattern their document listing eighteen grievances against men and society on the *Declaration of Independence*, which listed eighteen grievances against King George III. Their document, the *Declaration of Sentiments*, began with the words: "We hold these truths to be self evident; that all men and women are created equal." The document included demands such as the right to an education, the right to full participation in the church and the professions, the right to own and sell property, and the right to vote.

Another Waterloo landmark is the Scythe Tree, which is several miles west of Waterloo on Routes 5 and 20. It is a large Balm of Gilead tree, of the poplar family, in which three scythes were imbedded by Waterloo men leaving for war. The first scythe was placed in the tree by a Civil War soldier who didn't return from the war and the second two blades by two World War I military men who did return. This historical curiosity is marked by a nearby monument.

Waterloo, on the Cayuga-Seneca Canal, used a State grant, village labor, and volunteer labor to transform Oak Island in the canal into a welcoming area for the village. Oak Island provides docking areas for boaters including a handicapped-accessible dock, picnic areas, and a trail that includes a walking tour of the village.

AUBURN

....

This jewel, eleven miles in length,
    Is famed for scenery.
It lies two hundred forty yards
    Above the wind-vexed sea.

....

An old Algonkian village was
    Found at its northern rim.
The site is now a relic ground
    Whose history is dim.

And at its outlet, limpid, swift,
    The town of Auburn lies.
This paradise upon her hills
    Attracts all stranger's eyes.

....

And, every summer, artists come
    To paint this light-blue lake,
Whose beauty is alluring as
    Queen Nature's hand can make.

Owasco Lake by Edwin Becker

The City of Auburn, two and a half miles north of Owasco Lake, is a picturesque city with Historic District neighborhoods. It has grand old homes, such as Seward House, the home of William H. Seward, Secretary of State in the administrations of Abraham Lincoln and Andrew Johnson. Auburn is located at the junction of New York State Routes 5 and 20, and is directly south of New York State Thruway Interchange 40. The city is the home of varied enterprises, including manufacturers of plastics, bottling, steel, and transportation components.

Auburn has beautiful parks, such as Emerson Park and the Casey Park family sports complex, one of Central New York's most complete outdoor recreational facilities. Fort Hill Cemetery, the site of the early Native American fort, Osco, has a monument to Chief Logan, the famed Iroquois orator. Other Auburn attractions include the the Cayuga County Agricultural Museum, Cayuga Museum with its "Home of Talking Pictures" exhibit, Schweinfurth Memorial Art Center, and the Willard Chapel, the only chapel designed by Tiffany.

Captain John L. Hardenbergh, a member of the General Sullivan expedition in 1779, returned to Auburn, then Wasco, to build a log cabin and a grist mill behind the site of the present City Hall. He is known as the father of Auburn. Several mills sprang up on the Owasco Outlet, along with a stagecoach stop and tavern, and the settlement became known as Hardenbergh's Corners. In 1803, the name was changed to Auburn after "the loveliest village of the plain" in a poem by Oliver Goldsmith. By 1810, fourteen mills were operating along the Owasco Outlet, including mills that made linseed oil and sunflower oil.

Auburn donated land to the State for a state prison, and construction began in September 1816. Prison reform dictated individual cells for prisoners, and Auburn prison became the first prison in the United States to have a cell block. The first electric chair in the world was built at Auburn in 1890 to electrocute William Kemmler, a Buffalo murderer. Fifty-seven prisoners were electrocuted at Auburn before 1916, when executions were moved to Sing Sing. Among those executed at Auburn were Leon Czolgosz, who assassinated President McKinley at the Buffalo Exposition in 1901, and Chester Gillette, who gained fame when his case was dramatized in Theodore Dreiser's *An American Tragedy*.

The Auburn Theological Seminary was built in 1820-21 and admitted its first students in 1821. The seminary trained Presbyterian ministers until 1939, when it was closed and merged with the Union Theological Seminary in New York City. Willard Memorial Chapel was a part of the seminary.

The first Governor of New York State from Auburn was Enos Throop, who served from 1829 to 1832. His home, Willowbrook, was built in 1818, on the east side of the lake, just south of Auburn. Willard Seward Burroughs, inventor of the first marketed adding machine, began his career as a bank clerk in Auburn. William G. Fargo, founder of the Wells Fargo Company with Henry Wells, once worked as an agent at the Auburn railroad station. Harriet Tubman, who led over 300 slaves to freedom on the Underground Railroad, moved to Auburn after the Civil War, where she was active in the Women's Rights Movement.

SKANEATELES

Enchanting Skaneateles Lake
   Which nestles in the heights
Is nearly sixteen miles in length
   With sandy bathing sites.

Like Iceland spar, this crystal jewel
   Is famed for purity.
It lies eight hundred sixty feet
   Above the dull-green sea.

In flint-lock days, Moravians
   Who left their land to roam,
Located here at St. John's beach
   And built "The Pilgrims Home."
....

A famous author once remarked
That Skaneateles Lake,
Has all the charm and loveliness
That Nature's hand can make.

Skaneateles Lake by Edwin Becker

The village of Skaneateles, located at the northern end of Skaneateles Lake, has a population of over 8,000, and is known for its award-winning, restored downtown. The village boasts of preserved homes and shops, a scenic setting on the lake, and good restaurants, such as the Krebs and the Sherwood Inn.

The village has Austin and Thayer parks, the John D. Barrow Art Gallery, scenic cruises from the foot of the lake, Polo on Sunday afternoons during July and August, the Skaneateles Nature Trail, and band concerts in Thayer Park. Other activities include weekly sailboat races with regattas on Fourth of July and Labor Day weekends, "flares around the lake" on July 3rd, and antique shows, art exhibits, and flower shows.

The Skaneateles Festival, a high-quality regional chamber music festival with approximately eighty musicians, is held each year during August. Nearby is the Baltimore Woods nature preserve and an operating water-driven flour mill at New Hope, about two miles from the west shore of the southern end of the lake.

The first non-Native-American visitors to the site of the village, Moravian missionaries, came from Bethlehem, Pennsylvania, in 1750. They built "the Pilgrim's Hut" of logs on St. James Beach, near the current location of St. James Episcopal Church. The first settlers on the site of the village were Abraham Cuddleback, his wife, and their eight children, who arrived after a forty-three-day wagon trip from Orange County.

By 1797, a series of mills using the outlet for power had

been built along Skaneateles Creek, in Skaneateles, Mottville, and Skaneateles Falls. An artisan from Salem, Massachusetts, brought the New England influence to the architecture of the older homes in the village. He lived in Skaneateles from 1812 to 1820, and built many of the "Salem doorways" that still decorate many of the older houses.

Isaac Sherwood was an early settler who delivered mail on foot, then on horseback, and founded a stage coach company, the Old Mail Line, in 1809. The company had the contract for carrying mail between Utica and Canandaigua. By 1815, he had fifteen stage coaches in service passing through Skaneateles and stopping at the original 1807 Sherwood Inn.

Skaneateles was a stop on the Underground Railroad during the mid-1800s. Evergreen House at 98 West Genesee Street was a rest stop for slaves being escorted from the South to freedom in Canada. People who lived in the Skaneateles area in its early days include Henry Arnold, brother of General Benedict Arnold, the Revolutionary War traitor, and two members of the Roosevelt family, Nicholas and S. Montgomery Roosevelt. Henry Roosevelt, owner of a summer home on the lake, served in the Department of the Navy with his relative, Assistant Secretary of the Navy Franklin Delano Roosevelt.

CHAPTER 7
Northwest of Seneca Falls

Of all the spots on God's green earth,
The one I'd choose for my own
Would be the wonderful finger lakes
With their beauty of great renown
Sparkling waters and verdant hills
Nestled beneath azure skies.
To [those] who'd make this spot [their] home,
[They] would live in a paradise.
Indians say that God's own Hand
Planted His fingerprints here
To bless the land for His children
To show them His garden rare
And as I gaze at its beauty
I cannot help but feel awed
To think that this marvel of nature
Was blessed by the Hand of God.

From *Inspiration* by A. Glenn Rogers

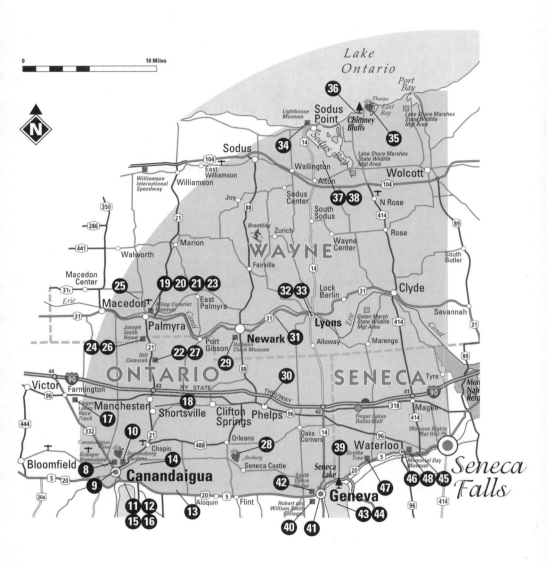

Map of Northwest of Seneca Falls

PLACES TO SEE / THINGS TO DO

Page No.

North of Geneva (continued)   Page No.

PLACES TO SEE / THINGS TO DO

CANANDAIGUA AREA

8) Granger Homestead and Carriage Museum

The Granger Homestead, located on a twelve-acre site at 295 North Main Street, Canandaigua, is a federal-style mansion completed in 1816. The mansion, which contains detailed carved moldings and mantelpieces, took two years to build at a cost of $13,000. Almost half of the twenty-three rooms have been restored.

Many of the furnishings on display in the restored rooms were owned by four generations of the Granger family. The period furniture includes the dining room table that Dolly Madison saved when the British Army burned the White House during the War of 1812. Upon request, visitors are shown a thirty-minute TV documentary, "The Statesman from Canandaigua," about Gideon Granger, the homestead's builder.

Gideon Granger was a Yale graduate, a lawyer, a Connecticut State Senator, father of the public school system in Connecticut, and the U.S. Postmaster General from 1800 until 1813 in the administrations of Thomas Jefferson and James Madison. Granger became familiar with the Finger Lakes Region when he was the agent for the State of Connecticut in settling Oliver Phelps' estate.

Granger moved to Canandaigua after he left Madison's administration, practiced law, and served a term as a New York State Senator. He died in 1822. His son, Francis, ran unsuccessfully for Vice President and served as Postmaster General in the abbreviated term of President William Henry Harrison. The Granger Homestead served as the Granger Place School for Young Ladies from 1875 to 1906. The Granger family lived at the homestead until the death of Miss Antoinette Granger, the last of the Granger family, in 1930.

The Carriage Museum contains over fifty horse-drawn

vehicles, including coaches, fire-fighting equipment, hearses, sleighs, sporting vehicles, and commercial wagons. The carriages were built in the period from 1820 to 1939, and many have been restored. The collection includes the half-moon carriage used by Jemima Wilkinson, "Publick Universal Friend," leader of a religious sect near Branchport during the late 1700s and early 1800s.

The Homestead, which is maintained by the Granger Homestead Society, is open Tuesday through Saturday afternoons from mid-May through mid-October. Additional summer hours are Sunday afternoons from June 1 through August 31.

9) Ontario County Historical Society Museum

The Ontario County Historical Society Museum, located at 55 North Main Street, was constructed in 1914 to preserve the County's unique heritage. The Museum features a series of thematic exhibits, a "hands-on" discovery center, and a research library on local history. The Ontario County Historical Society sponsors lectures, preservation activities, educational programs, special events, and a permanent exhibit on the history of Ontario County.

10) Sonnenberg Gardens and Mansion

Sonnenberg Gardens and Mansion, at 151 Charlotte Street in Canandaigua, is a fifty-acre estate that includes nine formal gardens, a Japanese garden, a greenhouse conservatory, ponds, statuary, and a forty-room mansion built by Mr. and Mrs. Frederick Ferris Thompson in 1887. The rusticated gray stone mansion, trimmed in red Medina sandstone, is a blend of Elizabethan, Richardson Romanesque, and Tudor architectural influences. Designed by Boston architect Francis Allen, the mansion has a prominent turret, half-timbered gables, and a covered carriage entranceway.

The Palm House is the centerpiece of the greenhouse complex and is constructed of 1,100 pieces of curved, frosted glass. The Peach House, which contains its original iron trellises, is now the Peach House luncheon restaurant. The Mansion houses two gift shops, and the Canandaigua Brands Company operates its winetasting room on the grounds of the estate.

The Thompsons purchased the property in 1863 from the Holberton family, who had named the house Sonnenberg (Sunny Hill) for a small town in Germany. The Thompsons retained the name, but replaced the house. Mrs. Thompson commissioned Ernest W. Bowditch, a highly regarded Boston horticulturist and landscape gardener, to design and oversee the construction of the gardens.

Bowditch's earlier accomplishments were the private gardens of Cornelius Vanderbilt and Pierre Lorillard, and the park system in Cleveland, Ohio. At Sonnenberg, he designed nine separate gardens, an aviary, and a deer park. The tenth garden, a beautiful Japanese garden, was designed by landscape architect K. Wadamori.

The Italian Garden is laid out in four large rectangles containing silver and red fleur-de-lis arrangements bordered by seventy-two hand-trimmed, cone-shaped yews. Adjacent to the Italian garden is the Blue and White Garden, called the "intimate" garden by Mrs. Thompson. Privacy is ensured in this garden, which is planted only with blue flowers and white flowers, by walls of hedges and vines.

The Pansy Garden, bordered by a wall of yews and a tall stone banquette, is accessed via an archway in the hedge from the Blue and White Garden, which is directly in front of it. The Pansy Garden, designed as a place for meditation and reflection, has a six-foot-high fountain that flows into a marble birdbath shaped like a pansy. The small Moonlight Garden, behind a row of cherry dogwood and bordered with privet hedges adjacent to the Pansy Garden, was planted with fragrant white flowers to be enjoyed by moonlight.

The Sub-Rosa or "Hidden" Garden, containing arborvitae, English ivy, juniper, lilacs, privet, and trumpet vine, is sur-

Sonnenberg Gardens and Mansion, Canandaigua

rounded by dense, square-clipped boxwood hedges. This garden, viewed as an "outdoor chapel," contains a fountain, a pool, four white marble busts of the seasons, and two marble lions. The Rose Garden is planted with over 2,600 white, pink, and red roses; the Old-Fashioned (Colonial) Garden is known for its variety of color. The Rock Garden has a stone lookout tower, shady wooded pathways, and a water cascade.

The Japanese Garden has brooks and lily ponds spanned by small bridges, two stone devil dogs (one smiling to greet friends, another scowling to fend off evil spirits), and a large bronze statue of Buddha, sitting in the lotus position. This garden has English yews and many varieties of trees, including bronze Japanese maples, Japanese umbrella trees, and red cedars.

Mrs. Thompson outlived her husband by twenty-four years; she died in 1923. The estate was sold to the U.S. Government, which built a Veterans' Administration hospital on the estate's farmlands and converted the mansion into nurses' quarters. Sonnenberg Gardens, Inc., a nonprofit educational corporation, was chartered by an act of Congress in 1972 to preserve the Mansion and Gardens for display to the public. Sonnenberg Gardens and Mansion are open daily from May through October.

11) Canandaigua Lake State Marine Park
Canandaigua Lake State Marine Park, located off South Main Street in Canandaigua at the northern end of the Lake, has boat launch facilities, a comfort station, and parking space for over 200 cars and trailers.

12) Kershaw Park
Kershaw Park, a City of Canandaigua park located on seven acres at the northern end of Canandaigua Lake, has a supervised swimming area, a small craft launch area, and a first aid station. The Park also contains a picnic area with barbecue grills, a sand-pit volleyball court, grassy play areas, and rest

rooms and dressing rooms that are open in spring, summer, and fall.

John "Jack" Kershaw, a member of the Board of Health and Public Safety for whom the Park is named, suggested that a park be constructed on the site in 1920. In 1931, Dr. Charles Booth promoted the implementation of Jack Kershaw's recommendation. Construction of the Park became a Works Progress Administration project during the Depression; the State provided the labor, and the City furnished the trucks and materials. The Park was officially opened on August 11, 1936, and was improved in 1995-96.

13) New York Pageant of Steam—Hopewell

The Annual Pageant of Steam, which began in 1961, is held in early August on Gehan Road in Hopewell, off Routes 5 and 20, three miles east of Canandaigua. Steam engines are demonstrated sawing lumber and threshing grain, and steam traction engines and tractors participate in daily parades. The multiple-day event also includes a display of over 600 gasoline engines and over 200 early gasoline-engine-powered tractors.

The Pageant features daily parades, wagon rides, steam whistle concerts, and a flea market. Live bands play on several nights. Antique tractor pulls are scheduled in the evenings. In a recent year, over 12,000 visitors attended the Pageant. Campsites with shower facilities are available on the grounds.

14) Canandaigua Speedway

The Canandaigua Speedway, located at the Ontario County Fairgrounds, is a DIRT (Drivers' Independent Race Track) track. Races are held Saturday evenings, and selected other evenings, from early April through August.

15) Boat Rides on the *Canandaigua Lady*

The *Canandaigua Lady*, which can accommodate 150 passengers (130 for dining) on her upper deck and in her lower cabin, is a replica of a nineteenth-century paddlewheel steamboat. The vessel has a beam of twenty-four feet and a length of eighty-eight feet, or one hundred feet if the gangplank at the bow and the paddlewheel at the stern are included in the measurement.

The lower cabin is air conditioned and has full bar service, a dance floor, and rest rooms. The *Canandaigua Lady* offers dinner cruises, lunch cruises, supper cruises, a Sunday brunch, Sunday breakfast, and narrated boat tours.

Special event cruises can be booked, such as anniversary or birthday cruises, corporate or private charters, fall foliage cruises, fund raisers, field trips, school party cruises, tour groups, moonlight cruises, or wedding cruises. The ticket office for the *Canandaigua Lady* is located at 169 Lakeshore Drive, Canandaigua.

16) Captain Gray's Boat Tours

Captain Gray's Boat Tours, which began service in 1972, offers narrated tours of Canandaigua Lake daily from late morning until mid-evening from the Inn on the Lake dock at the foot of Main Street in Canandaigua. Captain Gray's Boat Tours offers one-hour, two-hour, and around-the-lake cruises as well as specialty cruises for events such as bridal and baby showers, group meetings, family and class reunions, and wedding rehearsals.

17) Finger Lakes Race Track—Farmington

Finger Lakes Race Track, located in Farmington at the intersection of Routes 96 and 332 (about six miles north of Canandaigua) opened on May 23, 1962. The track offers an over 170-day thoroughbred racing season. Hall of Fame jockeys, including Steve Cauthen, Angel Cordero, and Bill Shoemaker, have ridden at the Finger Lakes Race Track.

Finger Lakes Race Track offers an average of ten races per day from early April until the first week of December. The major races include the Finger Lakes Breeders' Cup, the New York Oaks, the New York Derby, and the New York Breeders' Futurity. Total wagering in 1995 was over $172,000,000.

Concession stands are located throughout the facility, and a limited menu with table seating is available in the Paddock Room. A full luncheon menu is offered in the air-conditioned, glass-enclosed Terrace Dining Room. Parking for the handicapped is near the clubhouse entrance, and handicapped access to all levels is provided by an elevator in the lower grandstand.

18) The Wild Water Derby—Manchester / Shortsville

The first Annual Wild Water Derby sponsored by the Twin Cities (Manchester and Shortsville) Lions Club was held in April 1976. The Derby has been held on three and a quarter miles of whitewater of the Canadaigua Lake outlet between Littleville and Manchester, on Route 21 south of the New York State Thruway. In this section the outlet is whitewater rapids for only a few days in the early spring, when the floodgates between Canandaigua Lake and the outlet are opened to reduce the high lake level. When the lake level has dropped and the floodgates are closed, the course provides an easy canoe trip. Later in the summer, the water is too low for good canoeing.

In early April, however, the whitewater over the course of the derby is rated Class III, and is possibly Class IV at the peak rapids at Shortsville. Classification of rapids varies from Class I (easy) to Class IV (possible risk to life). In his book written over forty years ago, *Canoeable Waterways of New York State*, canoeing authority Lawrence Grinnell described the stretch of the outlet used for the Derby:

> Just before the bridge at Littleville, one and one-half miles above Shortsville, is a partly destroyed dam, which still backs up water. Below this dam are impassable cataracts.

Between Littleville and Manchester, the stream descends sharply from a plateau in a succession of steep, boulder-strewn rapids, some definitely too shallow, or otherwise impossible to run at this stage. Steep banks make line-downs impractical. The descent could be dangerous at high water. The stream is still too steep and rocky to put in at Manchester bridge and re-embark one-quarter mile below this bridge, thus making the total portage from Littleville of about three and one-quarter miles.

Derby participants are divided into five classes:

- kayaks (the smallest class)
- two-man canoe — men's class
- mixed canoe class — man-woman or all-woman teams
- inflatables — plastic and rubber manufactured craft and inner-tube rafts
- homemade rafts

The fifth class, homemade rafts, has the most variety — from well-built craft to, on one occasion, a platform tied to fifty-gallon barrels that originally contained apple concentrate from South America. Beer barrels, casks, and kegs are also used as flotation devices. Some participants emphasize the artistic quality of the raft. Entries have included a craft decorated as a sea monster with a crew dressed as Vikings. Personal flotation devices (life jackets) are required for all entrants, and kayakers must wear helmets. Many entrants also wear wet suits. Time to complete the race ranges from twenty minutes to just under thirty minutes.

Until 1998, the Derby was the main fund-raising event for the Twin Cities Lions Club. A new sponsor is being sought.

PALMYRA

19) Alling Coverlet Museum

The Alling Coverlet Museum, located at 122 William Street in Palmyra, houses the largest collection of coverlets in the United States. The Museum, which is administered by Historic Palmyra, Inc., contains coverlets collected by Mrs. Harold Alling for over thirty years. The Museum is located in a two-story brick building donated by Mrs. Henry Griffith.

One of the notable coverlets on display is the woven coverlet "American Tapestry," an approximately eighty-inches by ninety-inches bed cover woven of homespun wool and linen. Coverlets were made to be used, but they were also heirlooms. The flax and wool were raised by the early pioneers, cleaned, sorted, and spun prior to weaving the coverlet. Dyes were made from local flowers, roots, and weeds.

Most coverlets were made by professional weavers, who wove in geometric patterns; they sometimes used as many as twenty-four harnesses. Later, they used the French Jacquard loom controlled by punched cards to make more complicated patterns. Coverlets made by housewives were usually made on four-harness looms using the overshot weave.

Historic Palmyra, Inc., operates a gift shop in the Coverlet Museum that offers hand-crafted items and books about textiles. The Alling Coverlet Museum is open afternoons from June through mid-October and at other times by appointment.

Historic Palmyra, Inc., is a nonprofit organization dedicated to community service, historic preservation, and the operation of the Alling Coverlet Museum, the Palmyra Historical Museum, and the William Phelps General Store Museum.

20) Palmyra Historical Museum

The Palmyra Historical Museum, located at 132 Market Street, houses antiques, children's toys, Palmyra memorabilia, and Victorian period rooms. The Museum takes visitors back to an earlier time when Palmyra was a manufacturing center that used the Erie Canal to transport products, including agricultural implements, carriages, printing press equipment, and sleighs.

21) William Phelps General Store Museum

The William Phelps General Store Museum, 140 Market Street, is furnished with original Phelps family artifacts. The Museum provides a snapshot of a 1890s general store.

22) Hill Cumorah and the Moroni Monument

The brochure "Welcome to Historic Mormon Country" includes the following explanation of Hill Cumorah, four miles south of Palmyra:

> In A.D. 421, Moroni, the last survivor of a great civilization that inhabited the Americas from 600 BC to AD 420, buried in this hill a set of gold plates on which was recorded the history of his people. By commandment of God, Moroni returned as an angel and delivered the plates to Joseph Smith in 1827. Joseph Smith translated the plates as the *Book of Mormon*, a companion scripture to the Bible. The *Book of Mormon* tells of the visit of Jesus Christ to the ancient Americans.

Hill Cumorah is a prominent drumlin, formed by glacial activity, in the region north of the Finger Lakes. It is the site of a spectacular outdoor religious pageant, "America's Witness for Christ," performed each summer by a cast of over 600 for audiences of over 100,000 people. The significance of Hill Cumorah is explained through exhibits, paintings, and video presentations in the Visitor Center, which is open year-round. Free guided tours are conducted daily.

Hill Cumorah and the Moroni Monument, Palmyra

23) Historic Grandin Building

The Historic Grandin Building in Palmyra was constructed in 1828, three years after the completion of the Erie Canal. E. B. Grandin supervised the printing of the first edition of the *Book of Mormon* in 1830. This first edition consisted of 5,000 leather-bound 590-page copies. The Visitor Center, which is open year-round, offers free displays, films, and guided tours.

24) Joseph Smith Home

Joseph Smith, the first president of the Church of Jesus Christ of Latter-Day Saints, and his father and brothers built this frame house in Palmyra in 1820. He lived in the house from his nineteenth to his twenty-second year. The Home, located south of Route 31 and west of Route 21, has been restored to its original condition with period furnishings. The Visitor Center has free displays, films, and guided tours year-round.

25) Martin Harris Farm

Martin Harris was an early follower of Joseph Smith and a strong believer in the *Book of Mormon*. He mortgaged his farm to finance the first edition of the *Book of Mormon*, which was printed at the historic E. B. Grandin Building in 1830. An 1850 Erie Canal cobblestone house is now located on the former Harris farm in Palmyra. The Visitor Center is open year-round; it offers displays, films, and free guided tours.

26) The Sacred Grove

The Sacred Grove, located south of Route 31 and west of the Joseph Smith Home in Palmyra, was the site of a visitation at which Joseph Smith learned from Heavenly Beings that he should join no established church.

When Joseph Smith was fourteen, he had wondered which of the local churches he should join. He noted a passage in the Bible, James 1:5, "If any lack wisdom, let him ask of God." Smith walked westward from his home on a beautiful spring morning into a grove of trees nearby. He knelt in prayer in the grove, and had a vision: "I saw a pillar of light. When the light rested upon me, I saw two personages, whose brightness and glory defy all description, standing above me in the air. One of them spoke unto me, calling me by name and said, pointing to the other, 'This is my Beloved Son; hear him.'"

Seven years later Smith was directed to the gold plates buried in Hill Cumorah, from which he translated the *Book of Mormon*.

27) The Hill Cumorah Pageant

The Hill Cumorah Pageant is held in mid-July at Hill Cumorah, four miles south of Palmyra on Route 21. Recognized as America's largest outdoor drama, the Pageant is attended annually by over 100,000 people from around the world. It is based on the *Book of Mormon* and tells the story of of the rise and fall of an ancient civilization on this continent between 600 BC and AD 420.

The Pageant features a cast of 600 and 1,400 costumes, a high-tech digital sound recording of the Mormon Tabernacle Choir, and a 100-voice children's choir with the Utah Symphony Orchestra in the Salt Lake City Tabernacle. The Pageant has attention-getting special effects, such as explosions, fireballs, volcanos, and the simulation of a prophet burned at the stake. Staging includes fifteen-foot water curtains, a quality outdoor sound system, and thirty- and fifty-foot light towers using more than 500,000 watts of power.

Critics have made the following observations of the pageant:

- "A pageant performed with the spirit of a George Lucas techno-dazzler and the scope of a Cecil B. DeMille epic."—The New York *Times*
- "Staging the Mormon Pageant on this holy site, with the statue of Moroni glittering atop the hill, roughly equals staging Oberammergau at Lourdes, except that this

show has a distinctly American-style flash and grandeur." — Rochester *Democrat and Chronicle*

- "One of the most dramatic moments in the production takes place when the resurrected Christ appears 30 feet in the air and slowly descends to the highest point of the gigantic seven-level stage." — Buffalo *News*
- "As always, the pageant promises glittering exotic costumes and an extensive sound and light show." — Denver *Post*

The Hill Cumorah Pageant, which is one hour and fifteen minutes long, has been presented by the Church of Jesus of Latter Day Saints since 1937. The performance begins at dusk. No admission is charged, parking is free, and seating is provided for over 8,000 (or bring blankets or lawn chairs). Interpreters are provided for the hearing impaired, and French, German, and Spanish earphone translations are available.

NORTH OF GENEVA

28) Amberg Wine Cellars

Amberg Wine Cellars, at 2412 Seneca Castle Road, northwest of Geneva, was established in 1990. It is run by the Amberg family, who have been grape growers in the Seneca Lake area for decades. They have supplied root stock to area growers for over thirty years as Amberg's Grafted Grape Vine Nursery. The original winery, which burned down in 1996, was located in the old barns of a farm established in 1795. The Winery was rebuilt in 1997. Seneca Castle Road is approximately four miles west of Geneva, off Routes 5 and 20; the Winery is near the intersection of Seneca Castle Road and County Road 23. Amberg Wine Cellars also has a retail store west of Geneva on Routes 5 and 20.

The Winery produces both varietal wines and blends. Their vineyards are planted with Chardonnay, Pinot Noir, Riesling,

Chambourcin (a French-American hybrid red), and Traminette and Vidal Blanc (hybrid white) vines. Amberg Wine Cellars currently produces more than 5,000 gallons annually of Chardonnay, Riesling, Pinot Noir, and blends, including Blanc, Burgundy, and Pearl. Amberg Wine Cellars also offers a popular wine, Gypsy, which is a blend of Traminette and Riesling, and Red Panda, a semi-sweet red wine.

Winemaker Eric Amberg acquired his winemaking expertise at wineries in California, Germany, and New York State after earning his degree in enology at Fresno State University in California.

29) Hoffman Clock Museum—Newark

The Hoffman Clock Museum, which is located in the Newark Public Library at the corner of Mason and High Streets in Newark, has over 100 horological items on display—mainly nineteenth-century American clocks. The collection has fifteen clocks made in New York State, and includes Dutch, English, French, German, and early Japanese clocks as well. The collection includes a 1760 enamelled watch, an 1815 banjo clock, and an 1875 oriental clock.

The Museum's exhibits provide an opportunity to learn about the history of timekeeping. They introduce visitors to the development of timekeeping technology and clock styles. The unique collection of timepieces has something for everyone—young and old, novice and expert. Each travel season, a particular facet of timekeeping is highlighted in a special display.

The core collection was assembled by Augustus and Jennie Hoffman of Newark. The Hoffman Foundation, established in 1950, was organized to preserve the Hoffmans' collection for the education and enjoyment of the community. The Museum is open daily during regular library hours, Monday through Saturday. However, the Library and the Museum are closed Saturdays during July and August. Arrangements for group tours of the Museum may be made with the curator. Admission to the Museum is free.

30) Sauerkraut Festival—Phelps

Phelps, the home of the annual Sauerkraut Festival since 1967, was a center for cabbage growing and sauerkraut factories for much of its history. The annual Sauerkraut Festival is held at the Phelps firemen's field on Ontario Street in early August. The Festival provides music, parades, and food, including plenty of sauerkraut.

Previous years' festivals have included an early evening children's parade, children's night on the midway, and a DJ on Thursday. Friday's activities are midway rides, a block dance at the American Legion on Main Street with music of the 1950s, 1960s, and 1970s, and live music at the Festival grounds. Saturday's activities have included:

- arts and crafts
- festival parade
- a bike rodeo
- fireworks
- midway rides
- chicken and pork barbecues
- cutting of the sauerkraut cake
- continuous live music
- special music events, such as bagpipers and cloggers
- a 20K race over country roads from Phelps to Clifton Springs and back

Events scheduled for Sunday have included arts and crafts, bike tours, a custom car show, a chicken barbecue at the American Legion, live music, and midway rides.

31) Blue Cut Nature Center—Lyons

Blue Cut Nature Center, which is located just west of Lyons, is a wildlife refuge and nature study center spread over more than forty acres of meadow, swamp, woodland, and drumlins (hills or ridges of glacial drift). Blue Cut has been the name of the locale since railroad tracks were built through the area in 1853. A cut made through a drumlin revealed Vernon Shale that had a bluish cast when exposed.

The Nature Center has three trails:

TIME STUDY TRAIL (Blue Trail)—The theme of this trail is that everything changes; nothing is permanent. It begins in a 30-year-old pine forest and travels up a drumlin formed 11,000 years ago. Erosion, tree growth rings, and weathering are examples of factors visible from this trail.

FORESTRY TRAIL (Green Trail)—This is a forest management trail that winds through a mixed pine plantation. Examples of pruning, thinning methods, and timber cruising are provided along this trail.

WILDLIFE TRAIL (Orange Trail)—Wildlife management techniques are emphasized along this trail, including control of aquatic plants, field border plantings, fish stocking, shrub plantings, and strip mowing. It begins in a marsh, travels by a pond, and continues through a hardwood stand to an open field.

32) Wayne County Historical Society Museum—Lyons

The Wayne County Historical Society Museum, at 21 Butternut Street in Lyons, is located in a brick Italianate house and an attached stone building that served as the sheriff's residence and county jail for 107 years. The Museum has exhibits on Erie Canal times, the early glass and pottery industries, Indian life, prehistoric times, and Wayne County military history.

Visitors can enter a replica of a general store in the circa 1910 barn located behind the Museum. The Museum also displays a collection of diverse transportation artifacts, including an 1860 coach and the only known surviving wooden canal horse bridge. The second floor contains exhibits of the rural history of Wayne County, including displays of carpentry, coopering, farming, ice harvesting, and lumbering.

33) Liberty Erie Canal Cruises—Lyons

Cruises are provided on the 49-passenger *Liberty* from Village Park in Lyons. Several cruises are offered:

- a "coffee and Danish" cruise lasting an hour and a half
- a buffet lunch cruise
- excursions to Creagger's Island, Newark, or Port Gibson, of two to four hours duration
- a buffet dinner and evening cruise
- a narrated canal study trip covering Ganargua Creek, Clinton's Ditch, Erie Canal, Barge Canal, and the dry-dock in Lyons

Most public cruises pass through a canal lock, either at Lyons or Newark. The *Liberty* is available for charter cruises.

SODUS BAY AREA

34) Sodus Bay Lighthouse Museum—Sodus Point

The Sodus Bay Lighthouse Museum, operated by the Sodus Bay Historical Society of 7066 N. Ontario Street, is located on Lake Street in Sodus Point. The nonprofit institution, which was chartered by the state in 1979, is supported by contributions and memberships.

The Sodus Bay region has been known for its commercial fishing, ice industry, grain exports, lumber trade, and shipbuilding. The first non-Native American settlers entered the area in the late 1700s, and Sodus Bay became a busy harbor for exporting farm products and other commodities. Congress appropriated $4,500 for the construction of a lighthouse and keeper's house on the site in 1824; Ishmael Hill was the first lighthouse keeper.

Congress appropriated $14,000 in 1869 to replace the original structures, which had deteriorated beyond the need for maintenance. That lighthouse was used from 1871 until 1901. West pier, constructed in 1834 at the new entrance to

Sodus Bay Lighthouse Museum, Sodus Point

the bay, was a more favorable location for the beacon and light that were installed in 1901. The lighthouse on West Pier was used as a residence for maintenance personnel until 1984.

The lighthouse served an area with heavy traffic of both commercial and pleasure boats. A railroad connecting Sodus Point with the coal fields of Pennsylvania was completed in 1872, along with a small coal loading trestle at the west end of the bay. In the five-year period 1861-1865, seven and a half million tons of coal were shipped using the trestle; the trestle was expanded considerably in 1927. The wooden trestle caught fire and was destroyed when it was being dismantled in 1971.

The area served by the lighthouse, which has been a popular summertime recreation site since the 1850s, is used by boaters, campers, fisherman, and picnickers. It is also a center for winter sports such as ice boating, ice fishing, and snowmobiling. The Sodus Bay Lighthouse Museum, which is open from May 1 through October 31, Tuesday through Sunday, contains many nautical artifacts and items of local history. Its D. Russell Chamberlain Memorial Library is open during Museum hours. The Museum is also open by appointment for adult group tours, bus tours, and school group tours.

35) Thorpe Vineyard and Farm Winery — Wolcott

The Thorpe Vineyard and Farm Winery, located at 8150 Chimney Heights Boulevard in Wolcott, produces Chimney Heights brand wines, including Cayuga White, Chardonnay, Estate Blanc, and Pinot Noir. The vineyard was planted in 1978; the first harvest was in 1983. Additional varieties have been planted including Marechal Foch, Melody, Pinot Gris, and Riesling. The winery produces over 1,000 cases a year.

Chimney Bluffs State Park, on Lake Ontario

36) Chimney Bluffs State Park—on Lake Ontario

Chimney Bluffs State Park, an undeveloped State park known as a "natural park," is accessible off East Bay Road, two and a half miles east of Sodus Point. The natural park, which consists of pinnacles and spires that have been carved out by hundreds of years of water and wind erosion, extends along the Lake Ontario shoreline for over a mile.

The Park can be viewed from a hiking trail inland from the bluffs, and from a narrow strip of beach between the bluffs and Lake Ontario. Since the chimney bluffs can be easily damaged by foot and vehicle traffic, hiking on the bluff faces and off-road vehicle use are prohibited.

37) Alasa Farms—Alton

Alasa Farms, located at 6450 Shaker Road in Alton, is a contraction of the names of two former owners, Alvah Strong and Asa McBride. It is currently a 700-acre working farm that includes twelve acres of barns, dwellings, and other buildings. The central area is surrounded by pastureland, woods, 65 acres of orchards, and 200 acres of tillable crop land.

The farm tour includes a visit to the horse barn that used to house the hackney ponies. Varnished wainscoting is part of the interior woodwork of this magnificent barn. Grazing horse, sheep, and goats can be seen during a stroll around the fifteen acres of pasture on the farm. Children have the opportunity to feed and pet some of the animals in a petting corral behind the barn.

The Alasa Farm Museum is located in the Farm's only remaining large Shaker barn, which was constructed over 150 years ago from timber harvested from surrounding forests. The barn contains a corn crib, livestock quarters, and a hog scalding cauldron used by the Shakers. The Museum houses artifacts from an archaeological dig on the farm and a display of farming equipment.

For an additional fee, visitors can tour the Main Dwelling House, now a private residence. The home contains some original window glass and Shaker pegboard and staircases. The third floor has been renovated in the Shaker tradition with authentic Shaker furniture. The Shaker Heritage Antique Show, which is held on Alasa Farms in July, features many out-of-state dealers offering Shaker originals as well as reproductions and fine Americana.

38) Sodus Shaker Festival—Alton

One day every other summer, Alasa Farms returns to its heritage as a Shaker Community, a nineteenth-century utopian society. Alasa Farms hosts the Sodus Shaker Festival in July in even-numbered years.

Members of the United Society of Believers in Christ's Second Coming were known as Shakers, because of the shaking and quivering dances they performed during religious services. They bought the tract of 1,400 acres in 1826 and built the Shaker Dwelling House in 1834. The house, which was inhabited by sixty people, had an ice-house wing on the east side. The cluster of simple white buildings is located on a ridge overlooking Sodus Bay, south of Sodus Point and east of the hamlet of Alton.

The Shakers lived simply; they were known for the simplicity of the design of everything they built, from early washing machines to dressers, ladder-back chairs, and tables. They sold baskets, brooms, brushes, and furniture, and are credited with being the first to market seeds commercially in packets.

In 1836, the Sodus Shaker Community moved to Groveland, south of Mt. Morris. Until 1892, 150 Shakers lived on 1,800 acres of rich Groveland farmland containing over thirty buildings, including barns, homes, mills, and a church. Their community was sold in 1893 to the Craig Colony for Epileptics. It is now the Livingston County Correctional Facility.

Sodus Shaker Festivals feature authorities on various aspects of Shaker life, craftsmen demonstrating Shaker crafts and selling Shaker reproductions, and Shaker music and dances.

GENEVA

39) Seneca Lake State Park

Seneca Lake State Park is located on 141 acres on Routes 5 and 20, one mile east of Geneva, along the northern end of Seneca Lake. The City of Geneva reclaimed an area of brush, marsh, and trees, and developed a city park on the site in 1922. In 1935, bones, projectile points, and tool artifacts were found, and archaeologists determined that they dated from a pre-Iroquois Lamoka culture about 4,000 years ago. Geneva transferred the city park lands to the State of New York in 1957 to develop Seneca Lake State Park, which was established in 1962.

The Park has electrical hookups, pavilions, picnic areas with tables and fireplaces, playgrounds, playing fields, pay telephones, hot showers, and flush toilets. The Park has over 200 seasonal boat slips, over twenty transient boat slips, a boat launching site, and marine sewage pumpout facilities. Swimming is restricted to the designated lifeguard area. The Park's season is from April 1 through October 23.

40) Hobart / William Smith Colleges

Hobart College is an independent liberal arts college for men and William Smith College is an independent liberal arts college for women; the two colleges form a coordinate system. Students of the colleges take all classes together and are taught by a single faculty, but have separate student governments, athletic programs, and administrative support. Hobart College, founded in 1822, has over 1,000 students, and William Smith College, founded in 1908, has over 800 students.

The 170-acre campus, which borders Seneca Lake in Geneva, has over twenty-eight classroom and administrative

Statue of Elizabeth Blackwell at Hobart / William Smith Colleges, Geneva

buildings, forty-seven residence halls, and a 105-acre nature preserve and an outdoor laboratory located nearby. In sports, Hobart College is known particularly for its lacrosse team, which has won the NCAA Division III lacrosse title on many occasions and now plays in Division I; William Smith College consistently ranks in the top ten in women's soccer.

41) Prouty-Chew Museum

Prouty-Chew Museum, owned and administered by the Geneva Historical Society, is located at 543 South Main Street, Geneva, at the intersection of Routes 5 and 20 and Route 14. The Museum also serves as the Geneva Historical Society's main offices. The Federal-style Prouty-Chew House was built in 1829 by Charles Butler, a Geneva Attorney.

The House was changed and enlarged by the Prouty family in the 1850s and 1870s. In 1969, the Chew family donated the house to the Geneva Historical Society, who restored it and furnished it in the two major architectural styles it represents, Federal and Victorian.

Changing exhibitions are offered throughout the year: art exhibits, costume exhibits of selections from the Museum's costume collection, and exhibits related to local history. The Museum also has a permanent exhibition called "Early Geneva, 1700-1830: The Development of Geneva through Photos, Text, Graphics, and Artifacts." The Museum offers special events, such as the Annual Antique Show and Sale at Rose Hill Mansion, a Christmas Open House, and fall and spring lecture Series.

42) The Smith Opera House

The Smith Opera House, 82 Seneca Street, Geneva, is both a movie theatre and a theatre for the performing arts. Its forty-two-foot by thirty-foot movie screen is the largest in central New York. The Opera House is one of only twenty-one "Great American Movie Palaces" left in New York, of which only five are still used as performing arts facilities (another of the five is Radio City Music Hall in New York City). Only about 300 of the once more than 3,000 theatres of this type in the United States still exist. The Smith Opera House was almost destroyed in 1981 to provide space for a parking lot but was saved by the Finger Lakes Regional Arts Council.

Due to the modifications that it underwent over the years, its architecture is an eclectic mixture of Art-Deco, Spanish-Baroque, and Victorian styles. The theatre's original facade was "Richardsonian" with a terra-cotta arch carved with the likenesses of Edwin Booth and William Shakespeare. The walls on the sides of the stage have golden cartouches with busts of Beethoven and Moliere. The theatre has excellent acoustics, and an unobstructed view of the stage is provided from all 1,500 seats.

Geneva philanthropist William Smith paid $39,000 in 1894 to fulfill his dream of building an opera house for the city. It opened on October 29, 1894, with James O'Neill, the father of playwright Eugene O'Neill, starring in the play "The Count of Monte Cristo." Other famous entertainers who have performed at the Opera House are Sarah Bernhardt, George M. Cohan, Tommy Dorsey, Isadora Duncan, Arthur Fiedler, Al Jolson, John Philip Sousa, and Ellen Terry.

The Smith Opera House was used as a vaudeville house / playhouse until the early 1900s, when it was donated to Hobart College. Hobart sold it to help endow William Smith College at its founding in 1908. Schine Enterprises bought the building in 1929, and totally renovated it as the flagship of the Schine chain of theatres. Architect Victor Rigaumount designed a ceiling of stars in an evening sky, used Art Deco-style signs and trim, and chose Victorian-style light fixtures.

Performances at the Smith Opera House in recent years have included acrobats from the Peoples' Republic of China, Berkshire Ballet's Nutcracker, the Rochester Philharmonic Orchestra, Bruce Springsteen, the Syracuse Symphony Orchestra, and the U.S. Air Force Band of the East. The Smith Opera House is the home of the Finger Lakes Symphony

Orchestra and the Geneva Theatre Guild.

43) Boat Rides on the *Seneca Dreamer*

The Seneca Boat Company operates the *Seneca Dreamer*, a 149-passenger paddle-wheeler tour and dining boat from Lakeshore Park, Geneva. The Seneca Boat Company provides scenic narrated cruises, dinner cruises, sunset cruises, and moonlight cruises from May to October.

44) Seneca Lake Whale Watch

The first annual Seneca Lake Whale Watch, held in August 1994 in Geneva's Lakeshore Park, attracted 11,000 people. The annual multiple-day festival provides a diversity of quality music, food, and fun. The goal of the festival's promoters is to operate in "something for everyone mode." The festival offers continuous entertainment on multiple stages, a wine tent for sampling Finger Lakes wines, an children's area with special performances and readings for young whale watchers, hands-on demonstrations, a juried arts and crafts area offering the wares of over sixty vendors, fireworks, street performers, strolling musicians, and a variety of food from over fifteen area restaurants.

The Seneca Lake Whale Watch may be the only freshwater whale watch held in the inland waters of America. Organizers refuse to be discouraged by the absence of whale sightings in the Finger Lakes. They point out to skeptical festival-goers that no whale watch can promise actual sightings. The official whale watching vessel is the *Seneca Dreamer*, a 149-passenger paddle-wheeler.

WATERLOO

45) Hunt House

The home of Jane and Richard Hunt, 401 East Main Street, Waterloo, was in the Hunt family until 1919. The new owner replaced the front porch with a two-story, neo-classical porti-

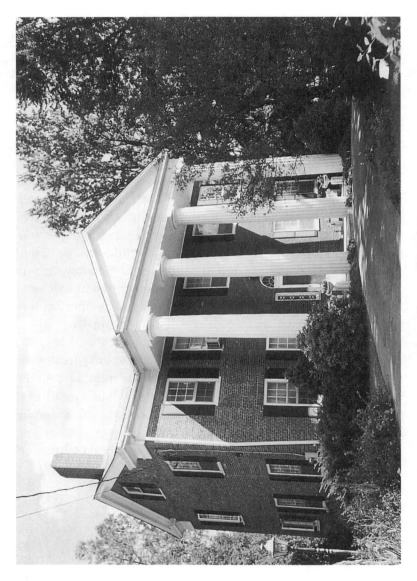

Hunt House, Waterloo

co and removed the west wing. The planning for the first Women's Rights Convention held on July 19-20, 1848, in Seneca Falls was done at the Hunt House on the preceding July 9.

Jane Hunt invited Lucretia Mott and Elizabeth Cady Stanton to tea along with Martha Wright (Lucretia Mott's sister) and Mary Ann M'Clintock, a Quaker abolitionist from Waterloo. The five women discussed their frustration with the limited rights of women and the discrimination they had experienced in the abolitionist and temperance movements. They prepared a notice about the Convention that appeared in the Seneca County *Courier* on July 14.

46) M'Clintock House

The five women—Jane Hunt, Mary Ann M'Clintock, Lucretia Mott, Elizabeth Cady Stanton, and Martha Wright—who did the planning at the Hunt House on July 9 for the first Women's Rights Convention held on July 19-20 in Seneca Falls decided to reconvene at the home of Mary Ann and Thomas M'Clintock at 16 East William Street, Waterloo, on July 16 to prepare an agenda for the Convention.

The women listed their grievances and proposed resolutions to resolve them. Elizabeth Cady Stanton was the principal author of the *Declaration of Sentiments* patterned on the *Declaration of Independence*. The *Declaration of Sentiments* began with the lines: "We hold these truths to be self-evident; that all men and women are created equal." The mahogany table around which they sat to prepare their agenda is now in the Smithsonian Institution.

47) The Scythe Tree

In October 1861, twenty-six-year-old James Wyman Johnson attended a recruiting rally in Waterloo at which two Grand Army of the Republic recruiting officers and the Rev. Dr. Samuel Gridley, pastor of the local Presbyterian church, spoke to gain recruits for Mr. Lincoln's army. Wyman

M'Clintock House, Waterloo

Johnson, waking early the morning after the rally, wrestled with the decision of whether to volunteer or to stay and help his parents run the farm. He went to the barn, took his scythe off its hook, and began to cut a field of tall grass, while mulling over his decision. Finally, he decided that it was his duty as the oldest son to volunteer. His brother and two sisters could help his father and mother run the farm.

He told his parents of his decision, placed his scythe in the crotch of a Balm of Gilead sapling (a tree of the poplar family), said "Leave this scythe in the tree until I return," and walked to Waterloo to join Company G of the 85th New York Volunteers. He fought in the Battle of Fair Oaks and was captured in a battle at New Berne, North Carolina. He was released in an exchange of prisoners and returned to the front. At Plymouth, near Albemarle Sound, he was wounded in the thigh and taken to the Confederate Hospital at Raleigh, where he died of his wounds.

Wyman Johnson's parents refused to believe that their son was dead and hoped that he would return to take his scythe from the Balm of Gilead tree. In 1916, the grave of Wyman Johnson was found in a Confederate cemetery in Raleigh. His remains were moved to the National Cemetery in Arlington, Virginia. That same year, the Scythe Tree was struck by lightning, but neither the tree nor the scythe blade suffered any damage. The wooden handle of the scythe had long since rotted away.

In 1918, Scythe Tree Farm was owned by the C. L. Schaffer family. Both sons of the family, Raymond and Lynn, volunteered for service in World War I. Raymond joined Company F, 33rd Engineers, and his brother enlisted in the U.S. Navy. They both placed their scythes in the crotch of the Balm of Gilead tree before they left for training camp. Raymond and Lynn returned home safely from the war and removed the handles from their scythes in the tree, but left the blades in place, several feet above Wyman Johnson's blade.

Scythe Tree Farm is located two and a half miles west of

Waterloo at 841 Waterloo-Geneva Road (Routes 5 and 20). The owners have always allowed public access to the tree. All three scythe blades can be seen extending from the tree, but less than six inches of the blade placed there in 1861 are still visible.

48) Memorial Day Museum

The Memorial Day Museum is located at 35 E. Main Street, Waterloo. The Museum was built as a home in the 1830s and extensively renovated in the 1860s, when two large wings were added. Eight rooms of the twenty-room brick mansion are open to the public.

In May 1866, Waterloo was the site of the first Memorial Day celebration to honor local soldiers who died in the Civil War. The Museum displays items pertinent to Memorial Day, the Civil War, World Wars I and II, and the Korean Conflict. The Museum is open afternoons, Tuesday through Friday, from Memorial Day until Labor Day.

CHAPTER 8

Northeast of Seneca Falls

Six long slim lakes of larkspur blue,
No gems have such entrancing hue.
Like storm clouds in an azure sky,
They've charmed me when their waves were high.
They've charmed me when they were serene,
These precious jewels inlaid in green.
When viewed, at night, from points afar,
How beautiful their lit towns are!
Health-giving sport their fishing makes,
These world-famous Finger Lakes.
Here tourists flock, for Nature brings
The loveliest of outdoor things.

The Finger Lakes by Edwin Becker

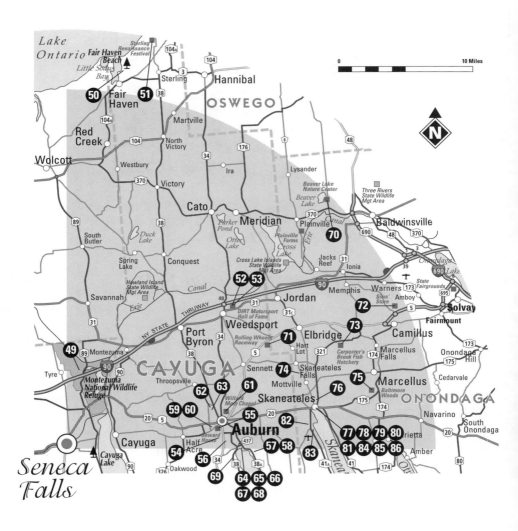

Map of Northeast of Seneca Falls

PLACES TO SEE / THINGS TO DO

PLACES TO SEE / THINGS TO DO

49) Montezuma National Wildlife Refuge

The Montezuma National Wildlife Refuge, established in 1937, is located at 3395 Routes 5 and 20, east of Seneca Falls. It is bounded by the Erie Canal in the north, the Cayuga Lake outlet to the Erie Canal in the east, and Cayuga Lake and the Cayuga-Seneca Canal to the south. The western boundary, comprised of Route 89, Lay Road, and Durling Road, is irregular.

The Refuge is maintained by the U.S. Fish and Wildlife Service, Department of the Interior, primarily as a feeding, nesting, and resting habitat for migratory waterfowl. Over 282 species of birds have been seen in the refuge, including Canada geese, herons, mallards, northern harriers (marsh hawks), osprey, rails, redwing blackbirds, shorebirds, snipe, songbirds, teal, terns, and wood ducks.

The largest concentrations of water fowl can be seen during migration; 140,000 Canada geese have been observed in April and 150,000 ducks in October. The spring migration of waterfowl such as Canada geese has reduced in number in recent years. However, several hundred Canada geese maintain a year-round home at the refuge and can be seen making excursions to and from off-refuge feeding areas.

Muskrats, white-tailed deer, and woodchucks can also be observed in their habitats in the Refuge. Muskrats are controlled to provide the necessary combination of open water and vegetation for food and cover for the waterfowl. Since muskrats use water plants to construct their houses and for food, too many muskrats deplete plant cover for the waterfowl and too few muskrats allow the plants to take over the open water.

The prime times for viewing wildlife are early in the morning and late in the day (the Refuge is open from sunrise to sunset). A three-and-a-half-mile auto-tour route, two twenty-foot observation towers, and a two-and-one-fifth-mile nature trail give ample opportunity for observing wildlife. Esker Brook Nature Trail, west off Route 89, is a mildly sloping loop that follows Esker Brook; it is an excellent location for finding songbirds.

The Visitor Center provides a diorama exhibit, leaflets, and a small information room, as well as rest rooms and public telephones. A two-level observation deck with a spotting telescope is available at the back of the Visitor Center on the second level. The observation deck overlooks the 2,700-acre Main Pool, one of two large pools and five small pools in the refuge. The water level in the Main Pool is maintained at about two and a half feet for most of its area, but a portion of it is one-foot deep for the use of mallards, pintails, and teal.

The other large pool is the 1,340 acre Tschache (pronounced "shocky") Pool, which contains a great blue heron rookery and is a bald eagle nesting and feeding area. In 1980, only one breeding pair of bald eagles nested in New York State. A program to build up the bald eagle population was started in 1976 at the Montezuma Refuge by releasing young birds into the wild. Montezuma's efforts have been crucial in increasing the State's eagle population.

The five small pools in the Refuge are the East Pool, the West Pool, May's Point Pool (known for shorebirds in the spring and fall), the North Spring Pool, and the South Spring Pool. The East Pool, along the outlet from Cayuga Lake to the Erie Canal, has a dam and locks at its southern end. The West Pool is part of the Cayuga-Seneca Canal, and the South Spring Pool has a scenic overlook.

Fish, including carp, brown bullhead, northern pike, and walleye, are abundant in the canals and rivers on the periphery of the refuge. Fishing and boating are not allowed in the refuge, but three public fishing sites and a boat launch nearby allow access to the Erie Canal from Cayuga Lake and the Clyde River.

Prior to 1900, the Montezuma Marsh extended north for twelve miles from Cayuga Lake and was eight miles wide at its widest point. Its importance as a refuge for wildlife was not recognized, and much of it was drained to make arable farms. By 1911, there were only 100 acres left undrained. It was eventually purchased by the federal government and became part of the National Wildlife Refuge System in 1934. It was established as the Montezuma National Wildlife Refuge in 1937 and was gradually expanded to over 6,432 acres.

NORTH OF AUBURN

50) Fair Haven Beach State Park

Fair Haven Beach State Park is located on 865 hilly, rocky acres one mile north of Fair Haven on Route 104A. Elevation in the park ranges from 245 feet to 360 feet. The Park has a beautiful lakeshore, lakeshore bluffs, flat and wide expanses, inland Sterling Pond, and woodlands. Fair Haven Beach State Park contains thirty-three cabins, 191 campsites (44 electric, 147 non-electric; RVs allowed), three pavilions (two reservable), and picnic areas with tables and fireplaces. It also has playing fields, a playground, and hiking trails, including self-guided nature trails.

The Park has a boat launching ramp, boat rentals, a camp store, concession stand, and pay telephones, as well as fishing, swimming off the lakeshore within the designated lifeguard area, and bathhouse facilities. Hot showers, flush toilets, a marine sewage pumpout station, and a trailer dumping station are available in the Park. Camping is permitted from mid-April to the end of October; a camper recreation program is provided. The recreation building is available for use all summer and can be reserved in the off-season. Fair Haven Beach State Park is open all winter for cross-country skiing, hiking, and snowmobiling. Eight cabins with wood-burning stoves are available during the winter.

Cayuga and Seneca Indians who canoed and fished on Little Sodus Bay in the mid-1600s called it "Date-ke-ashote." In the last half of the seventeenth century, French traders used it as a landing site in trading with the Indians for furs. The French called Little Sodus Bay, "Chroutons," or passage that leads to the Cayugas. Commercial activity in the area increased significantly in 1873 when the the harbor was developed and the Southern Central Railroad was completed. Coal was brought in by rail for shipment via Lake Ontario, and outgoing shipments included apples, ice, milk, and wood products.

Many cottages were built along the lake around 1900, and the area became a popular resort area. The Parks Commission was formed in 1923, and the construction of buildings and roads began in 1927; the Civilian Conservation Corps built additional buildings, campsites, roads, and trails in the 1930s.

The Park contains two examples of wave-eroded drumlins, which are hills formed by glacial drift. Beaches separate Sterling Marsh, Sterling Pond, and other backwater areas from Lake Ontario. The sheltered wetlands are home for amphibians, beavers, ducks, fish, geese, muskrats, and aquatic plants.

51) Sterling Renaissance Festival

The Sterling Renaissance Festival, located at 15431 Farden Road in Sterling, east of Fair Haven, recreates festival time at the English village of Warwick during the reign of Queen Elizabeth I, about the year 1585. The comedies of Shakespeare and other playwrights of the period are performed on the Bankside Stage and Wyldwood Stage.

The Festival, which was established in 1977, features period arts and crafts, entertainment, food, and music in a thirty-five-acre natural, wooded setting. The period artisans and craftspeople demonstrate the making of books, glass objects, hair garlands, wax seals and ornaments, jewelry, leather crafts, prints, and stained glass.

Over fifty artisans display their crafts. The grounds are populated with beggars, jugglers, knaves, lords, ladies, minstrels, monks, puppeteers, shopkeepers, and wenches. Over 600 actors, crafters, entertainers, food service people, and gamers participate in the activities.

Visitors may come in their own Elizabethan costumes, rent costumes from the village seamstress, or stay dressed as they are. Entertainment includes fire eating, juggling, magic, music, and dancing and jousting in the lanes and on the stages. Examples of English food are fish and chips, marinated steak-on-a-stick, peasant bread, spinach pies, turkey legs, and hot apple dumplings with ice cream.

Admission is charged, but once inside the grounds there is free entertainment, outdoor theatre, and street performances, including live jousting. Other activities are Shakespearean plays, street theatre, and children's productions, such as puppet shows, storytelling, and the Theatre of Fools. Over eighty stage and street performances are ongoing at no extra charge. The season is from early July until mid-August. The day's events open with Queen Elizabeth's parade at 10:00 a.m.

52) DIRT Motorsport Hall of Fame and Classic Car Collection — Weedsport

The Drivers' Independent Race Tracks (DIRT) Motorsport Hall of Fame and Classic Car Museum is located at the Cayuga County Fairgrounds on Route 31, one mile from New York State Thruway Exit 40. It displays over thirty modified racing cars and more than fifty classic cars. The Hall of Fame and Museum, which opened in 1992 to preserve the history of modified dirt racing and to display classic cars, is the filming site of a weekly show that is nationally-televised, "This week on DIRT."

The Jack Burgess National Parts Peddler Theatre Room shows films of old-time races. A worldwide finders' network provides classic car enthusiasts with a way of finding rare and collectible classic cars. An on-site gift shop offers apparel, collectors' items, and souvenirs. The Museum is open all year; a nominal admission fee is charged.

53) Cayuga County Fair Speedway—Weedsport

The Cayuga County Fair Speedway is located at the Cayuga County Fairgrounds on Route 31 near Weedsport, one mile from the New York State Thruway exit 40. It is a DIRT (Drivers' Independent Race Track) track with a three-eighths mile clay oval. Races are held every Sunday night from May through September.

AUBURN

54) Fort Hill Cemetery

Fort Hill Cemetery in Auburn is the site of an earthen fort built by the Mound Builders, or Alleghans, who preceded the Cayuga Indians in the area. Their Fort Osco on the site of Fort Hill Cemetery had embankments for defense and an earthen altar for the worship of the sun. The burial mounds were outside the walls of the fortress, about 275 yards north of Fort Hill.

The Alleghan village of Osco appears to have been their easternmost settlement. Their name was given to the Allegheny Mountains and to the Allegheny River. They were driven from the region in the thirteenth century by the Iroquois.

The Cayuga village of Wasco was the birthplace in 1727 of Cayuga Chief Logan, or Tah-gah-jute, who was a celebrated orator of the Iroquois Confederacy. In 1852, a fifty-six-foot stone obelisk was erected on the site of an Alleghan altar mound in Fort Hill Cemetery in memory of Chief Logan.

Tah-gah-jute was the second son of Shikellimus, a distinguished sachem of the Cayugas, who was appointed Indian agent as a friend of the white man. Tah-gah-jute received the name of Logan when he was baptized in honor of James Logan, secretary of the Province. He embraced not only Christian doctrines but also the pacifism of the Quakers. He and his wife, Alvaretta, the daughter of Ontonegea, were married by a missionary, Reverend Zeisberger.

228

He ceased being a pacifist when his wife and children were killed by Colonel Cresap, the English leader of a band of ruffians. Logan went on a rampage until thirty scalps hung from his belt. He made one of his more famous speeches just after this incident, in a conference with the British governor of Virginia, at the signing of the Treaty of Lord Dunmore:

> I appeal to any white man to say if he ever entered Logan's cabin hungry and he gave him not meat; if he ever came in cold and naked, and he clothed him not. During the close of the last long and bloody war Logan remained idle in his cabin, an advocate of peace. Such was my love for the whites, that my countrymen pointed, as they passed, and said, "Logan is the friend of the white men." I had even thought to have lived with you, but for the injuries of one man, Colonel Cresap, the last spring, in cold blood and unprovoked, murdered all the relations of Logan, not sparing even my wife and children.
>
> There runs not a drop of my blood in any living creature. This called on me for revenge. I have sought it. I have killed many. I have fully glutted my vengeance. For my country, I rejoice at the beams of peace. But do not harbor a thought that mine is the joy of fear. Logan never felt fear. He will not turn on his heel to save his life. Who is there to mourn for Logan? Not one.

The inscription on the stone obelisk in Fort Hill Cemetery in memory of Chief Logan is from this speech, "WHO IS THERE TO MOURN FOR LOGAN."

Seward House, Auburn

55) Seward House

Seward House, 33 South Street, Auburn, was built in 1816-17 by Judge Elijah Miller, William H. Seward's father-in-law. The Federal-style mansion, a registered National Historic Landmark, was expanded in 1847 and in 1860. Each room in the thirty-room house, over half of which are open to the public, is furnished only with original family pieces and the gifts and memorabilia collected by Seward in his travels.

The only residents of the house have been four generations of the Seward family. General William H. Seward II, a brigadier general in the Civil War, inherited the house from his father. He headed the Auburn banking firm, William H. Seward & Company. William H. Seward III made a gift of the house, upon his death in 1951, to the Fred L. Emerson Foundation in memory of his grandfather and father. The Foundation Historical Association, an affiliate of the Emerson Foundation, was established to maintain and operate the house as a public museum.

William H. Seward, who was born in the hamlet of Florida, Orange County, New York, became Judge Miller's junior law partner in 1823. He graduated from Union College in 1820, continued with the study of law, and passed his bar exam before joining the law office of Judge Miller. Seward already knew the judge's daughter, Frances, as she was a schoolmate of his sister. They were married in 1824. The judge, who had been a widower since Frances was an infant, consented to the wedding on the condition that she would not leave his home while he lived. Seward, who moved into the house when they were married in 1824, once said, "I thus became an inmate of her family."

The public career of William H. Seward began with his election to the State Senate in 1830. He served two terms (1839-43) as the Governor of New York, and was elected to the U.S. Senate. He was a founder of the Republican Party and was considered to be the leading Republican candidate for the Presidential nomination in 1860. However, Abraham

Lincoln won the nomination and the election and asked Seward to serve as his Secretary of State. Seward continued in that cabinet position in the administration of President Andrew Johnson after the assassination of Lincoln in 1864.

As Secretary of State, he is most frequently remembered for the purchase of Alaska from Russia for $7,000,000, or about two cents an acre. It was known as "Seward's Ice-box" or "Seward's Folly" at the time, but it is now recognized as a phenomenal bargain.

The parlor of Seward House contains the gilded furniture, upholstered with its original tapestry material, from the parlor of the Seward's Washington home. The fireplace mantel in the parlor was built by a sixteen-year-old journeyman painter and carpenter, Brigham Young, who later inherited the leadership of the Mormon Church from its founder, Joseph Smith.

The dining room table expands to seat twenty-four. Guests were served on some of the sixty place settings of crested Imperial Sevres china, which was a gift from Prince Napoleon Bonaparte, nephew of the Emperor. The dining room also contains china that was a gift from Emperor Maximilian of Mexico and a copper samovar given to Seward by Baron Edward Stoeckl, Russian Minister to the United States, with whom he negotiated the purchase of Alaska.

The guests who dined at Seward House included Presidents John Quincy Adams, Martin Van Buren, Andrew Johnson, and William McKinley. Other luminaries who dined with Seward were Henry Clay, General Custer, Admiral Farragut, General Grant, and Daniel Webster.

The impressive drawing room contains many family portraits, including one of the Seward's daughter, Frances Adeline Seward, painted by Emanuel Leutze. A large painting of a Portage Falls scene by Hudson River School founder, Thomas Cole, hangs over the rosewood Steinway grand piano. Paintings by Henry Inman also hang in the mansion. The drawing room is graced by a Greek amphora, which is over 2,000 years old, that was found on the island of Cyprus.

The spiral staircase leading upstairs from the front hallway was made of laurelwood and manzanita that was a gift from the California Pioneer Society given in appreciation of Seward's pivotal efforts on the Senate floor in 1850 to have California admitted to the union as a free State. The staircase leads to the Diplomatic Gallery that has on display Seward's collection of over 130 prints and photographs of diplomats, generals, and world rulers.

The well-known Emanuel Leutze painting of the Alaska Purchase Treaty is prominently displayed in the gallery as is a slender mahogany desk used by a member of the first United States Congress. That Congress assembled in Federal Hall in New York City in 1789, prior to the inauguration of George Washington.

A large bust of Seward by Daniel Chester French, sculptor of the Lincoln Memorial, stands in the small north library. This library also contains the couch on which Seward was relaxing after a ride in his carriage, when he passed away about 4:00 p.m. on October 10, 1872. He had complained of having difficulty breathing.

Seward House also has an exhibit about Harriet Tubman. She was a nurse, scout, and spy for the Union forces during the Civil War, and a leader of the Underground Railroad who helped over 300 slaves escape to freedom. When Harriet, who lived at 180 South Street, was out of town, Mrs. (Frances) Seward, who was also an abolitionist, hid fugitive slaves in two rooms at the back of the Seward House near the kitchen. Harriet Tubman was active in the Women's Rights Movement after the Civil War.

In addition, the Seward House has many letters, such as the one from Abraham Lincoln appointing Seward Secretary of State, original costumes dating from 1820, Civil War memorabilia, and some early Alaskan artifacts. Free guide service is available. Seward House is closed during January, February, and March.

Harriet Tubman House, Auburn

56) Harriet Tubman House

The Harriet Tubman House is a white frame house with long verandas at 180 South Street, Auburn. Harriet Tubman personally led over 300 slaves to freedom on the Underground Railroad, which guided slaves from the South to Canada and liberation. She was also a nurse, scout, and spy for the Union forces during the Civil War.

After the Civil War, she moved to Auburn and lived in a home obtained for her by her friend, William H. Seward. Later, she came into possession of another property with twenty-six acres of land and two substantial houses. After Harriet's death, on March 10, 1913, the two houses fell into disrepair. One of the houses was taken down, and the other one was renovated by the African Methodist Episcopal Zion Church (A.M.E. Zion Church). The A.M.E. Zion Church has built a library building on the property to house much of the available reference material on Harriet Tubman.

The Harriet Tubman House is open on Tuesdays through Fridays and at other times by appointment.

57) Cayuga County Agricultural Museum

The Cayuga County Agricultural Museum is located across Route 38A from the main entrance to Emerson Park, at the northern end of Owasco Lake. The Museum features farm implements dating from 1860 to 1930—the years of farming's greatest changes—and antique buggies, sleighs, and tractors. The farm equipment ranges from hand-held tools to horse-drawn tools to tractors, and spans all of the major farm crops over the four seasons.

The spring wing has fitting tools and plows; the summer wing has cultivators and planters. The fall wing has corn and hay harvest equipment; the winter wing has ice harvesting equipment and lumbering equipment. Wheat-harvesting equipment manufactured by the D. M. Osborne Company is also on display.

The Museum has a a blacksmith shop, a creamery, a general store, a veterinarian's office, a village square, and a wood and wheelwright shop, as well as a 1900 farm kitchen and an herb garden. The goal of the Museum is to take the visitor back to the rural way of life at the turn of the century. The Museum is open Saturday and Sunday afternoons in June and Wednesday-Sunday afternoons in July and August.

58) Owasco Teyetasta (Iroquois Museum)

The Owasco Teyetasta is located on Route 38A across from Emerson Park, adjacent to the Cayuga County Agricultural Museum. The Museum offers exhibits of Iroquois prehistory and history, including the Point Peninsula culture, the Owasco and Cayuga cultures, and a 12,000-year-old mastodon skeleton.

59) Cayuga Museum of History and Art

The Cayuga Museum of History and Art, 203 Genesee Street contains exhibits of historic and contemporary art and artifacts. It is housed in the mansion that was the home of Theodore Willard Case, pioneer in motion picture sound synchronization. Theodore Case and William Fox formed the Fox-Case Movietone Corporation, which later became Twentieth Century Fox.

The Museum has Indian collections and period rooms, as well as collections of domestic textiles and costumes, folk art, military and medical artifacts, and objects representative of North American industry. Local nineteenth-century artists are featured in the Museum.

The Case Research Laboratory was located in Theodore Case's mansion. The sound studio was located in the carriage house. The Laboratory created the first commercially successful sound-on-film system, invented by Case and E. I. Sponable. This system was used by de Forest Phonofilms Company from 1922-25 and by Fox Films from 1926-37. It preceded the Warner Brothers disc system.

The Case Research Laboratory collections include the

sound projector that set the standards for today's film industry, the blimp box that housed the camera man, De Forest
amplifiers, experimental light cells, laboratory equipment,
and Western Electric amplifiers. The collection also includes
many test films made at the laboratory during the development of talking films. The Museum is open Tuesday through
Sunday afternoons and on Monday holidays; it is closed
Thanksgiving Day and Christmas Day.

60) Schweinfurth Memorial Art Center
The Schweinfurth Memorial Art Center, located at 205
Genesee Street, has exhibitions highlighting regional fine art,
contemporary crafts, photography, architecture and design,
and children's art. The Art Center has a museum shop and a
regional arts information center. It offers concerts, lectures,
workshops, and special events.

The Center hosts several regionally-renowned events each
year, including a national Juried Quilt Show in November and
December. The Art Center is open Tuesday through Friday
afternoons, Sunday afternoon, and all day Saturday. In
November and December, it is open Monday through Friday
afternoons. Tours are available with advance notice.

61) Willard Memorial Chapel
The Willard Memorial Chapel, at 17 Nelson Street, Auburn,
was built for the Auburn Theological Seminary in 1892-94 as
a memorial to Dr. Sylvester D. Willard and his wife, Jane
Frances Case, from their daughters. At the same time the
chapel was being constructed, the Seminary received a
bequest from former professor R. B. Welch for the construction of a new classroom building. All that remains today of
the Auburn Theological Seminary is the Willard Memorial
Chapel and the adjoining Welch Memorial Building, with
over 8,000 feet of usable space.

The two Romanesque Revival buildings are built of gray
Cayuga County limestone trimmed with red portage stone and

Willard Memorial Chapel, Auburn

joined by an enclosed walkway. The architect was A. J. Warner of Rochester, and the builder was Barnes and Stout of Auburn. Both buildings are on the New York Register of Historic Places and the National Register of Historic Places. The Auburn Theological Seminary closed it doors in 1939 and became part of the Union Theological Seminary in New York City.

One well-known family associated with the Auburn Theological Seminary was the Dulles family. Reverend Allen Macy Dulles moved to Auburn with his family in 1904 to teach at the seminary and to serve as pastor of the Second Presbyterian Church. One of Reverend Dulles' sons, John Foster Dulles, served as Secretary of State, and another son, Allen Welch Dulles, was Director of the Central Intelligence Agency.

The Willard Memorial Chapel, which seats 250, is unique in that the entire chapel and its furnishing were designed by Louis Comfort Tiffany. Tiffany is known for decorating the mansions of bankers and captains of industry and, in 1881, redecorating the reception rooms of the White House. Many buildings and museums have a Tiffany lamp, plaque, or window, but the entire interior of the Willard Memorial Chapel was designed by Tiffany, including the ceiling, chairs, chandeliers, floors, glass mosaics, pews, walls, windows, and the memorial plaque. Harold Jaffe, president of the Louis Comfort Tiffany Society, calls the Chapel "the only complete religious building extant in the United States designed by Louis Comfort Tiffany."

A gilt bronze and mosaic glass memorial tablet dominates the wall to the left of the entrance. It is an 18-foot by 9-foot bas-relief of an angel with extended wings in the center, looking upward toward the memorial inscription to Dr. and Mrs. Willard. St. John the Baptist and the Holy Spirit are on one side of the angel, and Hope and Charity are on the other side. The angel is holding a scroll with the inscription, "And now bideth Faith, Hope, and Love, these three, but the greatest of these is Love." The memorial plaque is surrounded by a border of Tiffany mosaic.

The largest Tiffany "Favrile" glass window in the chapel, directly above the memorial plaque, displays Christ sustaining St. Peter on the waves of Lake Genesareth. Tiffany derived the name "Favrile" from the Anglo-Saxon word for "handmade." Nine Mooresque-style chandeliers designed by Tiffany that hang from the vaulted wood ceiling are made of jeweled and leaded glass, are mounted in bronze, and have crystal pendants hanging from them.

A row of seven oak chairs, inlaid with glass and metal mosaic, is behind the carved oak / gold-stenciled pulpit. Singing was accompanied by a large Steere and Turner tracker organ. Other features of the chapel include fourteen opalescent windows, mosaic floors, and oak wainscoting.

The interior of the Willard Memorial Chapel was almost auctioned off in the late 1980s, but was saved by the Community Preservation Committee of Auburn. The Seventh-day Adventist Church, owners of the Chapel from 1957 until 1988, decided to build a new church that would be more economical to heat. The Chapel was sold to an antique dealer, who planned to dismantle and sell the interior. However, the Community Preservation Committee prevailed upon him to sell the Chapel to them for $500,000 (even though authentic Tiffany lamps sold for $480,000 in 1987).

The preservation committee plans to continue the Chapel's use as a place of interfaith worship and a setting for functions such as concerts and weddings. Tours that focus on its art, architecture, and history are conducted on Tuesday through Friday afternoons and by appointment. The Chapel doesn't provide tours during January, February, and March. A 22-minute video, "The Willard Memorial Chapel Story," traces the history of the Chapel from its beginning as a part of the Auburn Theological Seminary.

62) Auburn Doubledays Class A Baseball

The Auburn Doubledays, a Short Season (78-game schedule) Class A farm team for the Houston Astros, are a member of the New York-Penn League (NYP League). The young players are on rung two of the ladder to the major leagues. They have to climb through Long Season A, Advanced A, AA, and AAA ball before they arrive in the big leagues. Tug McGraw played at Auburn before he moved up to the majors.

The NYP League, with fourteen teams (including Elmira and Watertown), have eight teams in New York, two in Pennsylvania, and one each in Vermont, Ontario, Massachusetts, and New Jersey. In addition to having the opportunity to watch good baseball, fans are entertained on promotion nights by entertainers such as baseball clown Max Patkin and the San Diego Chicken.

63) Casey Park

Casey Park is a 44-acre family sports complex, located on N. Division Street in Auburn, has an olympic-size swimming pool and a mini-pool, a soccer field, basketball courts, tennis courts, platform tennis courts, and two lighted softball fields. It also has an outdoor amphitheatre, bike trails, fitness trails, bocce courts, horseshoe pits, picnic areas, and a playground.

Casey Park has an indoor artificial ice-skating rink that is open from November to April. The Park, one of Central New York's most complete recreation areas, is open year-round.

64) Emerson Park

Emerson Park, an Auburn City Park at the northern end of Owasco Lake, is the principal access point for the lake. It is located on Route 38A, just south of Auburn. The Park has a swimming beach, picnic facilities, playgrounds, a ballroom, a pavilion, and children's rides, including a carousel. The Merry-Go-Round Playhouse, which offers excellent summer theatre, is also located in the Park. The Cayuga County Agriculture Museum is located directly across Route 38A from the main entrance to the Park.

The Park also has canoe and paddleboat rentals and a public boat launch. Emerson Park has extensive lawns along the Lake, and fishing is permitted for bass, perch, northern pike, and lake trout.

65) Merry-Go-Round Playhouse

The Merry-Go-Round Playhouse, which opened in 1959, is a nonprofit regional theatre that presents musical, contemporary, and youth productions. The Playhouse, a showcase for professional repertory theatre, offers musicals from June to late August. The 328-seat theatre, the largest of its kind in Central New York, is located in Emerson Park, on the lakefront.

66) Auburn Concert Series

The Syracuse Symphony usually performs an annual concert series in Auburn. Concert selections include classics, opera, and pops. The Symphony also provides summer concerts in Emerson Park along the lakefront.

67) Antique / Classic Boat Show

The Antique / Classic Boat Show, which began in Auburn in 1987, is held in late July or early August in Emerson Park, Route 38A, just south of Auburn, along the northern end of Owasco Lake. Owners bring over fifty antique / classic boats, with their polished brass and varnished mahogany or teak, from the Northeast, the Midwest, and Canada. One-of-a-kind canoes, rowboats, old launches, steamboats, runabouts, and rum runners from the Thousand Islands have been entered in past shows. Awards are presented in a traditional ceremony.

An example of an entry in earlier shows is the 1915 Ingeson steam launch Eagle. The slender, 21-foot craft, with its red and white striped canopy, was one of the most popular boats in the Show as it cruised the lake accompanied by a steady hiss of steam and an occasional blast from its highly polished brass whistle.

In previous shows, there have been a chicken barbecue on Saturday afternoon and a pancake breakfast on Sunday morning. On both days of the Show, the children's rides (including a carousel) at Emerson Park are open, and there is swimming off the sandy beaches. Canoes and paddleboats are available for rental.

68) Finger Lakes Antique Car Show

The Finger Lakes Antique Car Show is held in late July at Emerson Park, Route 38A, just south of Auburn. The Show has over 400 entries from the United States and Canada.

69) Springside Inn—Historic Restaurant and Inn

The Springside Inn is located on Route 38, on the west side of Owasco Lake, just south of Auburn. It is a fine restaurant, a bed and breakfast inn, and an outstanding location for special events. The main public dining room, the Surrey Room, has an old-world charm enhanced by its massive beams, cathedral ceiling, turn-of-the-century hanging lamps, and stone fireplace.

In 1851, the Reverend Samuel Robbins Brown, pastor of the Dutch Reformed Church of the Owasco Outlet (Sand Beach Church), opened a school at the Springside Inn, and called it the "Springside" school. In 1858, Dr. Brown became the first American missionary to Japan. An assistant ran the school until 1867 when it was sold to become a private residence.

The Springside passed though several owners and was purchased in 1919 by Captain John A. Holland, an Englishman married to a MacDougall from Auburn. The Hollands ran it as a summer resort until the 1940s, when it became a year-round hotel / restaurant.

In 1941, the Stephen J. Miller family purchased the Springside Inn. The second generation of the Miller family continued the operation of the Inn.

Camillus Erie Canal Park

NORTH OF SKANEATELES

70) Beaver Lake Nature Center—Baldwinsville

Beaver Lake Nature Center, located two miles west of Route 370 on East Mud Lake Road, Baldwinswille, is a major resting place for thousands of Canada geese in the spring and the fall. The Nature Center has a 200-acre lake, which can be viewed from a floating boardwalk, and miles of woodland trails for cross-county skiing and hiking. The Center provides interpretive programs presented by professional naturalists to aid in exploring the natural world. Visitors can also learn from state-of-the-art exhibits in the modern Visitor Center.

71) Rolling Wheels Track—Elbridge

The Rolling Wheels Track is located on Route 5 in Elbridge, north of Skaneateles. It is a Drivers' Independent Race Track (DIRT) track with a five-eighths-mile clay oval. The track is open from April to September.

72) Camillus Erie Canal Park

Camillus Erie Canal Park, located on Devoe Road in Camillus, is a 300-acre park with seven miles of navigable canal and towpath trails. The Lock Tender's Shanty Museum and the Sims Store Museum, located at "Camillus Landing," are replicas of actual buildings; they contain authentic artifacts, memorabilia, and photographs of the Erie Canal. The Nine Mile Creek Aqueduct is within the park, along with flower gardens, nature trails, and picnic areas.

The Sims Store Museum is the point of departure for boat rides on the canal, which are offered on Sunday afternoons from May through October. The Park is open daily year-round. Tours of the park are given by appointment.

73) Carpenter's Brook Fish Hatchery

Carpenter's Brook Fish Hatchery, which is located approximately eight miles north of Skaneateles on Route 321, is open for tours and has a special 16-foot by 24-foot kids' fish pool and traveling display. The Hatchery produces more than 100,000 brook trout, brown trout, rainbow trout, and walleye pike annually. The Hatchery has a picnic area with tables and benches.

74) Wooden Toy Factory

The t. c. timber factory (formerly Skaneateles Handicrafters) is at 4407 Jordan Road between Mottville and Skaneateles Falls, several miles north of Skaneateles. Marshal Larrabee, the founder of Skaneateles Handicrafters, did not intend to spend his life as a toy maker; he thought he was going to be a banker. He graduated from the University of Pennsylvania's Wharton School of Business during the Depression and accepted a position at the Trust & Deposit Bank in Syracuse.

The following year, shortly after marrying his wife, Elizabeth, he was told that he had tuberculosis. Since there were no drugs to treat the disease in the 1930s, he spent the next ten years in bed. As soon as he could spend a few minutes a day out of bed, he asked for a band saw, a circular saw, a drill press, and a lathe. Elizabeth had challenged him to build a small train that a child could hold in his or her hand. Their daughter, Ethel, received the first train that Marshal made, and it was a hit.

For the next several years, Larrabee made thirty small trains as Christmas gifts for the children of the family's friends and neighbors. Fully recovered in 1940, Larrabee took a box filled with his wooden trains to Chicago to talk with the senior buyer at Marshall Fields. She agreed to buy all that he could make. Over the next forty years, the work force increased from two, Marshal and Elizabeth, to over 100 employees.

Their first trains included an engine, coach, flat car, and tank car, connected with hooks and eyes from the local hardware store. Maple was used because it is a fine-grained wood that is easy to work, and it does not sliver easily. Also, it is readily available in the southern tier of New York State and the northern tier of Pennsylvania.

Marshal Larrabee sold the business in 1980. It is now called t. c. timber and is owned by Habermaas, a German company. The wooden toys are still made as Larrabee made them, except that the hooks and eyes that used to connect the cars of the trains are now small magnets. An outlet store is operated by t. c. timber at the factory.

75) Baltimore Woods—Marcellus

Baltimore Woods is a 160-acre nature preserve located in rolling hills one mile south of the village of Marcellus, about six miles northeast of Skaneateles. The nature preserve is on the west side of Bishop Hill Road, which runs between Marcellus and Route 20. Baltimore Woods has a pavilion, log cabin, herb garden, wildflower garden, and over four miles of self-guided trails.

Baltimore Woods is owned by Save the County, an organization founded in 1971 to preserve the green spaces of Onondaga County. Several trails are maintained throughout the year, and are open to the public at all times. Volunteer naturalists conduct guided tours upon request.

Programs offered by the nature preserve include a Fall Festival, Maple Syrup Festival, summer day nature program for children, teacher workshops, and a volunteer naturalist program. Baltimore Woods also has Friday Night Nature Walks, Herb Sale Day, visits by naturalists to schools, school visits to the center, and many other seasonal programs.

76) Skaneateles Nature Trail

The Skaneateles Nature Trail follows Skaneateles Creek, just north of the village of Skaneateles. Skaneateles Creek flows northward from Skaneateles to the Seneca River / Erie Canal; it empties into the Canal near Cross Lake.

John D. Barrow Art Gallery, Skaneateles

SKANEATELES

77) Austin Park

Austin Park, on Austin Street in Skaneateles, has baseball fields, basketball courts, picnic areas, and tennis courts, all with outdoor lighting. Allyn Arena in the park provides artificial ice for open skating, figure skating, and hockey for six months of the year.

78) Thayer Park

Thayer Park is a pleasant village park along Genesee Street (Route 20) in Skaneateles, which offers scenic views of the northern end of Skaneateles Lake and of the beautiful homes on the slopes of the west side of the lake. During the summer, band concerts are presented at the gazebo, and the Park features craft fairs and outdoor art shows.

79) John D. Barrow Art Gallery

The John D. Barrow Art Gallery adjoins the village of Skaneateles Library, and admittance to the Gallery is through the library. The Gallery displays over 300 oil paintings by John Barrow in two exhibition rooms. Some of Barrow's smaller paintings are mounted on special frames on the lower walls of the Gallery, serving as striking wainscoting.

John Barrow moved to Skaneateles with his family when he was fourteen. He was sent to England for his education and returned to Skaneateles at the age of nineteen. He lived twenty years of his adulthood in New York City to be near other artists, but spent most of his life in Skaneateles, where he died at the age of eighty-two in 1906.

Barrow was a member of the Hudson River School of painters and is considered one of America's "second generation" of landscape artists. Most of his paintings were landscapes, including many of the Finger Lakes Region, but he was also a portrait painter. His well-known portrait of Abraham Lincoln is currently owned and displayed by the

Chicago Historical Society.

The village of Skaneateles Library is a gray stone building on East Genesee Street that originally served as a law office. John Barrow financed an annex to the library building in 1900 to be used as a gallery to exhibit his art. By 1970, the Gallery became run-down and had to be closed. Through the efforts of the Skaneateles Historical Society and art-oriented townspeople, $40,000 was collected to renovate the Gallery. It was reopened in 1977.

Since 1977, over 100 severely damaged paintings have been restored with the help of local groups and individuals. The restoration work continues. The Gallery is operated by a management committee and dedicated volunteers. A unique feature of the Gallery is that it displays most of the lifetime output of one artist.

80) Skaneateles Historical Association Museum
—The Creamery

The Skaneateles Historical Society Museum, 28 Hannum Street, was previously the Skaneateles Creamery Company's creamery building. It was deeded to the village of Skaneateles in 1989, and the Historical Society renovated the building and opened the Museum in 1992.

The Museum houses hundreds of local artifacts, a gift shop, and a meeting room used by the Historical Society and other local organizations. The expanding archives and research department includes photo and newspaper files, biographical records, and cemetery records. The Museum offers many permanent exhibits, including a fascinating display on the area's teasel (a thistle-like plant used to produce a napped surface on fabrics) industry, as well as changing displays.

The Skaneateles Historical Society Museum is open year-round on Friday afternoons and on Thursday and Saturday afternoons during the summer.

81) Skaneateles Art Exhibition

The Skaneateles Art Exhibition is held in October at several sites in the village. Paintings, sculptures, and ceramics are on exhibit throughout Skaneateles. Music and dance performances are also scheduled during the week of the Exhibition.

82) Skaneateles Polo Club

The Skaneateles Polo Club plays at 3:00 p.m. every Sunday in July and August at a playing field on Andrews Road, just west of its intersection with West Lake Road (Route 41A). The match is played rain or shine, but play is discontinued if the field becomes slippery. It is played with two teams of four players each on a field three times as long and three times as wide as a football field.

Play consists of hitting a hard, white three-inch ball at speeds approaching 100 miles per hour with a four-foot cane mallet, while riding a polo pony at up to forty-five miles an hour. The duration of the match is forty-five minutes, made up of six periods (chukkers) of seven and a half minutes each. An announcer describes the play.

The polo ponies are thoroughbreds, quarter horses, or mixed thoroughbred / quarter horses. The intensity of the play is such that one pony has the energy for about two chukkers; most players ride three ponies per match. Serious riders have four, five, or six ponies available for each match. Polo ponies are selected based on agility, courage, endurance, speed, and temperament; it takes at least two years to train one thoroughly.

Polo is considered a contact sport, but the fact that the rules are designed to protect the horse takes some of the danger out of the match. Riders are allowed to bump another horse to spoil a shot, but if the opponent's horse is knocked off balance, a "dangerous riding" foul is called.

The word polo is a derivation of the Tibetan word for ball, "pulu." Its place of origin is uncertain, but it was played in Persia over twelve centuries ago. The Chinese claim that their ancestors played polo in 1000 BC. Initially, it was used less for play than for conditioning for war. The Arabs learned the game from the Persians; later, it became popular in Greece, India, and England.

James Gordon Bennett, Jr., owner and editor of the New York *Herald*, introduced polo to the United States in 1876, the year of the first championship match. Harvard was the first college to have an organized polo team, and the U.S. Polo Association was formed in 1890. Polo was once considered to be the sport of royalty, or of wealthy people, but there are now over 225 polo clubs in the United States with a total membership of more than 2,200 players. Many players learn polo in college or at polo clinics.

The Skaneateles Polo Club was formed in 1962 by Donald H. Cross, Tim Gridley, and Peter J. Winkelman. In recent years, matches have attracted crowds of 200 to 300 spectators. It is a pleasant way to spend a Sunday afternoon while watching the action from a lawn chair, socializing, and sharing a picnic basket.

83) The Skaneateles Festival

The Skaneateles Festival is a regional chamber music festival that began in 1980 and offers a four-week season during the month of August. The Festival is a combination of work and play for the approximately eighty musicians who live together at Brook Farm or stay as guests in other private homes. Many bring spouses, children, and friends with them.

The musicians rehearse during the week and give four concerts each week: Wednesday, Thursday, and Friday evenings at St. James Episcopal Church, 94 East Genesee Street, and Saturday evenings at Brook Farm, weather permitting. For a stage, the musicians use the veranda of the beautiful house with the tall, white pillars. Seating is on the lawn at Brook Farm and concertgoers bring their own lawnchairs and blankets. The concerts are moved to St. Mary's of the Lake Church, 81 Jordan Street, Skaneateles, in inclement weather on Saturdays.

Two of the founders of the festival are David and Louise Robinson, owners of Brook Farm. The Festival, which was once known as the "best kept secret in the East" has gained a national reputation.

The Festival organizers have no difficulty attracting talented musicians. It is a small, intimate event that provides an opportunity for interaction between concertgoers and musicians. Composers are encouraged to attend the Festival to give the musicians and the audiences a chance to meet them and learn more about their work.

84) Mid-Lakes Navigation Ltd.

Mid-Lakes Navigation Co., Ltd., 11 Jordan Street, has offered Skaneateles Lake cruises since 1968. Their original dinner cruise is a three-hour excursion on a classic wooden boat, the *Barbara S. Wiles*, or the double-decked sixty-foot *Judge Ben Wiles*, with its mahogany trim and brass fittings.

The Sunday Brunch Cruise is a three-hour excursion offering hearty brunch fare; the luncheon cruise (Monday through Friday) is a two-hour cruise. Both are on the *Judge Ben Wiles*. Mid-Lakes Navigation also offers one-hour cruises on the *Judge Ben Wiles* on Monday through Friday and on the *Barbara S. Wiles* on Saturday and Sunday.

A thirty-two-mile U.S. mailboat cruise, which lasts three and a half hours, is provided daily, except Sundays and holidays, on the *Barbara S. Wiles*. Mail is delivered to cottages around the lake on this cruise, one of the last water routes for mail delivery in the U.S.

When Captain Peter Wiles took over the mail route in 1968, the route had been in operation for over 100 years, going back to the time of the steamboats on Skaneateles Lake. It is a family business run by the Wiles family.

Mid-Lakes Navigation, Ltd., also offers cruises that originate in Syracuse and pass through the area north of the lakes. The Syracuse to Buffalo cruise on the 149-passenger *Emita II* departs from Cold Springs Harbor near Syracuse. Highlights of the cruise include:

- the Montezuma National Wildlife Refuge and six locks
- docking at Newark—overnight lodging nearby
- stopping at Palmyra to inspect the 1825 aqueduct
- docking at Brockport's Harvester Park—overnight lodging nearby
- Medina Aqueduct and double locks at Lockport
- docking at North Tonawanda—return to Syracuse by chartered motorcoach

In addition, Mid-Lakes Navigation offers cruises from Buffalo to Syracuse, Syracuse to Albany, and Albany to Syracuse via the Erie Canal on the *Emita II*. They also offer cruises on Onondaga Lake and the Erie Canal near Syracuse on the *City of Syracuse*. Mid-Lakes Navigation also rents Lockmaster Hireboats on the Erie Canal.

85) The Krebs—Historic Restaurant

The Krebs, located at 53 West Genesee Street, has been in continual operation, May through October, since 1899. In 1899, Fred R. Krebs and his wife, Cora, began to serve three meals a day to their neighbors for $8.00 a week. They soon expanded to a small restaurant with a capacity of twenty-five patrons. By 1915, customers either had to make reservations or wait two hours to be served. In 1920, the Krebs was serving 3,000 meals on Saturdays and Sundays during the summer, and was operating at capacity for the rest of the week.

The restaurant, which has a capacity of 150, is located in a large white frame house that has been expanded several times. From a description of The Krebs in their wine list:

> There are no menus used at The Krebs—
> instead we feature our traditional meal which
> includes a first course (fresh fruit cup, shrimp

cocktail, tomato juice, melon), a choice of soup (clear broth or creamed soup), lobster a la newburg (made from Mrs. Krebs' secret recipe). [Other courses include] English sliced roast prime rib, pan fried half broilers of chicken, white potatoes, candied sweet potatoes, fresh vegetable, beef gravy, creamed mushrooms, and toast points, sweet rolls, and a choice of homemade sweet rolls and ice cream. Also included are a choice of salads, relishes, homemade bread and rolls, and a platter of brownies and angel food cake accompanies all desserts.

Two smaller meals are also offered for those who feel that they cannot eat a full seven-course meal. The format of these two [four-course] meals is basically the same as the traditional meal but are slightly abbreviated to please the lighter appetite. One features the lobster a la newburg, served with a side of wild rice, and the other, the roast prime rib and chicken entrees. A children's menu is also available. Vegetables and desserts change with the seasons and availability. All food is prepared on the premises, the emphasis being placed on quality.

The Krebs Original Sunday Brunch is served every Sunday during the season and consists of a choice of first course (fresh fruit cup, juices, and melon in season), choice of cereal or French onion soup, creamed chicken and baking powder biscuits, scrambled eggs and sausage, roast beef hash, sweet rolls, muffins, and hot pop-overs. There are homemade jams

> or jellies on the table and coffee s served con-
> stantly. To top off the brunch, there are waffles
> served with hot syrup and sherbet.

In 1946, the upstairs living quarters of Mr. and Mrs. Krebs were converted into sitting rooms and a cocktail lounge and furnished with Early American Tavern furniture. The restaurant is furnished with antiques, with linen table cloths and fresh flowers on the tables and lace curtains in the windows. The Krebs has attempted, successfully, to keep the restaurant the way it was in the early 1900s. The restaurant has been the Krebs family through three generations.

86) The Sherwood Inn—Historic Restaurant and Inn

The Sherwood Inn, located at 26 West Genesee Street, Skaneateles, was built as a stagecoach stop and tavern in 1807. The Inn has twenty guest rooms / suites, all with telephones and private baths; many have a view of the northern end of Skaneateles Lake. The Sherwood Inn has an extensive menu that offers American cooking with a continental touch.

The Inn has several formal dining rooms and a summer dining area on a screened-in porch where diners can watch the sailboats on the lake. Casual fare is served in their tavern in a friendly atmosphere that is mixed with jazz on Sunday afternoons. The Inn has ample conference rooms to accommodate business guests, including a cherry-paneled room adjacent to the main dining room and the West Porch.

The attractive lobby has a fireplace and is furnished with Stickley furniture, a baby grand piano, and oriental carpets. Antiques and period furnishings from the early 19th century through Victorian times provide a decor that is consistent with the Inn's past.

The Sherwood Inn has a small library and "the Boat," a restored 1946 Chris Craft, which can be reserved by guests for rides on the Lake.

CHAPTER 9

Southeast of Seneca Falls

CAYUGA LAKE

....

This jewel, forty miles in length, is rich in history.
It lies one hundred thirty yards above the deep, green sea.
And circling its irregular shore are thirteen village sites, where
Redskins once built council fires and held impressive rites.

And here's the isle called "Frontenac" where flambeax used to
glow. It was an indian burial ground two thousand years ago.

....

Red Jacket, famous orator, canoed this haze-blue lake.
He often stood upon the shore and saw the billows break.

....

From *Out of the Finger Lakes Country* by Edwin Becker

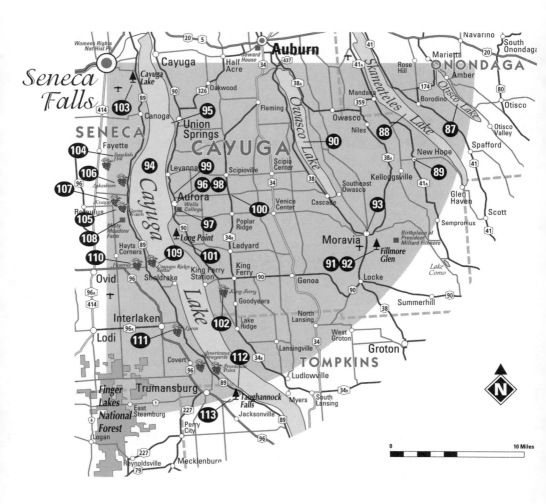

Map of Southeast of Seneca Falls

PLACES TO SEE / THINGS TO DO

Cayuga Lake—West Side (continued)   Page No.

PLACES TO SEE / THINGS TO DO

EAST OF SENECA FALLS

87) Otisco Lake

The Indian word Otisco means "waters dried away." The origin of the word is thought to be a sudden lowering of the water level in the distant past. Otisco Lake is 5.4 miles long and three quarters of a mile wide at its widest point; it has an average width of just over a half mile. It is sixty-six feet deep, has a volume of 21.1 billion gallons, and serves a watershed of thirty-four square miles.

Syracuse suburbs and the New York State Fairgrounds in Geddes use the lake as a public water supply. No water treatment plants discharge into the lake. The hamlets of Amber, Bay Shores, Rice Grove, and Williams Grove dot the periphery of the lake. The watershed includes many dairy farms.

88) Skaneateles Lake

The name Skaneateles is derived from the Indian word Skane-a-dice, which means "long lake." Skaneateles Lake is a spring-fed lake with an inlet, Grout Brook, near Glen Haven at the southern end of the lake; two inlets on the west side of the lake, Bear Swamp Creek and Harrold Brook; and three inlets on the east side, Shotwell Brook, Five Mile Brook, and Ten Mile Brook. The outlet is Skaneateles Creek at the northern end of the lake, in the village of Skaneateles.

Skaneateles Lake is fifteen miles long, nine-tenths of a mile wide on the average, and two miles wide at its widest point. At 350 feet deep, it is the third deepest Finger Lake (Seneca and Cayuga are deeper), has a volume of 424.5 billion gallons, and serves a watershed of seventy-three square miles. The lake is 867 feet above sea level, and is the highest of the major Finger Lakes. The Lake has an AA water purity rating, has no waste treatment plants discharging into it, and is the public water supply for Syracuse and some of its suburbs. It is the clearest of the major Finger Lakes, has the fewest plant species, and is the least productive for wildlife.

89) New Hope Mill

New Hope Mill is located in the hamlet of New Hope, about two miles west of Skaneateles Lake, off Route 41A, near the southern end of the lake. The Mill is located adjacent to a twenty-six-foot waterfall on Bear Swamp Creek, which supplies the power for the Mill. Almost no energy is lost in the operation of the Mill, and no pollution results from its use. Next to the Mill, a covered bridge spans Bear Swamp Creek.

The Mill's twenty-six-foot diameter, three-foot-wide over-shot waterwheel is one of the largest in the eastern United States. It was rebuilt from a wheel obtained in Hagarstown, New Jersey. The blades of the wheel are made from noncorrosive metal sheets that were originally intended for use in fenders for Brockway trucks.

The antique water turbine is twelve feet tall, has a water wheel with a diameter of three feet, generates seventy horsepower, and is ninety-two percent efficient. Instead of bearings, the shaft of the turbine is encased in lignum vitae, a heavy, durable wood whose resin provides its own lubrication. It requires no oil or grease and only requires maintenance every thirty years. The need for maintenance is due to the wear of the wood directly under the shaft. If water in Bear Swamp Creek is too low to turn the wheel and the turbine, the backup power is a water-cooled Fairbanks Morse diesel engine.

The sifter used by the Mill was reissued in 1892; it has four layers of silk within a hickory frame. Elevator cups mounted on a canvas strip move grain to the top of the sifter, which has a design similar to a spiral staircase. Although this sifter was built in 1892, contemporary sifters are based on the same design.

New Hope Mill was built by Judge Charles Kellogg in 1823. The hamlet, whose previous name was Sodom, took its name from the Mill. Few of the early residents of the hamlet liked to say that they were from Sodom.

A museum room contains early mill equipment and old ledgers and record books from the Mill. For safety reasons no tours of the Mill are given, but a video is shown in the museum room that describes the operation of the Mill. Also, an open house is scheduled once a year in the early fall; the owners spend considerable time eliminating safety hazards that might put visitors at risk. That is the one time during the year that visitors can see the old granite and burr stones actually grinding the grain.

The Mill sells about a dozen quality pancake mixes, bread mixes, syrups, spreads, spices, and baking supplies. New Hope Mills flour is unbleached and unenriched, and it contains no artificial ingredients. The owners feel that since they haven't taken any of the natural nutrients out in milling the flour, there is no need to add ingredients to "enrich" it. Summer wheat is used to make a courser, harder flour used in baking bread, and winter wheat is used to grind a finer, softer product for pastry flour.

90) Owasco Lake

The name Owasco is derived from the Indian word Wasco, which means "outlet" or "floating bridge." A second derivation of the name Owasco is from the Indian word Osco meaning "crossing place." The Owasco Inlet, which flows by the village of Moravia, is at the southern end of the lake. Dutch Hollow Creek and Sucker Brook flow into the east side of the lake. The Owasco River, at the northern end of the lake, flows through the City of Auburn to the Seneca River / Erie Canal near Port Byron; it is the Owasco Lake outlet.

Owasco Lake, the smallest of the six major Finger Lakes, is 11.1 miles long, 1.3 miles wide at its widest point, and has an average width of .9 mile. It is 177 feet deep at its deepest point, and has a volume of 212 billion gallons. It has a 208-square-mile watershed; the Lake is 710 feet above sea level.

Owasco is known as a good lake for trout fishing. The City of Auburn operates a public boat launching facility, just off Route 38A, at the northern end of the lake. The City of Auburn and the village of Moravia use the lake as a public water supply.

MORAVIA

91) Fillmore Glen State Park

Fillmore Glen State Park, established in 1925, is located on Route 38, one mile south of Moravia. The 938-acre park is named for the thirteenth President of the United States, Millard Fillmore, who was born in 1800 at Summerhill, about six miles southeast of the park. A replica of his birthplace has been constructed in the park.

Fillmore Glen State Park has hiking trails that cross Dry Creek on eight bridges. The trails offer striking views of gorges and unique geological formations, such as the Cowsheds Ledge, the Pinnacle, and waterfalls. The Cowsheds Ledge, adjacent to Lower Falls, is a large recess in the cliff made when weak shale eroded away under a ledge of limestone. Cowsheds Ledge received its name when cattle used the recess to cool off on a hot day. The Pinnacle is located in section of the park in which stones have been eroded into rectangular formations.

Fillmore Glen State Park has a greater variety of plant life than any other State Park in the Finger Lakes Region. It was this abundant flora that initially motivated Dr. Atwood, a local physician and amateur botanist, to lobby for the establishment of a public park at the glen. The trails were officially opened in 1921 and a plaque embedded in stone was unveiled to dedicate the event. The plaque is located at the trailhead near the first bridge.

The Park has over fifty-seven campsites (no utilities; RVs allowed), a playground, playing fields, picnic areas with tables and fireplaces, pay telephone, hot showers, flush toilets, and a trailer dumping station. The Park also has swimming in a stream-fed gorge pool, bathhouse facilities, and fishing in the Owasco inlet; special events, including family film night and guided nature hikes, are scheduled. A golf course adjoins the Park.

92) Fillmore Antique Car Show

An antique car show is held the Sunday of Labor Day weekend in Fillmore Glen State Park, Route 38, just south of Moravia. The Show has hundreds of entries, many trophies, a chicken barbecue, and a flea market.

93) St. Matthew's Church

St. Matthew's Church, Church Street, Moravia, is the church in which Millard and Abigail Fillmore were married on February 5, 1826. Millard Fillmore became the thirteenth President of the United States upon the death of President Zachary Taylor.

St. Matthew's Church was completed in 1898; it was the third church built by the Episcopalian parish since the founding of Moravia by New England settlers in 1822. In 1908, Father William Sutherland Stevens became rector of the church. He planned and coordinated the interior decoration of the church during his thirty-six-year ministry. He wrote to England for photographs of the Gothic interpretation of each saint to be carved as part of the master plan he envisioned. The carved wood statues were commissioned as memorials, one at a time.

The photographs he selected became the pattern for the woodcarvers in Hans Mayer's studio in Oberammergau, Bavaria, Germany. In 1910, the first statue was carved, which was Christ the Good Shepherd holding the pastoral symbols of the lamb and the staff. Below the central figure are carvings of the saints that symbolize the Anglican communion of the Episcopal Church: St. Hugh of England, St. Patrick of Ireland, St. Ninian of Scotland, and St. David of Wales.

265

St. Matthew's Church, Moravia

On the sides of these four statues, at a slightly higher level, are the carved figures of St. Mary the Virgin and St. Matthew. All of these statues are mounted in the retable that forms the back of the altar. The lectern has carvings of Moses, Isaiah, David, and St. John the Baptist. The litany desk has Old Testament figures on one side and New Testament figures on the other side. Over the entry to the apse is a carving of the crucifixion, flanked by St. Mary and St. John with St. Peter and St. Paul on the ends.

Complementing the carvings from Oberammergau are designs and reliefs carved by Charles Hall from the village of Tyrone, between Keuka and Seneca Lakes. Hall used the shop at the church that Father Stevens, a experienced organ builder, used to build the organ. Hall did many carvings of the flora of the region as well as the traditional symbols such as the Tudor rose and the acanthus, which are used on Corinthian columns.

Hall fashioned the swirling designs on the mahogany and oak pulpit from the drawings of William Blake. He also did all of the oak paneling and the retables behind the altar as well as the spired crown over the base of the baptismal font. Many of the church's window lights were donated as memorials. The stations of the cross, gifts of an anonymous donor in the 1930s, were modeled on hand-carved originals from Spain.

Father Stevens used pipes from all over the world in building the organ. However, he completed his tenure at St. Matthew's in 1944, and was unable to complete the construction of his organ by the time he left Moravia. His "echo organ" was purchased by the National Cathedral in Washington. Visitors are welcome to St. Matthew's for Sunday services, and tours may be arranged at other times by calling the Rectory.

CAYUGA LAKE

94) Cayuga Lake

The Indian name Cayuga means "boat landing." Many people

recognize Cayuga Lake because of the line "Far above Cayuga's waters" in the Cornell University alma mater. In addition to the Cayuga Inlet at Ithaca, the lake is fed by five tributaries at the southern end: Cascadilla Creek, Fall Creek, Salmon Creek, Six Mile Creek, and Taughannock Creek.

Cayuga Lake outlets into the Cayuga-Seneca Canal, which joins the northern end of Seneca and Cayuga Lakes and connects with the Erie Canal just north of Seneca Falls. Lake Ontario can be accessed from Cayuga Lake via the Erie canal, Cross Lake, and the Oswego Canal.

The longest of the Finger Lakes, Cayuga Lake is forty miles long, three and a half miles wide at the widest point, and has an average width of one and three quarters miles. It is 435 feet deep at the deepest point (off King Ferry), which makes it second only to Seneca Lake in depth. At 384 feet above sea level is the lowest of the Finger Lakes.

Because of its low elevation, the lake has many marshes, particularly at the northern end, extending into the Montezuma National Wildlife Refuge northeast of Seneca Falls. It was known as Gweh-u-qweh, "the lake at the mucky land," by the Cayuga Nation and "lake of the marshes" by the Mohawks. Cayuga Lake has just under ninety-six miles of shoreline.

CAYUGA LAKE—EAST SIDE

95) Frontenac Island / Union Springs

Frontenac Island, a small island located off the east shoreline near the village of Union Springs, is one of the two islands in the Finger Lakes (the other is Squaw Island at the northern end of Canandaigua Lake). In 1939 and 1940, a Rochester Museum and Science Center expedition, directed by the State Archaeologist, Dr. William R. Richie, discovered the burial sites of an ancient people who inhabited the island over 5,000 years ago.

Frontenac's neighbor, Union Springs, was founded in

1800; Quakers were among the founding families. During the 1800s, Union Springs had the largest gypsum quarry in the country. While the plaster industry flourished, gypsum was shipped from Union Springs to Ithaca for processing and for further shipment along the Atlantic Coast.

The Tallcot Bookshop, 28 South Cayuga Street (Route 90) in Union Springs, has one of the most comprehensive collections of regional books and books about New York State available anywhere.

96) Aurora

The village of Aurora is on the east side of Cayuga Lake, about fourteen miles south of the northern end of the Lake. It is the home of Wells College, founded in 1868 by Henry Wells—a founder of the Wells Fargo and American Express Companies, and of the Aurora Inn. Adjoining the campus of Wells College is Pumpkin Hill, which overlooks Paine's Creek gully and Moonshine Falls. The entire village of Aurora is included in the National Register of Historic Places.

In 1779, the Cayuga Indian village of Deawendote, on the site of Aurora, was destroyed by a 600-man contingent of General Sullivan's Army. Colonel William Butler's men destroyed the village's fourteen log houses and all of its crops and orchards. The Cayuga Indian name Deawendote meant village of constant dawn, so named because of the long ridge behind the village to the east that prolongs the sunrise. Aurora was first settled by white men in 1786. It was the county seat of Cayuga County from 1799 until 1809, when the county government was shifted to fast-growing Auburn. Aurora was the site of the first steam-powered flour mill east of the Hudson River.

97) Wells College

Wells College is four-year, nonsectarian women's college with an enrollment of over 450. It is located on a 360-acre wooded campus in the village of Aurora. The College was

Aurora Inn

founded in 1868 as the Wells Seminary for the Education of Young Women on 111 acres, which were donated by Henry Wells of the Wells Fargo Company. The name was changed to Wells College in 1870.

Henry Wells donated his home, Glen Park, as the first building for the College. The College also runs a conference center that uses some of the campus facilities. A nine-hole golf course designed by Robert Trent Jones is located east of the campus.

98) The Aurora Inn

The Aurora Inn, established in 1833 as the Aurora House, is located on Route 90, a short walk from Wells College. The Inn has 15 guest rooms, all decorated with a country theme. The Inn was used as a residence hall for two years when the main Wells College building burned down in 1888.

The Aurora Inn is an old stagecoach stop and the tall paintings in the main foyer and parlors are reminiscent of old-time country inns. The dining room, which offers traditional American fare, overlooks Cayuga Lake; the view includes a stone wall that was once the foundation of a steam grist mill. The Aurora Inn Tavern offers lighter food, including soups, salads, and sandwiches.

In 1845, the well-known anthropologist Lewis Henry Morgan sat in the parlor of Aurora House and told Henry Rowe Schoolcraft an Onondaga Indian legend. Schoolcraft passed the legend on to Henry Wadsworth Longfellow and the legend became Longfellow's epic poem, "The Song of Hiawatha."

99) MacKenzie-Childs Ltd.

MacKenzie-Childs Ltd., located at 3260 Route 90 in Aurora, was founded by Victoria and Richard Mackenzie-Childs in 1983. It is housed in a nineteenth-century estate that overlooks Cayuga Lake. Their products, including Majolica dinnerware (hand-formed terra cotta, glazed white and elabo-

Howland Stone Store Museum, Sherwood

rately hand-painted), Bistroware (hand-made of terra cotta with satin white glaze), MacLachlan porcelain ware, glassware (hand-blown and hand-painted), furnishings, trimmings, tiles, linens, and floor cloths that are painted free-hand, are created by hand by over 350 craftsmen.

The showrooms are open Monday through Saturday. Reservations are required for studio tours. The Shop, which is housed in a antique hand-hewn chestnut barn, sells "one-of-a-kind works of MacKenzie-Childs, happy accidents, and surplus production materials with infinite possibilities." The estate also includes a canteen, a museum of MacKenzie-Childs history, and a reading room. In 1993, MacKenzie-Childs Ltd. opened their American flagship store at 824 Madison Avenue (corner of 69th Street) in Manhattan.

100) Howland Stone Store Museum
The Howland Stone Store, located at the intersection of Route 34B and Sherwood Road, is a Greek Revival cobblestone building built in 1837 by Slocum Howland, a Quaker entrepreneur and wool buyer. Howland, who arrived in the area in 1798 with his parents Benjamin and Mary Howland, was a banker and landowner who was active in the antislavery and temperance movements.

The building was used as a store from 1837 until 1881. Slocum Howland was one of the first to sell the cast iron plows invented by his brother-in-law, Jethro Wood of Moravia. In 1881, the store became a warehouse.

The Howland Stone Store Museum contains a collection of memorabilia and over 100 posters from the Women's Rights Movement. Included in the collection are botanical specimens, Native American objects, and items collected in Europe and North Africa by Slocum's daughter, Emily Howland, and her niece, Isabel Howland.

Emily Howland was an educator who was active in the abolitionist, temperance, women's rights, and world peace movements. She founded and provided the funds for the

Sherwood Select School, which was the forerunner of the Emily Howland School in Sherwood today.

By 1869, when the Women's Rights Movement split into two factions, the American Woman Suffrage Association and the National Woman Suffrage Association, Emily had decided to devote her life to social change. She had close friends in both associations, and she also was active in the antislavery movement.

In 1891, Emily became the first woman bank director in New York State. She was frustrated by being granted increased fiscal authority while not being allowed to vote. On June 7, 1894, she asked the Suffrage Committee of the Constitutional Convention in the Assembly Chamber at Albany, "Have we a representative government when one half the people have no voice in it?"

In 1904, Emily told a convention of the National American Woman Suffrage Association, "Our cause came straight from the antislavery cause. All its early advocates were also advocates of freeing the [African-American] race in bondage. Let us not forget them now. Neither a nation nor an individual can be really free 'til all are free."

In *The World of Emily Howland: Odyssey of a Humanitarian*, Judith Colucci Breault observes that:

> Emily's contribution to the nineteenth woman's movement did not arise, however, out of her participation in the local and county women's suffrage campaigns. Instead, through her interest in education, her writing, her philanthropy and her relations with leading feminists, Emily performed a unique and valuable service to the women's movement....
>
> Although not considered a major historical figure, she does deserve recognition and attention when examining the history of social

movements, reforms and humanitarianism in the United States. Yet her unique importance does not lie only in her role of chronicler-participant in the reformist events of her over eighty critical years in the life of the nation. Her most significant historical contribution may ultimately rest in her delineation of a world in which she, as a woman, struggled to lead a satisfying, fulfilling life.

Emily Howland died on June 29, 1929. The words she chose for her tombstone were:

EMILY HOWLAND

NOVEMBER 20, 1827   JUNE 29, 1929

I STROVE TO REALIZE MYSELF AND TO SERVE

Her niece, Isabel Howland added the words:

PURPOSES NOBLY FULFILLED

The Howland Stone Store Museum, which is owned and operated by the Friends of the Howland Stone Store, is open Sunday afternoons from June through September.

101) Long Point State Park
Long Point State Park, on Lake Road, off Route 90, south of Aurora, on the east side of Cayuga Lake, has fourteen tent / trailer sites (three electric) and a picnicking area. Boating facilities in the Park include a dock, two boat launches, and a marine pumpout station.

102) King Ferry Winery
King Ferry Winery, located on the east shore of Cayuga Lake

sixteen miles north of Ithaca, is owned and operated by Peter and Tacie Saltonstall. Peter is the winemaker and Tacie is the marketing manager. The Winery specializes in wine made from the European varieties of grapes such as Chardonnay, Riesling, Gewürztraminer, Merlot, and Pinot Noir. The first two varieties are the most winter hardy of the European varieties.

King Ferry Winery pays particular attention to the Chardonnay and Riesling varieties. Peter Saltonstall is attempting to blend his Chardonnays to obtain the creamy, complex, and rich flavor of the Chardonnays made in Meursalt, France, in southern Burgundy. Peter ferments about seventy-five percent of his Chardonnay in French Vosges oak barrels; the oak imparts a slight creaminess and a touch of smokiness to the wine. The barrels hold about sixty gallons, which is an ideal size because of the ratio of the inside surface area of the barrel to the volume of the wine.

The Winery produces over 2,000 cases annually, most of which are sold at the winery. Their wine is sold in restaurants and wine stores in New York City—the major but as yet underdeveloped market for Finger Lakes wine—and in area restaurants and wine stores. King Ferry Winery labels their wine Treleaven; the Saltonstalls bought the property for their vineyards and winery from the Treleaven family.

CAYUGA LAKE—WEST SIDE

103) Cayuga Lake State Park

Cayuga Lake State Park, established in 1928, is located three miles southeast of Seneca Falls, off Route 89, at 2678 Lower Lake Road. Oak-shaded lawns and sandy beach areas extend along the Lake in this 141-acre park. The terrain is flat at the lakeshore, and slants slightly uphill toward the campgrounds; the Lake off the swimming area is barely five feet deep. The Park has a boat launching ramp; fishing is a popular activity.

The Park has 286 campsites (250 non-electric, 36 electric;

RVs allowed), fourteen cabins, flush toilets, hot showers, and a trailer dumping station. The Park also has a bath house, a concession stand, a recreation building, and three pavilions, as well as playing fields, a playground, and picnic areas with tables and fireplaces. The Park, which is accessible to the mobility impaired, is open all winter for cross-country skiing, hiking, ice-fishing, sledding, and snowmobiling.

104) Swedish Hill Vineyard

Swedish Hill Vineyard, 4565 Route 414, Romulus, eight miles south of Seneca Falls, is owned and operated by Dick and Cindy Peterson. Dick is responsible for the vineyard, Cindy is the marketing manager, and their son, Dave, is the winemaker. Swedish Hill Vineyard produces over 90,000 gallons of wine each year. Varieties grown in their over 35-acre vineyard include Aurora, Cabernet Franc, Cabernet Sauvignon, Catawba, Chardonnay, Lemberger, Merlot, Ventura, and Vignoles.

Swedish Hill Vineyard makes wine from European varieties, such as Chardonnay, Riesling, Merlot, and Cabernet Sauvignon; from French-American hybrid varieties, including Aurora, Baco Noir, Marechal Foch, and Vignoles; and from native American grapes, such as Catawba. The Svenska series of blended wines—a red, a white, and a blush—are also popular. Swedish Hill Vineyard also produces an award-winning Blanc de Blanc champagne. Swedish Hill has tours daily and is known for many special events throughout the year.

105) Goose Watch Winery

Goose Watch Winery, located fifteen minutes south of Seneca Falls at 5480 Route 89, Romulus, is owned by Dick and Cindy Peterson. The winetasting room is in a beautifully restored century-old barn situated in Goose Watch Farm's chestnut grove. The Farm also has an aquaculture trout operation.

Goose Watch Winery produces premium wines from

European grape varieties such as Merlot, Pinot Gris, and Pinot Noir; hybrid varieties including Melody and Traminette, which makes a Gewürztraminer-type wine; and native varieties such as Diamond and Isabella, from which they make Rosé of Isabella. The Winery also makes Pinot Noir Brut Rosé Champagne and a dessert wine, "Finale" White Port.

Visitors to Goose Watch Winery are invited to bring a picnic lunch to enjoy on the deck or snack on local cheese and other delicacies, including smoked trout produced on Goose Watch Farm. The Winery offers horse-drawn wagon vineyard tours on weekends. Goose Watch Winery, located a half mile north of Dean's Cove on the western shore of Cayuga Lake, is accessible by boat. Docking is available.

106) Lakeshore Winery

Lakeshore Winery, at 5132 Route 89, Romulus, on the west side of Cayuga Lake, is owned and operated by John and Annie Bachman. Lakeshore Winery produces wine from many grape varieties including the European varieties Cabernet Sauvignon, Pinot Noir, and Riesling. Lakeshore Winery also offers wine made from French-American varieties, such as Baco Noir, Cayuga, and Vignoles (Ravat 51). Two of their popular wines are Aunt Clara and Uncle Charlie, blended wines that include the native variety, Catawba.

Isaac Philips Roberts, founder of the College of Agriculture at Cornell University, was born in the house on the Winery property on July 24, 1833. A New York State historical marker on Route 89 below the Winery notes that event.

Lakeshore Winery provides special activities for visitors, including the Lakeshore Nouveau Weekend in early November to celebrate the harvest just completed. The Winery favors sitdown winetastings with food served between individual tastings to emphasize the fact that wine is food. Picnic facilities are available. The Lakeshore Winery winetasting room has a large stone fireplace that is used during the late fall, winter, and early spring.

107) Knapp Vineyards

Knapp Vineyards, at 2770 Ernsberger Road (County Road 128), Romulus, off Route 89 on the east side of Cayuga Lake, is owned and run by Doug and Susie Knapp. Doug, a past president of the New York State Wine Grape Growers Association, is the winemaker, and Susie is responsible for marketing. Knapp Vineyards produces over 25,000 gallons of wine each year. They specialize in the classic European varieties, including Chardonnay, Riesling, Pinot Noir, Cabernet Franc, and Cabernet Sauvignon. Knapp Vineyards also makes wine from the French-American hybrid varieties, such as Vignoles and Seyval Blanc.

The Knapps continue to try new things and have added Nebbiolo, an Italian red, to their wine offerings. Their popular wildflower series of blended wines spotlights three endangered species: Dutchman's breeches, Lady's Slipper, and Cardinal Flower, which are displayed on the labels. The winery has a distillery license, which allows them to offer Brandy, Grappa, Port, and Aviñac.

Knapp Vineyards is also known for its fine restaurant, which is open from April through December featuring American cuisine and a variety of European dishes. The emphasis is on fish and meat from the region and on locally grown vegetables.

108) Misty Meadow Farm

Misty Meadow Farm is a clean, modern 200-acre working hog farm overlooking the west shore of Cayuga Lake off Route 89. Fred and Anne Sepe and family raise over 1,600 lean, long hogs for the market annually on their "farrow-to-finish" swine operation at 2828 Vineyard Road, Romulus. An opportunity to see real farm life is provided during a fifty-minute guided tour that starts with a short orientation highlighting the sights in each barn. Background information about pigs, the farm, the swine industry, and the general subject of agriculture is also provided.

The tour includes the breeding area, the gestating area where sows await giving birth, the farrowing house with sows nursing litters of piglets, the old barn with its "adolescent" pigs, and the finishing barn where hogs are grown to market size. Children can pet and play with a variety of young animals at "Old McDonald's Pen." The Misty Meadow Farm has a Farm Shop offering local crafts, gifts, pig collectables, souvenirs, and frozen cuts of Misty Meadow's premium USDA-inspected pork. Lunch is available at the Farm Kitchen Restaurant, an enclosed pavilion overlooking the lake, from a menu which includes many pork products and other choices such as hamburgers.

The Sepes have hybrid stock bred to produce large litters of healthy, fast-growing piglets. Because the boars and sows are hybrids, the piglets are a variety of colors and shading. The hybrid pigs produce a leaner meat than their forebears did. Because Misty Meadow Farm is a working farm, it is not open to visitors all the time. Visitors are hosted, "between morning and evening chores, after planting and before harvest season."

109) Cayuga Ridge Estate Vineyard

Cayuga Ridge Estate Vineyard was purchased by Tom and Susie Challen of Ontario, Canada, in 1991. Tom had been winemaker for Paul Masson & Co., Ltd., winemaker for the Horticultural Research Institute in Vineland Station, and viticultural technician for the T. G. Bright & Co., Ltd. Winery, all in Ontario.

Cayuga Ridge Estate Vineyard specializes in Chardonnay, Riesling, Cayuga, Chancellor, Pinot Noir, and Vignoles wines. Chancellor is one of the most notable French-American hybrid red varieties and is widely grown in France. Challen ages the Chardonnay and the Pinot Noir in French oak and the Chancellor in American oak barrels.

The winery is also known for the "serenade series": Duet and Trio. Duet is a blend of Cayuga and Vignoles; Trio, a blush rosé blend, is the drier of the two wines. Cranberry Essence, essence of cranberry combined with white wine, has been a popular offering. In recent years, Tom has planted additional Chancellor and Cabernet Franc vines.

Cayuga Ridge Estate Vineyard sponsors a vigneron (rent-a-grapevine) program. A participant in the program leases, tends, and harvests the grapes from ten, twenty, or thirty grapevines. A vigneron visits the vineyard about five times during the growing season and learns how to prune, tie, cluster-thin, and harvest their vines. At harvest time, they have a choice of taking or selling the grapes, or of paying the winery to make wine from their grapes.

In the past, Cayuga Ridge Estate Vineyard sponsored a food- and wine-matching activity in September and an early October event for visitors to experience the picking, crushing, and pressing of the harvested grapes. Picnic tables are available at the winery.

110) Hosmer Winery

Hosmer Winery, 6999 Route 89, Ovid, is on the western shore of the Cayuga Lake, twenty-two and a half miles north of Ithaca. The Winery is owned and operated by Cameron ("Tunker") and Maren Hosmer. Hosmer Winery specializes in Cayuga White and Riesling varieties, but makes twelve other wines, including Seyval Blanc, Chardonnay, and Pinot Noir. A popular addition has been Raspberry Rhapsody, a raspberry-flavored wine made by combining fresh raspberries with fermented grape wine.

Hosmer has a spacious wine-tasting facility located near the vineyards and a gift shop. Light food items are sold, and picnic tables are available. The Hosmers sponsor special events at the Winery, such as a "Spring Out" barrel tasting in April and Asparagus Days in May.

Taughannock Falls, near Trumansburg

111) Lucas Vineyards

Lucas Vineyards, at 3862 County Road 150, Interlaken, is eighteen miles north of Ithaca, off Route 89 on the west side of Cayuga Lake. Lucas Vineyards, the oldest winery on Cayuga Lake, is owned and operated by Bill and Ruth Lucas. Bill has spent many years as tugboat captain in the waters of the eastern seaboard, which explains the origin of the labels on their Tugboat Red and Tugboat White wines. Lucas makes wine from European varieties, such as Chardonnay, Gewürztraminer, and Riesling, as well as French-American hybrid varieties, including Baco Noir, Cayuga, DeChaunac, Seyval Blanc, Vidal Blanc, and Vignoles.

One of the visitors' favorites is Captain's Belle Blush, a blend of five French-American hybrid varieties. Blues wine is a blend of Cayuga and Seyval Blanc; Harbor Moon is a blend of Cayuga and Vidal Blanc. Lucas Vineyards also offers extra-dry, brut, and blanc de blancs champagne. The winery has a gift shop, and picnic facilities are available.

112) Taughannock Farms Inn—Trumansburg

The Taughannock Farms Inn is located off of Route 89 in the southeast corner of Taughannock Falls Park. The Inn was built in 1873 as a Victorian summer estate by John Jones, Jr., an owner of a nearby papermill. The Inn overlooks Goodwin's Point on the west side of Cayuga Lake. Mr. Jones envisioned a grand summer resort at the point, but he died before he could fulfill his dream. Taughannock Farms Inn has been a highly regarded restaurant since the 1940s. The Inn also operates as a Bed and Breakfast.

113) Taughannock Falls State Park—Trumansburg

Taughannock Falls State Park, established in 1924, is located on 783 acres, eight miles north of Ithaca on Route 89. The most notable attraction of this park is the 215-foot-high Taughannock Falls, the highest straight falls east of the Rocky Mountains and fifty feet higher than Niagara Falls. The setting of the falls is a 400-foot-high rock amphitheatre composed of Sherbourne Flagstone at the top half of the cliff and Geneseo Shale at the bottom half.

Trails for hiking are maintained through the woods and along the gorge. Also, the Park has two lookout areas, one at the end of a three-quarter mile trail at the base of the falls and one at a panoramic overlook that can be reached by car. The Park offers a swimming beach on the lake with a bathhouse and a concession stand. Fishing is permitted in the creek and in the Lake; facilities include tie-up docks, a boat launch, and a marine pumpout facility.

The Park has seventy-six campsites (16 electric, 60 with no utilities), sixteen cabins, flush toilets, hot showers, and a trailer dumping site. Also provided are playing fields, a playground, and picnic areas with tables and fireplaces. A camper recreation program is held in the summer.

CHAPTER 10

Southwest of Seneca Falls

GEM OF THE FINGER LAKES

Seneca, gem of the Finger Lakes, where once crept along
the lengthy shore, scores of barken Indian canoes; Where
tented cities of six nations dotted the low wooden slopes;
where, from the shore, Sullivan's vanguard heard the muf-
fled boom of the "lake guns" and where, in the legend of
the Senecas, were heard the beat of phantom drums!

....

And where Louis Philippe, French King, sailed in 1797
with his brothers—There is the Grape Region of the East,
This beautiful jewel in Central New York.

From *Poems of the Finger Lakes Region* by Edwin Becker

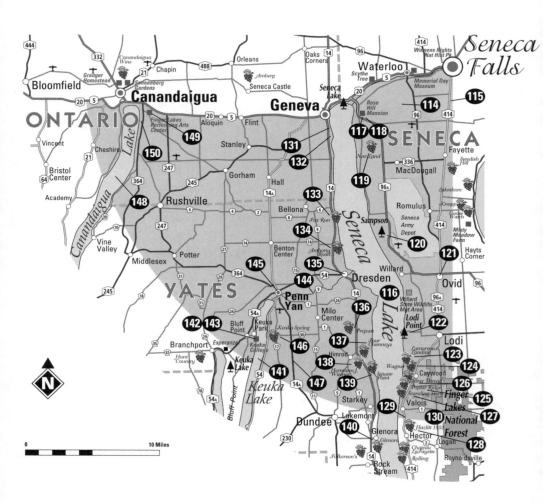

Map of Southwest of Seneca Falls

PLACES TO SEE / THINGS TO DO

PLACES TO SEE / THINGS TO DO

SOUTH OF SENECA FALLS / WATERLOO

114) Peter Whitmer Home—Fayette

On April 6, 1830, at the home of Peter Whitmer, Joseph Smith, the first president of the Church of Jesus Christ of Latter-Day Saints (Mormons), and five witnesses formally signed the papers to organize the restored Church of Jesus Christ. The five witnesses were Oliver Cowdery, Joseph's brothers Hyrum and Samuel H. Smith, and Peter Whitmer and his brother, David. The Home is a small, open-hearthed farm home in Fayette, two miles south of Waterloo, off Route 96. The Visitor Center is maintained by the Church of Jesus Christ of Latter-Day Saints.

115) Empire State Farm Days

Empire State Farm Days are held on more than 325 acres of the 4,000-acre Rodman Lott and Sons farm south of Seneca Falls in early August. It is the major farm show in the Northeast, with over 550 exhibits; between 75,000 and 100,000 visitors attend the three-day show each year.

Empire State Farm Days, the longest running outdoor agriculture trade show in the Northeast, began in 1933. The central focus of the show is on working farmers and the people who provide service and support to them, but there is something of interest to everyone. One of the managers of the show has observed, "Anyone who is interested in where their food and fiber comes from can learn a lot at Empire Farm Days."

Empire Farm Days displays the latest farm machinery and provides an opportunity to show children how farms are worked. Daily demonstrations of the latest agricultural techniques are given. In addition to agricultural topics, such as the discussion of the latest strains of hybrid corn, a visitor has the opportunity to learn about subjects such as health and safety and the latest in profit-management packages.

SENECA LAKE

116) Seneca Lake

Seneca Lake was named for the Seneca Indian Nation, one of the six nations of the Iroquois Confederacy, who used to inhabit the area. The word Seneca is derived from the Indian name assiniki, which means "place of the stone" or "stoney place." Seneca Lake has the steepest shoreline of all of the Finger Lakes, particularly at the southern end.

Two of the main inlets to Seneca are Catharine (pronounced Cathareen by natives) Creek at the southern end and the Keuka Lake Outlet, which becomes an inlet to Seneca Lake at Dresden. The Lake is also fed by many ravines, some of which have spectacular waterfalls, including the falls of Rock Stream at Glenora, the falls of Sawmill Creek at Hector, and the Silver Thread Falls of Mill Creek at Lodi Landing. Seneca Lake is also fed by many springs at the bottom of the lake. The Lake outlets into the Seneca River / Cayuga-Seneca Canal, which connects Seneca and Cayuga Lakes at their northern ends.

Seneca Lake is the deepest and the widest of the Finger Lakes, but not the longest; Cayuga Lake has that distinction. Seneca Lake is 632 feet deep (off Lodi Point) and thirty-five miles long. The bottom falls away quickly; in some locations, the depth is 50 to 100 feet just twenty feet from shore. The Lake is 3.2 miles wide at the widest point and has an average width of 1.9 miles. Seneca Lake has 75.4 miles of shoreline and a volume of 4.2 trillion gallons. Whitecaps can come up quickly on the Lake, particularly when driven by a south wind.

Due to the large water volume, Seneca Lake has a pronounced moderating influence on the air temperature around its periphery, which is the principal reason that the Lake has evolved into a prime grape-growing area. The moderating influence on the temperature lengthens the growing season. Severe winter conditions have less impact on non-winter-hardy grape varieties on Seneca Lake than on other lakes in the region. Seneca Lake has more wineries (over twenty) than any other Finger Lake. The Lake surface has iced over only nine times since the beginning of weather record-keeping.

Seneca Lake is rated as an excellent lake for fishing and is particularly known for lake trout. The National Lake Trout Derby is held at Geneva every Memorial Day weekend.

SENECA LAKE—EAST SIDE

117) Rose Hill Mansion

Rose Hill, an 1839 Greek Revival mansion, is located east of Geneva, one mile south of Routes 5 and 20 on Route 96A. The Mansion, owned and administered by the Geneva Historical Society, was declared a National Historic Landmark in 1988 by the National Park Service, for "possessing national significance in commemorating the history of the United States."

Rose Hill is one of the country's finest examples of Greek-Revival architecture. Six two-story Ionic columns support the central portico, and a cupola caps the central part of the mansion. The central section has symmetrical wings, with one-story Ionic columns.

Guided tours are conducted through twenty rooms decorated with wood and plaster moldings and furnished in the Empire style popular during the Greek-Revival period. The paint colors, draperies, and wallpaper used in the restoration of the Mansion are typical of the period, as is the wall-to-wall carpeting. Most of the furniture is made of mahogany, a popular wood of the time. The high-ceilinged rooms, with their large windows and hefty doors, are hung with the paintings of former owners, including a painting by Severin Rosen of Williamsport, Pennsylvania.

The French crystal chandelier in the huge banquet hall is one of a pair made about 1810. Its mate hangs in Lemon Hill, a restored mansion in Fairmont Park, Philadelphia. The stair-

Rose Hill Mansion, Geneva

way's mahogany railing curves upward for three floors, capped by a skylight.

The Jenny Lynd bedroom contains the original Jenny Lynd bed. The "Swedish Nightingale" was brought to the United States in 1850 by impresario and showman P. T. Barnum. A London theatre manager told Jenny that Barnum was a cheap showman with no friends of culture. To dispel the rumor, Barnum asked his friends, the Shelton family, to entertain Jenny at their home, Greystone, in Derby, Connecticut. The bed in the Jenny Lynd bedroom at Rose Hill is the bed in which Miss Lynd slept at Greystone; it was widely copied by cabinet-makers in a line of "Jenny Lynd" furniture.

An early owner of the Rose Hill estate was Dr. Alexander Coventry, who bought the land in 1792, and named the property Fairhill after his ancestral home in Scotland. He built his house, not on the high ground on which Rose Hill stands, but near the lake shore, adjacent to the marshes of the Seneca River. Considering the property unhealthy, Dr. Coventry sold the 900-acre Fairhill farm to Robert Selden Rose, a Virginia planter and lawyer, in the early 1800s. Rose built a plain house on the site of the present mansion in 1809, which was later moved a short distance north to become the present carriage house. The kitchen of the original Rose house, with its brick fireplace and beehive oven in the hearth, became part of Rose Hill Mansion.

Rose was elected to the State Assembly in 1811, 1820, and 1821 and was a member of Congress from 1823 to 1827. He was a principal of the Seneca Lock Navigation Company formed to improve navigation between Seneca and Cayuga Lakes, a trustee of Hobart College, and the first vice president of New York State Agricultural Society upon its founding in 1832. He died in 1835, and the farm was sold to General William K. Strong, a retired wool merchant from New York City. Strong built the mansion on Rose's hill in 1839. One of General Strong's guests at Rose Hill was President Martin Van Buren. After the death of his wife, Sarah Van Giesen of

Geneva, Strong returned to New York City to become vice president of the Bank of North America.

The farm reached its peak under the next owner, Robert J. Swan, who received the Mansion and 360 acres of the property in 1850 as a wedding gift from his father, a New York City merchant. Swan, who decided that he was more suited to agriculture than to his father's mercantile business, moved to the area to study farming with John Johnson, a neighbor of Rose Hill. Swan married Johnson's daughter, Margaret, and they began their forty-year residency at the mansion in 1850.

Swan, who turned Rose Hill into one of the most productive farms in the state, won the silver cups on display in the carriage house for his agricultural ability. He was awarded first prize for a premium farm in 1853 by the New York State Agricultural Society for comprehensive experiments in the use of drainage tiles to drain marshy land. He installed the first large-scale tile drainage system in the early 1850s.

He received another award in 1858, and he was one of the first to use the reaper successfully on his principal crop, wheat. He was one of the incorporators of the State College of Agriculture in 1853, and he played a significant role in establishing the New York State Agricultural Experiment Station in Geneva.

By 1965, Rose Hill had become run-down, and the Mansion, with two and a half acres of land, went on the market for $15,000. Swan's grandson, Waldo Hutchins, Jr., purchased it, along with fifteen acres in front to protect its view of the lake and five acres in the rear, as a gift to the Geneva Historical Society. The Historical Society restored the Mansion to its 1840s condition, and it was opened to the public on September 28, 1968. Hutchins dedicated the Mansion to his mother, Agnes Swan Hutchins, who was born and grew to adulthood at Rose Hill.

Rose Hill Mansion is open from May through October on Monday through Saturday and on Sunday afternoons. A nominal admission fee is charged.

118) Mike Weaver Drain Tile Museum

The Mike Weaver Drain Tile Museum, on East Lake Road just south of Rose Hill Mansion, is located in the restored home of John and Margaret Johnson. John Johnson introduced tile drainage to America in 1835. The Museum houses a collection of over 350 different styles of tiles dating from 100 BC until the present time.

The Museum has an orientation room on tiling and a research room containing many original documents and items of written material on tiling. The Johnsons' living room is furnished with many pieces of the original furniture. The Museum is open from May 1 to October 31 by appointment only. Call or visit Rose Hill Mansion for admission.

119) New Land Vineyard

New Land Vineyard, established in 1988 on fifty acres by Andy and Nancy Burdick, is located at 577 Lerch Road, five miles south of Geneva, on the east side of Seneca Lake. They chose the name New Land for their winery because Nancy's maiden name is Newland, and also because they gave the land a new purpose, from growing corn to growing grapes.

The Burdicks, who specialize in Vinifera wines, grafted their own vines in 1982 and planted their first three acres in 1983; by 1989, they had ten acres under cultivation. They have planted Chardonnay, Riesling, Gewürztraminer, Cabernet Sauvignon, Pinot Noir, Merlot and Sauvignon Blanc. They also have produced blended wines, such as their Merlot / Cabernet Sauvignon blend.

120) Sampson State Park—Romulus

Sampson State Park is located on 1,852 acres at 6096 Route 96A, Romulus, twelve miles south of Geneva. The terrain is flat and rolling woodlands crossed by ravines. It encompasses the former Indian village of Kendaia, which was eventually settled and developed by farmers. In 1942, the area became the Sampson Naval Training Station; after World War II, it was converted to Sampson State College for returning servicemen. The U.S. Air Force reopened it as a training station during the Korean War. The Air Force used it until 1955; in 1960, the State of New York purchased Sampson for use as a State Park.

The Park has 245 electric camping sites, picnic areas with tables and fireplaces, playing fields, a playground, hot showers, a trailer dumping station, and flush toilets. It also has a concession stand, a pavilion, and a recreation building. Pay telephones are available, and the Park is accessible to the handicapped. Sampson State Park has boat launch facilities and a marina with 126 berths (seasonal and transient).

The Sampson WW-2 Navy Museum is located in the original Navy brig (jail) facility at Sampson State Park. The Sampson Naval Training Station trained 411,429 men and women beginning in 1942. The Training Station also housed the largest Naval Hospital on the eastern seaboard. The Museum was created by the thousands of members of the Sampson WW-2 Navy Veterans organization, and funding was provided by the membership and from American Legion Posts and Veterans of Foreign Wars organizations around the country. Members of the Sampson WW-2 Navy Veterans organization and the U.S. Department of the Navy contributed the artifacts on display in the Museum.

121) The Three Bears—Ovid

Along Main Street (Route 414) in the village of Ovid are three identical red-brick Greek Revival buildings, differing only in size. The buildings are called Big Bear, Middle Bear, and Little Bear by area residents. They are the result of a power struggle between Ovid and Waterloo, each of which wanted to be the county seat of Seneca County during the 1800s.

The compromise was to build two county court houses and two county clerk offices, one set in each village. Every three years, the furniture, records, and heating stove of the county clerk's office were packed up and moved twenty-two miles. The larger village, Waterloo, finally won out, and is now the county seat of Seneca County.

Big Bear housed the county courtroom in Ovid, and the top floor has remained virtually unchanged since 1845. It is a bare-bones room with wooden benches that were filled with people who listened to a speech in 1857 by Horace Greeley, editor of The New York *Tribune*. The room still contains its original table and an extra-thick door to thwart eavesdroppers. The first floor of Big Bear later housed the county health and social services departments.

Middle Bear formerly housed the county clerk's office, then served as the library, and then became an office for the Seneca County Sheriff's Department. Little Bear was originally the county clerk's office, before it was moved to Middle Bear, and was used, after 1930, as the meeting place for the Ovid post of the Sons of the Union Veterans, a national fraternal organization that commemorates the lives of soldiers of the Civil War.

122) Lodi Point State Marine Park

Lodi Point State Marine Park is located on Lodi Point Road, off Route 414, two miles west of Lodi. It has marina facilities with over twenty-two berths for boats up to thirty feet long, a four bay-boat launch, and a pumpout station. Generous parking, picnic facilities, and a modern comfort station with potable water are available.

123) Lamoreaux Landing Wine Cellars

Lamoreaux Landing Wine Cellars, located at 9224 Route 414, Lodi, on the east side of Seneca Lake, is owned by Mark Wagner. Mark's family have been vineyardists for many years. Award-winning Lamoreaux Landing Wine Cellars, which is named for an old steamboat landing on the property, was established in 1990.

The Wine Cellar's annual gallonage is over 8,500. Their

goal is to produce wines for the premium and ultra-premium market. Lamoreaux Landing specializes in Vinifera wines, including Dry Riesling, Semi-dry Riesling, Gewürztraminer, and barrel-fermented Chardonnay, as well as Brut and Blanc de Blanc sparkling wine using the Méthode Champenoise.

Mark Wagner hopes to expand the appreciation of red Vinifera wine made in the Finger Lakes Region. The Winery produces a full-bodied Pinot Noir, which is in contrast to many of the light-bodied and medium-bodied Pinot Noir wines made in the region, as well as Cabernet Franc, Cabernet Sauvignon, and Merlot.

Lamoreaux Landing constructed a new winery in 1992 and an addition in 1996. The tall, narrow, multi-level central structure with four large square columns in front catches visitors' eyes as they drive along Route 414. It was designed by California Architect Bruce Corson, son of Cornell President Emeritus Dale Corson, in "Greek-revival barn" style.

124) Wagner Vineyards and Ginny Lee Café

The Wagner Vineyards Winery, established in 1979 at 9322 Route 414, Lodi, on the east side of Seneca Lake, is the only winery in the Finger Lakes region that is octagon-shaped. It is an efficient design with an earthen core used for fermenting and aging wine surrounded by the crushing and pressing facilities, fermenting tanks, bottling line, tasting room, and retail store. All of the Wagner wines are estate bottled, that is, they are made from grapes grown in the 250-acre Wagner Vineyards.

The Winery is known for quality wines including Chardonnay, Johannisberg Riesling, Gewürztraminer, and barrel-fermented Seyval Blanc, as well as Cabernet Franc, Cabernet Sauvignon, and Merlot. Wagner Vineyards also produces blended wine, such as Reserve Red, White, and Blush, and a semi-sweet Alta B., named for Bill Wagner's mother. Wagner's makes wine from a few native American varieties, such as Delaware and Niagara, and they also make a brut champagne using the Méthode Champenoise.

Wagner opened the Ginny Lee Café, named for his grand-daughter, at the winery in 1983, and it has proved to be a pop-ular addition. The café dining room was enclosed in 1990 with windows to the north, west, and south to take advantage of the spectacular view. Bill established the café to stress "the link between wine and food and the fact that wine is food."

In 1997, the Wagner Brewing Company, which initially offered four ales and two lagers, was added to Wagner Vineyards. The brewing company began with a twenty-barrel, German-style brewhouse with three vessels: a mash mixer / kettle, a lauter run, and a whirlpool.

125) Bagley's Poplar Ridge Vineyards

Bagley's Poplar Ridge Vineyards is located on Route 414, just north of the village of Valois, on the east side of Seneca Lake. The owner and winemaker of Poplar Ridge Vineyards is David Bagley, whose motto, as displayed on his wine labels, is "wine without bull." One of his goals is also displayed on his labels: "... to produce wines that people can enjoy and feel comfortable with on any occasion. We hate to see people intimidated by the pretentious attitudes ... that take all the fun out of wine."

Poplar Ridge Vineyards produces Johannisberg Riesling wine and wine made from French-American hybrid grapes, such as Cayuga White, Ravat 51 (Vignoles), and Seyval Blanc. The winery also produces Dave's Big Red (Cabernet Sauvignon and Carmine), Queen of Diamonds (Cayuga and Concord), and Valois Rouge (Chelois and Cayuga) and offers a white blend, Landlocked White, and a premium apple wine, One-Eyed Jack. Poplar Ridge Vineyards also has planted Baco Noir, Cabernet Franc, Malbec, and Merlot vines.

126) Silver Thread Vineyard

Silver Thread Vineyard, located at 1401 Caywood Road, Caywood, is an environmentally sensitive winery that produces wine from certified organic grapes. Their grapes are grown without the use of synthetic pesticides, herbicides, or chemical fertilizers. Silver Thread Vineyard specializes in dry Vinifera table wines. Chardonnay, Pinot Noir, and semi-dry Riesling are some of the wines for which they are known. The Winery also offers blends, such Good Earth White (Chardonnay predominates) and Medley (Riesling and Gewürztraminer).

The turtle image on Silver Thread Vineyard wine labels was carved on a rock along a woodland creek in the Region many centuries ago. The turtle was an earth symbol in the culture of the Iroquois Confederacy.

127) Standing Stone Vineyard
Standing Stone Vineyard, located at 9934 Route 414, Valois, is owned and operated by Tom and Marti Macinski. The Vineyard was named for the People of the Standing Stone for whom the early Dutch fur traders in the region searched. Standing Stone Vineyard produces Chardonnay, Dry and Semi-Dry Riesling, and Gewürztraminer wine, which is made in the Alsatian style.

Standing Stone Vineyard was one of the earliest vineyards in the region to grow the Cabernet Franc grape, from which they produce an award-winning Cabernet Franc wine. They also produce Merlot wine and Pinnacle, a red Vinifera blend. Standing Stone's Dry Vidal Blanc is aged in oak barrels, and they also make a popular Semi-Dry Vidal wine.

128) Hazlitt 1852 Vineyards
Hazlitt 1852 Vineyards is located on a farm that has been in the family since 1852 and is currently operated by fifth and sixth generation Hazlitts. It is located on Route 414 at Hector, ten miles north of Watkins Glen, on the east side of Seneca Lake. Until 1985, when Jerry and Elaine Hazlitt opened the winery, the Hazlitt farm supplied quality grapes to wineries in the region.

Hazlitt 1852 Vineyards makes wine from vinifera varieties, including Chardonnay, Riesling, Cabernet Sauvignon, and Merlot; French-American hybrids; and native grape varieties, such as Catawba from which they make the popular Red Cat wine. Their French-American hybrid wines include Baco Noir, Cayuga White, Chablis (a blend of Aurora and Seyval Blanc), Ravat 51 (Vignoles), Vidal Blanc, and L'Ambertille— a little-grown hybrid. The Winery's blends, including Cabin Fever, Schooner White, Schooner Red, and White Stag, are also popular.

Their winetasting room, with a horseshoe-shaped tasting bar and the smell of freshly-popped popcorn, has a friendly, relaxed atmosphere fostered by members of the Hazlitt family. The room is a compact museum of local history, with Seneca Indian artifacts, antique tools, and other local memorabilia. The Winery is open all year; heat is provided by a large Round Oak wood stove during the winter months.

129) Finger Lakes Dixieland Jazz Festival

The annual Finger Lakes Dixieland Jazz Festival, a benefit for Schuyler County Emergency Services, is held in late summer by the Valois-Logan-Hector Fire Company, on Route 414, Hector. The Festival, which began in 1975, starts at noon and features about eight dixieland bands; each plays for approximately a hour. A huge circus tent is erected on the grounds, and the festival goes on rain or shine.

The Fire Company prepares barbecued chicken, which is available by itself or as part of a dinner. A row of stands provides sort-order food items such as hamburgers, hot dogs, sausages, and beverages. Many of the area wineries have their wine for sale. The Hazlitt 1852 Winery is adjacent to the fire company grounds. Chairs are provided inside the tent, but many fans bring their own blankets and lawn chairs. A group of Dixieland enthusiasts marches around the tent twirling their parasols (or umbrellas) and having a good time, just like (or almost like) New Orleans.

130) Finger Lakes National Forest

The 13,232-acre Finger Lakes National Forest is in the area between the southern halves of Seneca and Cayuga Lakes. The National Forest began as the Hector Land Use Area in 1938, when about 100 marginal farms were purchased by the Federal Government and placed under the control of the Soil Conservation Service.

Many of the farms in the Hector Hills area had been farmed since General Sullivan's soldiers returned to the area to live after the Revolutionary War. By 1900, the farmers were dealing not only with soil depletion, but also with competition from larger, more fertile farms in the Midwest. The Resettlement Administration helped the farmers relocate to more productive locations or to take up more lucrative trades.

In the late 1950s, the multiple land use concept was applied to the Hector Land Use Area. It involves managing the use of forest resources for grazing, recreation, timber, watershed measures, and wildlife. The Hector Land Use Area became part of the National Forest System in 1983, and in 1985 became the "Hector Ranger District" of the Finger Lakes National Forest.

Recreation activities in the National Forest include:

- Car travel through the forest, much of it along ridges. Forest roads are maintained for summer use; selected roads are open in the winter.
- Blueberry picking. Five acres of wild blueberries adjacent to the Blueberry Patch Campground are managed for picking. Apples, raspberries, and other fruit are abundant throughout the Forest.
- Hunting and fishing. New York State hunting and fishing licenses are required, and all state laws are applicable.
- Observing nature and wildlife. A multitude of wildflowers and many varieties of trees, including basswood, black walnut, Norway spruce, oak, shagbark hickory, sugar maple, and white ash enhance the forest. Game-

302

birds, such as pheasants, ruffed grouse, and wild turkey roam the forest, and birdwatchers will see brown creepers, chickadees, eastern bluebirds, mourning doves redbreasted and white-breasted nuthatches, rufous-sided towhees (spotted towhees), and woodpeckers, including the uncommon pileated woodpecker.

- Camping in three developed campgrounds:

BLUEBERRY PATCH CAMPGROUND—picnic area, nine sites for tents or self-contained RVs, a hand-pump well, and vault toilets. A fee is charged for overnight use.

POTOMAC GROUP CAMPGROUND—a open picnic shelter, cooking grills, a hand-pump well, and vault toilets. It is intended for use by groups of ten to forty people; a fee is charged for reserved use of the site.

BACKGROUND TRAILHOOD—designed for picnicking or overnight camping by horseback riders. Facilities include parking spaces with hitching rails, cooking grills, and vault toilets.

- Cross-country skiing, hiking, horseback riding, and snow mobiling. Over twenty-five miles of interconnecting trails are maintained in the National Forest, including two miles of the Finger Lakes Trail, which connects to the Appalachian Trail, and the twelve-mile-long Interloken National Recreation Trail. A shelter is available at the southern end of the Interloken Trail.
- Twenty-five ponds have been constructed throughout the Forest to attract waterfowl and to provide limited public fishing. Free camping is allowed in the Forest, except in areas marked otherwise such as Blueberry Patch and Potomac Group Campgrounds.

Belhurst Castle, Geneva

SENECA LAKE—WEST SIDE

131) Geneva-on-the-Lake Resort

Geneva-on-the-Lake is a European-style vacation resort on the west shore of Seneca Lake at 1001 Lochland Road, on Route 14, south of Geneva's old-world historic district.

The white Italianate villa, which has been nominated for the National Registry of Historic Places, is a replica of the Lancellotti Villa in Frascati, Italy. It is located on ten acres with a formal, hedged garden, a seventy-foot swimming pool, tall pines, and a path through woods to the lakeshore. The garden is bordered by Greek and Roman statues of Venus, Hermes, and Venus de Milo; the swimming pool is surrounded by columns topped with clay jardinieres in the style of a Borghese garden.

Geneva-on-the-Lake has twenty-nine suites, nineteen with one bedroom and ten with two bedrooms. Each suite has a living room, kitchen, and a full bath or a bath and a half.

The villa was built in 1912 by the Nester family as a private residence. The Capuchin Monks bought the villa from the Nesters and between 1949 and the early 1970s used it as a monastery. The Schickel family of Ithaca and Ohio purchased the resort and authorized a $2,000,000 renovation.

Geneva-on-the-Lake has a dock, boathouse, moorings, and sailing facilities; guests may bring their own boat or rent one. The Resort has conference facilities for executive meetings of up to thirty-five people, with three conference rooms. Geneva-on-the-Lake has a four-diamond rating from the American Automobile Association. Also, it is a member of the Organization of Distinguished Inns and Historic Hotels.

132) Belhurst Castle—Historic Restaurant and Inn

Belhurst Castle, an inn and restaurant constructed of red Medina stone, is located on Route 14, just south of the Geneva city line. The Castle, with its twenty-five acres of sweeping lawn, gardens, and over 100-year-old maples, oaks, and pines overlooking the west shore of Seneca Lake, has been a home, a speakeasy, a casino, and a restaurant. Belhurst ("beautiful forest") Castle was constructed from 1885 to 1889 in Richardson Romanesque style, mainly of materials imported from Europe.

In 1885, Carrie Harron Collins, a newly married Cincinnati society figure and a descendent of Henry Clay, commissioned architect Albert W. Fuller to design the castle home in which she and her husband lived for forty years. Fuller designed it with turrets, a covered carriage entrance, a third-floor Victorian dancing room, and carved wood paneling for both private and public rooms.

After the death of Mrs. Collins in 1926, Belhurst Castle was purchased by a local gambler, Cornelius "Red" Dwyer. Born in Lyons, New York, the flamboyant Dwyer worked as a fireman on the railroad and moved in the milieu of plush gambling halls across the State during prohibition. He operated the Castle as a speakeasy with a gambling casino on the second floor. Many well-known performers, including Sophie Tucker, entertained guests during those years. The upstairs gaming rooms were closed in the early 1950s when Dwyer was summoned to hearings in Washington conducted by Senator Estes Kefauver.

Part of the Belhurst Castle is now operated as an inn with thirteen rooms, including two two-room suites. The spacious guest rooms, all with modern baths, are furnished with valuable antiques and oriental rugs, and most of them have working fireplaces.

Dinner is usually accompanied by piano music. As a pleasant after-dinner pastime, guests can sit in the ornate parlor, with its carved white Honduran mahogany moldings, quarter-cut cherry mantelpieces, and white oak banisters, and listen to the music. Or they may walk across the lawn, sit on the park benches overlooking Seneca Lake, and watch the boats go by. While relaxing, they can speculate on a tale in the brochure that describes Belhurst Castle: "Tales persist of the romantic past that began before the present structure was built—of the doomed romance of the runaway Spanish Don and his beautiful Italian opera singer ladylove who once lived here, of secret tunnels and hidden treasures buried in the walls or on the grounds, of ghosts and hauntings, Fact or fancy? No one knows."

133) Fox Run Vineyards

Fox Run Vineyards, owned by Scott Osborn and Andy Hale, is located at 670 Route 14, Penn Yan, town of Benton, eight miles south of Geneva on the west side of Seneca Lake. The Winery is located on a 110-acre farm, complete with a Victorian-style house with natural mahogany, cherry, and chestnut woodwork, and a circa 1860s barn. In 1984, the vineyard was started when Chardonnay and Riesling vines were grafted onto hardy rootstocks and planted in an eight-acre vineyard.

Fox Run specializes in the European varieties of grapes, particularly Chardonnay, Riesling, Merlot, and Pinot Noir. They also make Ruby Vixen, a rosy blush; Arctic Fox, a crisp, white table wine; Brut Sparkling Wine, made using the Méthode Champenoise; and Blanc de Blanc, a crisp, clean sparkling wine. Fox Run now has more than fifty acres under cultivation and has purchased over 100 additional acres of adjacent land to expand the vineyard further. Fox Run Vineyards has a gift shop and offers winery tours.

134) Anthony Road Wine Company

Anthony Road Wine Company is located at 1225 Anthony Road, Penn Yan, off Route 14, about seven miles south of Geneva. It was established in 1989 by John Martini and his wife, Ann, and their partners, Derek and Donna Wilber. John has been growing wine grapes in the region for many years, and is a former president of the New York Wine Grape Growers. Derek is an experienced winemaker who was formerly winemaker for Finger Lakes Wine Cellars.

Anthony Road Wine Company produces wine from European grape varieties, such as Chardonnay, Riesling, and Cabernet Franc, as well as French-American grapes, including Seyval Blanc and Ravat 51 (Vignoles). The Wine Company also offers blends, such as Poulet Rouge, Tony's Red, Vintner's Red, and Vintner's Select. Anthony Road produces over 9,000 cases of wine a year.

135) Robert G. Ingersoll Birthplace Museum—Dresden

Robert Green Ingersoll, the foremost orator of his day, was born on August 11, 1833, at Dresden. Later in life, Ingersoll lived in Peoria, Illinois, where he was a successful lawyer, politician, family man, and philanthropist. He was known as the "Great Infidel" because he didn't believe in any organized religion. However, those who knew him saw his positive side. A Rochester *Democrat* columnist wrote that "Robert G. Ingersoll is not orthodox in theory, but we should like to see a better Christian in practice ... It is really so nice an article of infidelity that a good deal of it might be passed around with entire safety."

His rousing "Plumed Knight" speech nominating James G. Blaine for President at the 1876 Republican National Convention made Ingersoll a national figure. Many famous people were awed by his oratorical ability. Mark Twain said about an Ingersoll speech: "It was the supremest combination of English words that was ever put together since the world began." Reverend Henry Ward Beecher thought that Ingersoll was "the most brilliant speaker of the English tongue of all men on the globe." Elizabeth Cady Stanton listened to him speak for three hours to 3,000 people, who afterwards called him back for a thirty-minute encore.

Ingersoll's creed was:

> Justice is the only worship.
> Love is the only priest.
> Ignorance is the only slavery.

Happiness is the only good.
The time to be happy is now,
The place to be happy is here,
The way to be happy is to make others so.

The Robert Ingersoll Birthplace Museum is located on Main Street in Dresden across the street from the U.S. Post Office. The house in which Ingersoll was born has been restored three times, in 1921, 1954, and 1987. Letters, artifacts, and memorabilia bring Ingersoll and his era to life. Visitors can view a short video on his life and times. The room in which he was born has been restored with authentic furnishings.

The Museum's Dresden Room spotlights other aspects of local history, including:

• Early settlement of the Finger Lakes Region
• Yates County and the area circa 1833
• Issues and events of Ingersoll's public life
• America from the Civil War until the Guilded Age

The Museum is maintained by the R.G. Ingersoll Memorial Committee, Box 664, Amherst, NY.

136) Prejean Winery

Prejean Winery, established in 1985, is located at 2634 Route 14, Penn Yan, just south of Dresden on the west side of Seneca Lake. Elizabeth Prejean and her son, Tom, run the Winery and tend the over thirty-three acres vineyards currently under cultivation. The vineyard has Chardonnay, Riesling, Gewürztraminer, and Merlot Vinifera vines as well as Cayuga, Marechal Foch, and Vignoles French-American hybrid vines.

Prejean Winery is known for its Gewürztraminer and is striving for excellence with its premium Chardonnay. The Winery also produces Cabernet Franc and Merlot and is increasing its planting of red grape vines. They produced 6,400 gallons of wine from their first crop in 1985 and, by 1992, production had increased to 12,000 gallons. Their over 6,000-square-foot facility, with a beautiful view of the lake, accommodates the crushing, pressing, aging, warehousing, tasting, and retailing needs of the Winery.

137) Four Chimneys Farm Winery

Four Chimneys Farm Winery, established by Walter Pedersen and Scott Smith in 1980, is located on Hall Road, just off Route 14 in Himrod, about fifteen miles north of Watkins Glen on the west side of Seneca Lake. It was the first organic winery in the Finger Lakes Region.

Four Chimneys has two goals in organic viticulture: to spare the wine drinker from harmful residuals in the wine from chemicals used in the vineyard and to safeguard the environment. They use a cover crop of clover between the rows of grapevines as a source of nitrogen, and pheromone traps (sexual scent attractors) and "sticky stakes" (fly tapes with color or scent attractors) instead of chemical insecticides. Most vineyardists add only two ingredients to the soil, usually nitrogen for the vines and potash for the grapes; Four Chimneys adds about twenty natural elements, including boron and manganese, to balance the soil and enhance the vigor of the vines.

The Winery also takes an organic approach to winemaking by using an extensive, progressive filtration system to prevent spoilage by refermentation of the cold-stabilized finished wine. Four Chimney's Reserve White is a blend of Chardonnay and Aurora. They also make wine from the native grape varieties, such as Golden Crown—a blend of Catawba, Delaware, and Niagara. Another wine made from a native variety is Eye of the Bee, which is made from Concord grapes and honey, from their own hives, to counter the foxy or grapey Concord taste.

The property includes an Italianate chateau with four

chimneys and a Victorian barn. The Winery has special events thoughout the summer, such as the Lake Seneca Chamber Music Series.

138) Hermann J. Wiemer Vineyard

Hermann J. Wiemer Vineyard, Inc., is located on Route 14, fourteen miles north of Watkins Glen, on the west side of Seneca Lake. The Winery makes wine from Vitis Vinifera grapes, the world's premier grapes. They specialize in Johannisberg Riesling, Chardonnay, and Gewürztraminer and produce a Naturel sparkling wine from Riesling grapes and a Blanc de Noir from Chardonnay and Pinot Noir grapes using the classic Méthode Champenoise. The Winery also produces Pinot Noir wine and a limited quantity of a Trockenberenauslese-style wine made from individual bunch-selected late harvest Riesling grapes affected with botrytis, the "noble mold."

Hermann Wiemer, whose family has been involved in the wine industry in the Mosel Valley in Germany for over 300 years, immigrated to the United States in 1968. He was raised in Berkastel Kues, where his father ran the agricultural exper-iment station. He received his education in the Rheinpfalz and Rheingau districts of Germany. From 1968 to 1980, Wiemer was the winemaker for Walter Taylor at Bully Hill Winery, which specializes in French-American hybrid wines.

While at Bully Hill, Wiemer received medals for his Chancellor Noir and Seyval Blanc wines, but he wanted to work with Vinifera grapes. He purchased 140 acres of land overlooking Seneca Lake in 1973 and planted ten acres with hand-grafted vines. By 1988, eighty-five acres were under cultivation. The Winery also has sixteen acres of Chardonnay and Riesling and over twenty acres of other Vinifera varieties planted near Dresden. Hermann J. Wiemer Vineyards wines have been selected to be served on first-class American Airlines domestic flights and international flights to Switzerland and Germany.

Hermann Wiemer also runs a successful vine nursery operation, one of the largest in the United States, with production averaging nearly 300,000 plants annually. Vitis Vinifera vines are less winter-hardy and more susceptible to the phylloxera root louse than other varieties, such as native American and French-American hybrid vines; therefore, they are grafted onto sturdier root stock. Grafted Vinifera vines from the Wiemer Nursery have been used to establish Vinifera vineyards across the country.

139) Squaw Point Winery

Squaw Point Winery is on Poplar Point Road, off Route 14, about ten miles north of Watkins Glen, on the west side of Seneca Lake. Traveling from the north, the Squaw Point barrel people (people made with a barrel as their body and flexible tubing as arms and legs) on the right side of Route 14, just north of the turn-off onto Poplar Point Road, mark the entrance road to the Winery. A four-story fire tower, topped with a windpower generator, stands adjacent to the Winery.

Squaw Point Winery owner David Miles claims that these oak barrel figures tell him when to pick the grapes and how to proceed with the crushing and pressing. He says that the "Prince of Frogs" on his wine labels, a frog dressed in a Renaissance costume, is in charge of the barrel people.

Squaw Point Winery groups its wines into three categories: Semi-dry—Chardonnay, Seyval Blanc, Cayuga White, and Leon and Friends (a red blend of Leon Millot, Baco Noir, and Foch) and Riesling; Semi-sweet—Cabo (a blend of DeChaunac and Leon Millot), Moonglow (a blush that includes Cayuga and Leon Millot), Morning Mist (a blend that includes Chardonnay and Cayuga), Sweetheart (a blend of Niagara and Cayuga), Irby (a red blend of DeChaunac and Colobel), and Ravat; and Exotic—Amity (a blend of Baco Noir and Catawba), Icedela, an ice wine made with Delaware grapes, and Spice (a blush wine). The Winery provides picnic tables.

140) Glenora Wine Cellars

Glenora Wine Cellars, the largest winery on Seneca Lake, overlooks the western shore of the Lake at 5435 Route 14, Dundee, about eight miles north of Watkins Glen. Established in 1977, Glenora initially specialized in white wines, but has expanded into award-winning sparkling wines and red Vinifera wines, such as Cabernet Sauvignon and Merlot.

Glenora's wine from Vinifera grapes includes Chardonnay and a Chardonnay Reserve that has undergone malolactic fermentation (a step that reduces the acid in the finished wine), Johannisberg Riesling with a touch of sweetness, as well as a Dry Riesling and a spicy Gewürztraminer. Their 1987 Chardonnay was served at the Inaugural Dinner of George Bush in 1989.

Glenora's sparkling wines are Brut (a Pinot Noir-Chardonnay blend aged two to three years), Brut Reserve (predominantly Pinot Noir blended with Chardonnay and aged three to four years), and Blanc de Blancs (made from Chardonnay and aged eighteen months). In 1990, their 1987 Blanc de Blancs was served at a reception to honor Her Royal Highness Princess Anne of Great Britain.

Glenora takes full advantage of the viticultural diversity of New York State by using grapes from vineyards on three of the Finger Lakes and from the North Fork of Long Island. Some of the grapes used to make Glenora's Cabernet Sauvignon and Merlot wines are from Long Island, which has a slightly longer growing season than the Finger Lakes Region. Merlot is the variety that the French blend with Cabernet Sauvignon and small percentages of other varieties, such as Malbec, to make a more mellow Bordeaux. Glenora also uses Chardonnay grapes from Long Island in some of their wines.

In addition, Glenora makes French-American hybrid white wines, Cayuga Blanc and Seyval Blanc, as well as First Blush, a blend of Baco Noir, Cayuga, and Pinot Noir. Glenora does not offer a winery tour, but they show a well-produced video of their winery operations.

Glenora Wine Cellars brings world-class jazz to the region each summer with their concert series. Musicians who have performed in the concerts include David Benoit, Ramsey Lewis, the Gary Burton Quintet, Stanley Jordan and Trio, the Branford Marsalis Quartet, Chuck Mangione, Dave Brubeck, and Herbie Mann. The concerts, which began in 1983, are held in the area behind the Winery. Most seating is on the lawn; many concertgoers bring a blanket or lawn chair. Food and wine are on sale.

KEUKA LAKE

141) Keuka Lake
Keuka Lake is called the "Lady of the Lakes" because of its natural beauty. The Indian name Keuka means "canoe landing" but it was called Crooked Lake by the early white settlers. It is unique among the Finger Lakes because it is Y-shaped with a scenic bluff over seven hundred feet above lake level between the two branches of the Y, and it is the only Finger Lake that outlets into another Finger Lake—into Seneca Lake at Dresden.

The inlet is at Hammondsport at the southern end of the twenty-mile-long lake, and the outlet is at Penn Yan at the northern end of the east branch of the Y. Branchport is at the northern end of the west branch, the branch with the deepest point in the Lake, 187 feet. Its average width is three-quarters of a mile, and it is two miles wide at its widest point—the widewaters area just south of the bluff. The shoreline of the Lake is just under sixty miles long. Keuka Lake is one of the cleanest of the Finger Lakes and is rated excellent for fishing.

142) Keuka College
Keuka College is a coeducational, non-denominational four-year college founded as the Keuka Institute in 1890. The college corporation was formed in 1888, and the 160-acre

Ketchum farm on the lake, four miles south of Penn Yan, was purchased as the site for the new educational institution. Portions of the old Ketchum farm were sold as building lots to aid in financing the construction of buildings. Ball Memorial Hall, the central campus building, was the first building constructed.

The College, founded as a coeducational institution, became a college for women in 1921, but resumed its coeducational status in the 1970s. The College provides over twenty-two degree programs and its excellent teaching faculty, low student-to-professor ratio, and Field Period experience provide an educational opportunity that is not widely available. The Field Period Experience Program distinguishes it from many other small, private colleges. For five weeks each school year, Keuka College students leave the classroom to try out a career possibility, develop professional skills, or fulfill a personal goal. This may take the form of independent research, group experience, or work in a professional organization.

The College's seventy-fifth anniversary was celebrated during the 1964-65 academic year with the dedication of the Arthur H. Norton Chapel. The religious center is located on the lake shore facing the other campus buildings; it is a visual focus for the entire campus. The Chapel was designed on the plan of a Latin cross. The soaring roof of heavy cedar shingles reaches a height of sixty-eight feet, with a cross-topped bronze spire reaching to 110 feet. The Chapel seats 650 and has a 2,469-pipe organ.

The outer walls are made of granite-faced, off-white masonry, and there are stained-glass windows, created by Gabriel Loire of Chartres, France, on three walls (above the entrance and in each transcept). The building material came from many places: the white marble in the chancel platform from Vermont, the Douglas Fir in the timber trusses from Oregon, the cedar in the ceiling decking from the Pacific Coast, the heavy cedar-shake shingles from Canada, and the blown-glass spheres in the chandeliers from Italy.

The College's Lightner Library has stack space for over 150,000 volumes and a reading room that accommodates 400 people. The Library also provides a comprehensive inter-library loan program. The Weed Physical Arts Center invites people of all ages to participate in its many programs, such as aqua exercise, swimming lessons, and other classes, along with summer athletic camps for youths. The Weed Center's gymnasium, pool, weight room, and waterfront are open to the public for a nominal fee.

143) Keuka Arts Festival

The Keuka Arts Festival, an annual event since 1977, is held on the Keuka College Campus at Keuka Park, four miles south of Penn Yan, off Route 54A. A group of local artists established the Festival to promote art in Yates County. In recent years, attendance has been over 10,000 for the two-day show.

Over 160 artists and artisans display their work about the second weekend in August, with exhibits of drawings, jewelry, needlework, paintings, photography, sculpture, and textiles, as well as flowers, herbs, and plants. Also displayed are works made of glass, leather, and textiles, along with demonstrations of activities such as basket-weaving, broom-making, portrait-painting, and wood-carving.

The Festival includes a children's theatre with group songs and stories, special programs such as juggling and sock puppets, educational exhibits, formal and informal musical entertainment, and an interfaith worship service at the Norton Chapel of Keuka College. Examples of the musical entertainment in recent years are a barbershop chorus and quartet, Ed Klute's Dixieland Band, the Dundee Steel Band, the Mansfield University Brass Quartet, the Seneca Chamber Players, the Silvertones Flute Choir, and the "Storm" variety band playing music of the 1940s to the 1990s.

The special events in past years have included a carousel-

horse carving demonstration, clowns, an Elizabethan drama-
tist, Karvel the Magician, a presentation of restored antique
cars by the Western New York Antique Car Society, an exhibit of renderings of automobiles by Ray Noble, the Western
New York Cloggers Association Appalachian / Irish Dancers,
and a wind-surfing demonstration.

An Invitational Art Show displaying the work of painters
and sculptors at the College's Lightner Gallery has also been
popular at past festivals. In 1991, the first annual Keuka Lake
Wooden Boat Festival was held on the lakefront at Keuka
College, as an adjunct to the Keuka Arts Festival.

144) Keuka Outlet Trail

The outlet from Keuka Lake drops about 300 feet in elevation
over its six-mile length from Penn Yan on Keuka Lake to
Dresden on Seneca Lake. The outlet, called Minneseta by the
Seneca Indians, today has the appearance of a trout stream for
most of its length. Over its history, the Keuka outlet has been
a navigable canal with twenty-seven locks, part of a railroad
bed, and the site of over eleven mills, factories and distilleries.

Among the first settlers to the area were twenty-five members of a religious sect in 1788 led by James Parker, a follower of Jemima Wilkinson, an evangelical, non-denominational preacher known as the Publick Universal Friend. The
sect, which originated in Rhode Island, decided to move to
the wilderness to get away from the world's temptations.
Initially, they chose a site called City Hill near Dresden, one
mile south of the outlet stream. Later, they moved to a site
located north of Branchport and named their settlement
Jerusalem or Friend's Settlement after their leader.

In 1790, the town of City Hill had a population of 260 people, which was more than Canandaigua and Geneva combined. The followers of the Publick Universal Friend built the
first mill on the Keuka outlet, about halfway between Penn
Yan and Dresden. They constructed it at the highest waterfall

(thirty-five feet high), on the future site of Seneca Mills. They purchased their millstones at New Milford, Connecticut, and hauled them upstream from Dresden on ox sleds.

By 1820, seven gristmills, one oil mill, fourteen sawmills, and several distilleries dotted the length of the outlet. Eventually, the outlet became the home of paper mills, plaster mills, potash mills, tanneries, and factories producing many other products, including chemicals (such as carbon bisulfide), corrugated cardboard, handles, hoops, shingles, wheel spokes, and tools. During the late nineteenth century and the early twentieth century, thirty to forty factories and mills operated at one time.

With the completion of the Erie Canal in 1825, canal-building became a popular activity. The Crooked Lake Canal along the outlet went into operation with twelve dams and twenty-seven lift locks in 1833. Because its expenses consistently exceeded its income, it was abandoned by the state in 1873. However, the outlet survived as a transportation corridor when the Fall Brook Railroad was built in 1884, partly in the canal bed and partly on the towpath. The Railroad spurred a new industry along the outlet, the manufacture of paper from straw. Most of the mills had closed by 1930 and the Railroad, which had become part of the Penn-Central System, was abandoned in 1972, after being severely damaged in the spring flooding that year due to Hurricane Agnes.

The railroad right of way was purchased by Yates County in 1981 at the urging of John Sheridan, the Yates County Attorney. He suggested using the railroad bed for a hiking trail, which is now called the Keuka Outlet Trail. A memorial to John Sheridan, consisting of a large boulder and a brass plaque, is located adjacent to the trail at the Seneca Millsite, near the the Trail's midpoint.

The Outlet Trail is approximately six feet wide for most of its length and is an excellent hiking trail; it slopes sightly downhill from Penn Yan to Dresden. The Trail has eleven millsite markers and is known for its flora and fauna, as well as its history. Several of the mill buildings remain, but most of them are noted by a marker, and, at some sites, a foundation.

145) Buckwheat Festival

The first annual Buckwheat Harvest Festival, held in Penn Yan in 1986, was a two-day festival. It has grown into a three-day festival, with a large number of activities, and visitors have numbered over 40,000. The Festival is held in late September at the Yates County Fairgrounds. It is sponsored by the National Buckwheat Institute in Penn Yan, home of Birkett Mills, one of the largest producers of buckwheat products in the world. Birkett Mills has been in continuous operation since 1824; the mill was constructed on the foundation of the original mill built in 1796 by David Wagener, father of Abraham Wagener, the founder of Penn Yan.

Buckwheat is a member of the rhubarb family, not the wheat family. It is higher in protein than any other plant, contains no cholesterol or fat, has twice as much vitamin B as wheat, and is rich in phosphorus and potassium. Among the food items made from buckwheat, in addition to buckwheat flour, are grits (the heart of choice buckwheat grain), groats (raw dehulled buckwheat grain), and kasha (ground roasted dehulled buckwheat kernels).

At each of the first two annual Buckwheat Harvest Festivals, a record-setting buckwheat pancake was prepared, twenty-five feet in diameter in 1986, and twenty-eight feet, one inch in 1987. The record set at the second festival is documented in the Guinness Book of Records, which listed Penn Yan as the place where the world's largest pancake was made using 2,000 pounds of pancake mix and 2,000 pounds of water.

Festival tent entertainment on Friday and Saturday evenings and on Saturday and Sunday afternoons has included popular musical groups such as Chubby Checker, Lee Greenwood, the Guess Who, Nik & the Nice Guys, Sha-Na-

Na, and the Skycoasters. Special Events have included arts & crafts, circus acts, a classic car show, a fireworks spectacular Friday night, the festival parade on Saturday morning, the "Kasha Klassic" 10K Run on Sunday morning, magicians, photo contests, and recipe contests.

Examples of children's entertainment at previous Festivals are an animated comedy musical show, a dress-up circus, the Greenwood Petting Zoo, a medicine show, midway rides, and puppet shows. The Buckwheat Harvest Festival is a community event with over 1,000 volunteers from almost fifty local non-profit agencies and clubs working together to make the annual event a success.

146) Keuka Spring Winery

The Keuka Spring Winery is located on East Lake Road (Route 54), three miles south of Penn Yan, in a historic setting with an 1840s homestead and a gambrel-roofed barn that contains a rustic winetasting room. Keuka Spring Winery, owned by Judy and Len Wiltberger, produces 2,000 to 3,000 gallons of wine each year from European varieties, such as Chardonnay and Johannisberg Riesling, as well as from French-American Hybrids, such as Seyval Blanc and Vignoles (Ravat 51).

The Wiltbergers planted their first vines in 1981 and produced their first wine in 1985. Keuka Spring makes three blends that have been very successful, Crooked Lake White; Harvest Blush, a blend of Pinot Noir, Seyval, and Ravat; and Harvest White, a semi-dry, German-style blend of Cayuga, Johannisberg Riesling, and Seyval. Picnic tables are provided on the grounds of the winery.

147) Windmill Farm and Craft Market

The Windmill is a large farm market / craft market opened by the area Mennonite community in 1987 on Route 14A, half way between Penn Yan and Dundee, about a ten-minute drive south of Penn Yan. Over 100,000 people visited the Market in its first year of operation. It is modeled on the Green Dragon of Ephrata, Pennsylvania, a huge farmers' market in Pennsylvania Dutch country. The Market has an atmosphere of friendliness and a standard of quality that attracts visitors from many states and Canada.

The Windmill currently houses over 250 vendors in both open and enclosed booths, with space planned for additional stalls. It is open every Saturday from May through December, including Memorial Day, Fourth of July, and Labor Day holidays. The Market offers many events during the season, including music, entertainment, special exhibits and attractions, such as the Dundee Steel Band, horse auctions, rodeos, and Tennessee Walker exhibitions.

A variety of fruit, vegetables, flowers, and plants are sold at the farm market. The Craft Market offers many items produced by the Amish and Mennonite communities, such as accessories, cedar chests, novelties, pottery, quilts, and stained glass. Food items include baked goods, barbecues, bulk foods, candy, cheeses, fresh pretzels, fried dough, homemade chili, ice cream, and meat products. In addition, there are antiques, collectables, a flea market for browsing, a pony wagon ride for children, and a winetasting.

CANANDAIGUA LAKE

148) Canandaigua Lake

The Seneca Indian name, Canandaigua, has been translated both as "a place selected for a settlement" and "the chosen place." The principal inlet to the lake is Naples Creek, at the southern end; the main outlet is the Canandaigua Outlet, at the northern end. Canandaigua Lake is fifteen and a half miles long and one and a half miles wide; it has a shoreline of just under thirty-six miles. The lake is 276 feet deep at its deepest point, and has a volume of 445.5 billion gallons.

Canandaigua Lake has a watershed of 174 square miles; nearly half of the watershed is forested with beech, birch,

Ontario County Courthouse, Canandaigua

hemlock, and oak. The Lake's water quality is high. The water is medium-hard and takes 13.7 years to cycle from the lake.

Squaw Island, a half-acre island at the northern end of the lake, is one of two islands in the Finger Lakes (the other is Frontenac Island in Cayuga Lake). It is owned by the State of New York and maintained by the Department of Environmental Conservation. It was named during the time of General Sullivan's campaign against the Six Nations of the Iroquois Confederacy in 1779, when the women and children of the Seneca village of Kanandarque, now the City of Canandaigua, hid on the island to escape from the soldiers.

149) Finger Lakes Performing Arts Center

The Finger Lakes Performing Arts Center, the summer home of the Rochester Philharmonic Orchestra, is located on the campus of the Finger Lakes Community College at 4355 Lakeshore Drive, off Routes 5 and 20, about a mile east of Canandaigua. The amphitheatre opened in 1983. Indoor seating is available, in addition to lawn seats outside the shell. Concert-goers bring lawn chairs and blankets, and sit on the hillside overlooking the amphitheatre. Picnicking is allowed on the grounds surrounding the shell; refreshments are also available at the Performing Arts Center.

A light classics series of concerts is offered on Saturday evenings during the summer. Two annual events are a July 4th Family Day Concert with fireworks and an 1812 Overture concert, complete with cannons and fireworks. Sunday Evening Pops Concerts are scheduled every summer, as well as rock concerts and many other performances.

150) Thendara Inn—Historic Restaurant and Inn

Thendara Inn is located four miles south of the City of Canandaigua on Route 364 (East Lake Road) on Canandaigua Lake. The fourteen-room Victorian house was built in 1900 by John Raines, State Senator, U.S. Congressman, and

Republican leader of Ontario County. Thendara, a Mohawk Indian word meaning "the meeting place," was built on a bluff on thirty-five acres overlooking Deep Run Cove. Raines was known as the sponsor of "Raines Law," which increased the tax on all hotels that served liquor but specified that only hotels, not bars or restaurants, could serve liquor on Sunday.

The Canandaigua Yacht Club purchased Thendara from the Raines family; it was used as their clubhouse and base for sailing events for many years. C. J. "Jimmie" Miller purchased Thendara in 1975 and converted it into an inn and restaurant. Thendara was renovated in 1988; care was taken to preserve the architectural details of the early 1900s. The Inn has three dining room and can accommodate tour groups, weddings, and receptions and provides catering service. The restaurant can accommodate over sixty people for conferences and retreats. Thendara also has a par three golf course, the Lakeside Links.

EPILOGUE

American Women in the 1990s and the Twenty-First Century

"A revolution has begun and there is no going back. There will be no unravelling of commitments—not today's commitments, not last year's commitments, and not the last decade's commitments. This revolution is too just, too important, and too long overdue."

Gertrude Mongella, Commission on the Status of Women, 1995

Monumental strides have been made in the status of women in the last half of the twentieth century. William H. Chafe summarizes those gains in his book, *The Road to Equality: American Women Since 1962*:

> As the nation prepared to greet the year 2000, there were few issues that seemed as critical to the future direction of American society as what happened to women. The changes over the preceding 60 years had been breathtaking. In 1940 the typical woman worker was young, single, and poor. By the mid-1990s she was married and middle-aged, and her job was indispensible for her family to claim middle-class status. On the eve of World War II only one in four women held jobs outside the home. Fifty years later the figure approached three in four. Divorces and remarriage took place in one of every two unions, as opposed to one in six in 1940. Women medical doctors and lawyers had become almost as familiar a sight as men doctors and lawyers....

These gains did not just occur; many women worked hard to make them happen. In *Moving the Mountain: The Women's Movement in America Since 1960*, Flora Davis refers to the efforts "in Washington and in various state capitals that brought together feminist lawmakers, attorneys, and lobbyists to work on legislation for women. Then there were the women's PACS, the feminist legal services, the women's policy institutes, and the women's caucuses and committees within most professional groups and many unions."

Davis also describes the ongoing activities of the Women's Rights Movement of the 1990s: "The movement had also branched out into global networks; it was linked to the women's peace movement, to the revived welfare rights movement, and to activists who had recently organized to fight for better treatment for women with AIDS. There had been an explosion of organizations for women of color and of groups focused on women's health and spirituality."

Women are making significant inroads in politics. Women voters played a significant role in re-electing Bill Clinton President of the United States in 1996. In 1997, Madeleine Albright became the first woman Secretary of State of the United States. In *Megatrends for Women*, Patricia Aburdene and John Naisbitt identified the trends that are propelling women into leadership positions in politics, including:

- New routes to power that bypass the incumbent-ridden U.S. Congress are increasingly discovered by women. As big-city mayors, state treasurers, and secretaries of state, women can mount successful races for the Senate and governorships.

- Term limits, redistricting, and retirements will help women break the iron lock on con-gressional incumbency.... But in the longer run, the growing demand for term limits will open hundreds of seats to women candidates.

- Money. No longer can it buy a race. Today's voter is too sophisticated to fall for a candidate whose main credential is money. Paradoxically, women are becoming superb fundraisers; qualified women will not lack financial backing.

- The domestic agenda. Education, abortion, the environment, day care—what were once called "women's issues"—concern everyone now. This is where women have experience, confidence, strong feelings, and clear positions.

• Women now dominate the electorate—and consistently support their own. Men give women high marks for honesty, and with anti-incumbent sentiment running high, are willing to give women a chance.

Significant gains have been made in women's sports since Title IX was passed in 1972 forbidding sex discrimination in schools that receive federal funding. In the twenty years following the passing of Title IX, the number of high school girls participating in interscholastic sports increased 500 percent, to two million. The number of college women participating in intercollegiate athletics increased from fifteen percent to thirty-three percent as more sports were opened to them. In the 1992 Winter Olympics, all five gold medals won by the United States were won by women, and nine of the eleven medals won by Americans were won by women.

Women are also making advances in business and industry. Women entrepreneurs are starting small businesses at a greater rate than men entrepreneurs. The glass ceiling still exists, although inroads are being made by women in obtaining equal pay for equal work. However, work content and work efficiency aren't the only issues. Stroock & Stroock Lavan surveyed 4,000 senior executives in the United States who observed that efficiency isn't the only factor in considering a woman for promotion. Other factors such as integrity, loyalty, networking ability, personality, and political skill are more important than efficiency by itself.

The days of the autocratic manager in command-and-control mode are nearing the end. One of the manager of the future's principal goals is to create a nurturing environment for personal growth. The characteristics of the "manager of the future" are surprisingly like the attributes known as women's leadership style. In *Reinventing the Corporation*, John Naisbitt compared the two sets of characteristics, including the following:

Traditional Management	Leadership/Women's Leadership
Objective: Control	Objective: Change
Relies on order-giving	Facilitating / Teaching
Rank	Connections
Knows all the answers	Asks the right questions
Limits and defines	Empowers
Issues orders	Acts as a role model
Imposes discipline	Values creativity
Hierarchy	Networking / Web
Military archetype	Teaching archetype
Punishment	Reward
Bottom line	Vision
Closed: Information = power	Openness
Drill sargeant	Master motivator
Command and control	Empowerment
Rigid	Flexible
Impersonal / objective	Personal

Over the long term, what can be done to make the status of women in society equal to that of men? What can be done to ensure that the capabilities of over fifty percent of the population are optimized? An answer to these two questions is suggested by Riane Eisler in her book, *The Chalice & the Blade: Our History, Our Future*. Eisler describes two distinctly different societies: dominator and partnership.

She observes that "the dominator model is what is popularly termed either patriarchy or matriarchy—the ranking of one half of humanity over the other. The second, in which the social relations are primarily based on the principle of linking rather than ranking, may best be described as the partnership model. In this model—beginning with the most fundamental difference in our species, between male and female—diversity is not equated with either inferiority or superiority."

Eisler adds that "if we are ever to have a truly pluralistic society, where people's differences are freely expressed, celebrated—and utilized for everyone's benefit, it must begin with a partnership between women and men." Her comments are supported by Gertrude Mongella in her article, "Moving Beyond Rhetoric" in *Women: Looking Beyond 2000*, "We have been saying right along that women and men must work together if we are to bring this world safely into the coming century...."

We can look back over history and find many examples where men and women have worked together as a team utilizing their complementary strengths. The synergy of their joint effort sparked achievements that were greater than the sum of their individual contributions.

Two of these teams are Antoinette Brown Blackwell, the first ordained minister in the United States, and her husband, Samuel Blackwell; and Lucretia Coffin Mott and her husband, James Mott, who were leaders in the antislavery movement as well as the Women's Rights Movement.

Antoinette Brown Blackwell expected Samuel Blackwell to share the household responsibilities with her when they married. Samuel supported her in her career as a minister. Frequently, Antoinette was away on the lyceum circuit giving speeches or delivering sermons. On those occasions, Samuel was in charge of the household and children. Antoinette became a prolific author. Samuel, a successful businessman, looked out for the family to allow his wife to have the time and the solitude to write.

Lucretia Mott, the elder stateswoman of the Women's Rights Movement, was used to thinking and speaking for herself because of her early experiences in Quaker meetings. James Mott was a successful businessman who shared his wife's interests and supported her efforts in the antislavery movement and the Women's Rights Movement.

They functioned as a team. Lucretia was the better public speaker, but frequently James had to do the speaking because on many occasions women were not permitted to speak in public, for example, at conventions. Lucretia's achievements were orders of magnitude greater than they would have been without the assistance of her husband.

In *The Chalice & the Blade: Our History, Our Future*, Eisler considers the partnership model a: "'win-win' rather than 'win-lose' view of power, in psychological terms, a means of advancing one's own development without at the same time having to limit the development of others." She has high expectations for the partnership model:

> The changes in woman-man relations from the present high degree of suspicion and recrimination to more openness and trust will be reflected in our families and communities. There will also be positive repercussions in our national and international policies. Gradually, we will see a decrease in the seemingly endless array of day-to-day problems that now plague us....
>
> In the world as it will be when women and men live in full partnership, there will, of course, still be families, schools, governments and other social institutions. But like the already emerging institutions of the egalitarian family and the social-action network, the social structures of the future will be based more on linking than ranking. Instead of requiring people to fit into pyramidal hierarchies, these institutions will be heterarchic, allowing for both diversity and flexibility in decision-making and action. Consequently, the roles of men and women will be far less rigid,

allowing the entire human species a maximum
of developmental flexibility.

Some wishful thinking may exist in the ideas expressed by Riane Eisler. However, we will all benefit if her hopes are achieved. Setting a goal that is somewhat idealistic and difficult to accomplish has considerable merit. Even if we get part of the way or most of the way toward achievement of the goal we will have accomplished something significant, and we will certainly have made notable improvements to the social conditions that exist today.

EPILOGUE POEM

The Times That Try Men's Souls

CONFUSION has seized us, and all things go wrong,
　The women have leaped from "their spheres,"
And instead of fixed stars, shoot as comets along.
　And are setting the world by its ears!
In courses erratic they're wheeling through space,
In brainless confusion and meaningless chase.

In vain do our knowing ones try to compute
　Their return to the orbit designed;
They're glanced at a moment, then onward they shoot,
　And are neither "to hold or to bind;"
So freely they move in their chosen ellipse,
The "Lords of Creation" do fear an eclipse.

They've taken a notion to speak for themselves,
　And are wielding the tongue and the pen;
They've mounted the rostrum; the termagant elves,
　And—oh horrid!—are talking to men!
With faces blanched in our presence they come
To harangue us, they say, in behalf of the dumb.

They insist on their right to petition and pray,
　That St. Paul, in Corinthians, has given them rules
For appearing in public; despite what they say
　Whom we've trained to instruct them in schools;
But vain such instructions, if women may scan
And quote texts of Scripture to favor their plan.

Our grandmother's learning consisted of yore,
    In spreading their generous boards;
In twisting the distaff, or mopping the floor,
    And obeying the will of their Lords.
Now, misses may reason, and think, and debate,
'Til unquestioned submission is quite out of date.

Our clergy have preached on the sin and the shame
    Of women, when out of "her sphere,"
And labored divinely to ruin her fame,
    And shorten this horrid career,
But for spiritual guidance no longer they look
To Fulsom, or Winslow, or learned Parson Cook.

Our wise men have tried to exorcise in vain—
    The turbulent spirits abroad;
As well might we deal with the fetterless main,
    Or conquer ethereal essence with sword,
Like the devils of Milton, they rise from each blow,
With spirit unbroken, insulting the foe.

Our patriot fathers, of eloquent fame,
    Waged war against tangible forms;
Aye, their foes were men—and if ours were the same,
    We might speedily quiet their storms,
But ah! their descendants enjoy not such bliss—
The assumptions of Britain were nothing to this.

Could we but array all our force in the field,
    We'd teach these usurpers of power,
That their bodily safety demands that they should yield,
    And in presence of manhood should cower;
But, alas! for our tethered and impotent state,
Chained by notions of knighthood—we can but debate.

Oh! shade of the prophet Mahomet, arise!
  Place woman again in "her sphere,"
And teach that her soul was not born for the skies,
  But to flutter a brief moment here.
This doctrine of Jesus, as preached by Paul,
If embraced in its spirit will ruin us all.

By Maria W. Chapman

(Read at the Women's Rights Convention in Rochester, NY, on August 2, 1848, in reply to a Pastoral Letter by the "Lords of Creation")

335

Matilda Joslyn Gage House, Fayetteville

CHRONOLOGY

1648 Margaret Brent of Maryland becomes the first
       woman in America to demand the right to vote.
1792 Publication in England of *A Vindication of the Rights
       of Women* by Mary Wollstonecraft.
1828 Frances Wright is the first woman in the United
       State to speak in public before mixed audiences.
1833 The American Anti-Slavery Society is founded.
       Women, who are not permitted to join, form the
       Philadelphia Female Anti-Slavery Society
       headed by Lucretia Mott.
1836 The Married Woman's Property Act is first intro-
       duced to the New York State Legislature.
       Ernestine Rose circulates a petition to support it.
1837 Angelina and Sarah Grimké give antislavery lectures
       before mixed audiences. The Massachusetts
       clergy expresses its objections in a Pastoral
       Letter.
1840 World Anti-Slavery Convention held in London.
       Lucretia Mott and Elizabeth Cady Stanton meet and
       discuss holding a women's rights convention.
       Ernestine Rose, Paulina Wright, and Elizabeth Cady
       Stanton work for the passage of the Married
       Woman's Property Act.
1843 Oberlin College admits women students.
1845 Margaret Fuller's *Woman in the Nineteenth Century*
       published.
       Lucretia Mott gives the first public suffrage speech
       in the U.S.
1847 Lucy Stone makes her first speech in public on the
       subject of women.
1848 Married Woman's Property Act is passed by the New
       York State Legislature.
       Planning meetings in Waterloo on July 9 and July 16
       for the first Women's Rights Convention.

First Women's Rights Convention held in Seneca Falls on July 19-20.

1849 Elizabeth Blackwell receives a medical degree from Geneva College.

1850 First National Women's Rights Convention is held in Worcester, Massachusetts.

1851 Susan B. Anthony and Elizabeth Cady Stanton meet in Seneca Falls.

Bloomer costume is introduced and publicized.

1852 Susan B. Anthony organizes the first Women's State Temperance Society after being denied participation in a Sons of Temperance society convention.

1853 Antoinette Brown is ordained as the first woman minister in the U.S.

1854 Elizabeth Cady Stanton makes her first address to the New York Legislature on the Married Woman's Property Act and women's suffrage.

1860 Elizabeth Cady Stanton again addresses the New York Legislature to request expansion for married women's rights and women's suffrage.

1863 National Woman's Loyal League established by Susan B. Anthony and Elizabeth Cady Stanton.

1865 Women petition Congress for inclusion of women's suffrage in the Fourteenth Amendment and are denied.

1867 Kansas referendum to remove "male" and "white" from voting requirements; both are denied.

Susan B. Anthony and Elizabeth Cady Stanton campaign in Kansas accompanied by George Francis Train, who offers to finance a woman suffrage newspaper.

1868 Publication of the *Revolution* begins.

Woman Suffrage Amendment is introduced to the U.S. Congress for the first time.

1869 The Women's Suffrage Movement splits in two: The "New York" element headed by Susan B. Anthony

and Elizabeth Cady Stanton form the National
Woman Suffrage Association, and the "New
England" contingent led by Lucy Stone forms
the American Woman Suffrage Association.

Territory of Wyoming grants women suffrage.

1870 In Wyoming, Esther Morris is appointed the first
woman Justice of the Peace.

American Woman Suffrage Association begins
publication of the *Woman's Journal*.

Publication of the *Revolution* is discontinued due to
financial difficulties.

1871 Victoria Woodhull presents a speech on women's
suffrage to the U.S. Congress.

1872 Susan B. Anthony is arrested for attempting to vote
in a national election.

1878 "Susan B. Anthony Amendment" introduced to
Congress in the final wording of the Nineteenth
Amendment ratified in 1920.

1880 Lucretia Mott dies in Pennsylvania.

Susan B. Anthony, Matilda Joslyn Gage, and
Elizabeth Cady Stanton begin writing *The History
of Woman Suffrage*.

Elizabeth Cady Stanton attempts unsuccessfully to
vote in Tenafly, NJ.

1890 The two suffrage organizations reunite as the
National American Woman Suffrage Association
with Elizabeth Cady Stanton as president.

Wyoming admitted to the Union as a women's suffrage State.

1892 Elizabeth Cady Stanton resigns as president of the
National American Woman Suffrage Association
and is succeeded by Susan B. Anthony.

1893 Colorado is the first State to grant women's suffrage
by ballot.

New Zealand is the first country to grant full woman
suffrage.

1900 Susan B. Anthony resigns as president of the National American Woman Suffrage Association and is succeeded by Carrie Chapman Catt.

1902 Elizabeth Cady Stanton dies in New Jersey.

1904 Carrie Chapman Catt becomes active in the international suffrage movement, resigns as president of the Suffrage Association, and is succeeded by Anna Howard Shaw.

1906 Susan B. Anthony dies in New York.

1912 Alice Paul founds the Congressional Union for Woman Suffrage, later called the National Woman's Party, in Washington, D.C.

1915 Carrie Chapman Catt resumes the presidency of the National American Woman Suffrage Association replacing Anna Howard Shaw.

1916 Jeanette Rankin of Montana is the first woman to be elected to the U.S. House of Representatives.

1917 Women granted full suffrage in New York and partial suffrage in seven other states.

1918 Woman Suffrage Amendment passes the U.S. House of Representatives

1919 Woman Suffrage Amendment passes the U.S. Senate.

1920 The Nineteenth Amendment is ratified by a majority of the States and becomes law.

BIBLIOGRAPHY

Aburdene, Patricia, and John Naisbitt. *Megatrends for Women*. New York: Villard, 1992.

Abzug, Bella, and Margaret Gallagher, Gertrude Mongella, et. al. Women: *Looking Beyond 2000*. New York: United Nations, 1995.

Archer, Jules. *The Unpopular Ones*. New York: Crowell-Collier, 1968.

Bacon, Margaret Hope. Valiant Friend: *The Life of Lucretia Mott*. New York: Walker, 1980.

Barker, Dudley. *Prominent Edwardians*. New York: Atheneum, 1969.

Bartlett, Elizabeth Ann. *Liberty, Equality, Sorority—The Origins and Interpretation of American Feminist Thought: Frances Wright, Sarah Grimké, and Margaret Fuller*. Brooklyn: Carlson, 1994.

Blackwell, Alice Stone. *Lucy Stone: Pioneer Woman Suffragist*. Boston: Little, Brown, 1930.

Bloomer, D. C. *Life and Writings of Amelia Bloomer*. Boston: Arena, 1895.

Breault, Judith Colucci. *The World of Emily Howland: Odyssey of a Humanitarian*. Millbrae, CA: Les Femmes, 1976.

Bryant, Jennifer Fisher. *Lucretia Mott: Guiding Light*. Grand Rapids: Eerdmans, 1996.

Buhle, Mari Jo and Paul. *The Concise History of Woman Suffrage: Selections from the Classic Work of Stanton, Anthony, Gage, and Harper*. Urbana: U of Illinois P, 1978.

Bullock, Ian, and Richard Pankhurst, eds. *Sylvia Pankhurst: From Artist to Anti-Fascist*. New York: St. Martin's, 1992.

Castle, Barbara. *Sylvia and Christabel Pankhurst*. New York: Penguin, 1987.

Catt, Carrie Chapman and Nettie Rogers Shuler. *Woman Suffrage and Politics: The Inner Story of the Suffrage Movement*. Seattle: U of Washington P: 1969.

Chafe, William H. *The Road to Equality: American Women Since 1962*. New York: Oxford UP, 1994.

Chevigny, Bell Gale. *The Woman and the Myth: Margaret Fuller's Life and Writings*. New York: Feminist Press, 1976.

Clarke, Mary Stetson. *Bloomers and Ballots: Elizabeth Cady Stanton and Women's Rights*. New York: Viking, 1972.

Coolidge, Olivia. *Women's Rights: The Suffrage Movement in America, 1848-1920*. New York: Dutton, 1966.

Cooper, Ilene. *Susan B. Anthony*. New York: Franklin Watts, 1984.

Cromwell, Otelia. *Lucretia Mott*. Cambridge: Harvard UP, 1958.

D'Ambrosio, Mary. "Matilda Gage." *Syracuse Magazine*. Mar. 1981: 33.

Davis, Flora. *Moving the Mountain: The Women's Movement in America Since 1960*. New York: Simon & Schuster, 1991.

Dunnahoo, Terry. *Before the Supreme Court: The Story of Belva Ann Lockwood*. Boston: Houghton Mifflin, 1974.

DuBois, Ellen Carol. *Feminism and Suffrage: The Emergence of an Independent Women's Movement in America*. Ithaca: Cornell UP, 1978.

Eisler, Riane. *The Chalice & the Blade: Our History, Our Future*. San Francisco: Harper & Row, 1987.

Flexner, Eleanor. *Century of Struggle: The Woman's Rights Movement in the United States*. Cambridge: Harvard UP, 1975.

Fowler, Robert Booth. *Carrie Catt: Feminist Politician*. Boston: Northeastern UP, 1986.

Gatley, Charles Nielson. *The Bloomer Girls*. New York: Coward-McCann, 1967.

Goldberg, Michael. *Breaking New Ground: American Women 1800-1848*. New York: Oxford UP, 1994.

Griffith, Elizabeth. *In Her Own Right: The Life of Elizabeth

Cady Stanton. New York: Oxford UP, 1984.

Gurko, Miriam. *The Ladies of Seneca Falls: The Birth of the Woman's Rights Movement*. New York: Macmillan, 1974.

Hallowell, Anna Davis, ed. *James and Lucretia Mott: Life and Letters*. Cambridge: Riverside, 1884.

Hays, Elinor Rice. *Morning Star: A Biography of Lucy Stone 1818-1893*. New York: Harcourt, Brace & World, 1961.

Hedglon, Mary. "Along the Way: Routes 5 & 20 Offer Slice of Finger Lakes Life." Rochester *Democrat and Chronicle*. 6 September 1992: 1-2D.

Irwin, Inez Hayes. *The Story of Alice Paul and the National Woman's Party*. Fairfax, VA: Denlinger's, 1977.

Johnston, Joanna. *Mrs. Satan: The Incredible Saga of Victoria C. Woodhull*. New York: Putnam, 1967.

Jump, Harriet Devine. *Mary Wollstonecraft: Writer.* New York: Harvester Wheatsheaf, 1994.

Kelley, Mary, ed. *The Portable Margaret Fuller*. New York: Penguin, 1994.

Kerr, Andrea Moore. *Lucy Stone: Speaking Out for Equality*. New Brunswick: Rutgers UP, 1992.

Klees, Emerson. *People of the Finger Lakes Region: The Heart of New York State*. Rochester: Friends of the Finger Lakes Publishing, 1995.

—. *Persons, Places, and Things Around the Finger Lakes Region: The Heart of New York State*. Rochester: Friends of the Finger Lakes Publishing, 1994.

—. *Persons, Places, and Things In the Finger Lakes Region: The Heart of New York State*. Rochester: Friends of the Finger Lakes Publishing, 1993.

Larson, T. A. *History of Wyoming*. Lincoln: U of Nebraska P, 1978.

Linkugel, Wil A. and Martha Solomon. *Anna Howard Shaw: Suffrage Orator and Social Reforme*r. New York: Greenwood, 1991.

Lumpkin, Katherine DuPre. *The Emancipation of Angelina*

Grimké. Chapel Hill: U of North Carolina P, 1974.

Lunardini, Christine A. *From Equal Suffrage to Equal Rights: Alice Paul and the National Woman's Party, 1910-1928*. New York: New York UP, 1986.

Marberry, M. M. Vicky: *A Biography of Victoria C. Woodhull*. New York: Funk & Wagnalls, 1967.

Mazel, Ella, ed. *Ahead of Her Time: A Sampler of the Life and Thought of Mary Wollstonecraft*. Larchmont, NY: Bernell, 1995.

Melder, Keith E. *Beginnings of Sisterhood: The American Rights Movement, 1800-1850*. New York: Schocken, 1977.

Mitchell, David. *The Fighting Pankhursts: A Study in Tenacity*. New York: Macmillan, 1967.

Munhall, Patricia L., and Virginia Macken Fitzsimmons. *The Emergence of Women into the 21st Century*. New York: NLN Press, 1995.

Nixon, Edna. *Mary Wollstonecraft: Her Life and Times*. London: J. M. Dent & Sons, 1971.

Pankhurst, E. Sylvia. *The Life of Emmeline Pankhurst: The Suffragette Struggle for Women's Citizenship*. Boston: Houghton Mifflin, 1936.

Peck, Mary Gray. *Carrie Chapman Catt: A Biography*. New York: H. W. Wilson, 1944.

"Proceedings of the Womans Rights Conventions Held at Seneca Falls and Rochester, N. Y." New York: Robert J. Johnston, 1870.

Reynolds, Moira Davison. *Women Champions of Human Rights: Eleven U.S. Leaders of the Twentieth Century*. Jefferson, N.C.: McFarland, 1991.

Robb, Carol S. *Equal Value: An Ethical Approach to Economics and Sex*. Boston: Beacon, 1995.

Romero, Patricia W. E. *Sylvia Pankhurst: Portrait of a Radical*. New Haven: Yale UP, 1987.

Sachs, Emanie. *The Terrible Siren: Victoria Woodhull*. New York: Harper & Brothers, 1928.

Sagan, Miriam. *Women's Suffrage*. San Diego: Lucent, 1995.

Sherr, Lynn and Jurate Kazickas. *Susan B. Anthony Slept Here: A Guide to American Women's Landmarks*. New York: Random House, 1996.

Stanton, Elizabeth Cady. *Eighty Years and More: Reminiscences 1815-1897*. New York: Schocken, 1971.

Sterling, Dorothy. *Lucretia Mott: Gentle Warrior*. Garden City: Doubleday, 1964.

Stoneburner, Carol and John. *The Influence of Quaker Women on American History: Biographical Studies*. Lewiston: Edwin Mellen Press, 1986.

Thornton, Willis. *The Nine Lives of Citizen Train*. New York: Greenberg, 1948.

Train, George Francis. *My Life in Many States and in Foreign Lands*. New York: Appleton, 1902.

Underhill, Lois Beachy. *The Woman Who Ran for President: The Many Lives of Victoria Lockwood*. Bridgehampton, NY: Bridgeworks, 1995.

Weatherford, Doris. *American Women's History*. New York: Prentice-Hall, 1994.

—. *Milestones: A Chronology of American Women's History*. New York: Facts on File, 1997.

Weisberg, Barbara. *Susan B. Anthony*. New York: Chelsea House, 1988.

Winner, Julia Hull. *Belva A. Lockwood*. Lockport, NY: Niagara County Historical Society, 1969.

Wolf, Doris. "Seneca Falls Touts Its 'Wonderful Life.'" Rochester *Democrat and Chronicle*. 19 December, 1996: 1A, 16A.

National Women's Hall of Fame, Seneca Falls

INDEX